GOD'S BOOK OF WISDOM

A DAILY DEVOTIONAL BUILT ON THE WISDOM OF PROVERBS

BELINDA BUCKLAND

CHRISTIAN FOCUS PUBLICATIONS

To Rachel,
my darling daughter.
My prayer is
that you may come
to a saving knowledge
of the Lord Jesus Christ
and that He may use
His Word
to mould you
into His image.

Contents

INTRODUCTION

Have you ever said to yourself, "How can I teach my children true wisdom in the midst of so much false teaching in the world? How can I give them practical advice that can guide them through all of the pit falls of life?" That's what this book is all about. God has given us the book of Proverbs as a guide to teach our children how to handle all of the practical relationships and responsibilities of life. This book will help you in using the book of Proverbs to teach your children the Wisdom of God.

When studying Proverbs we must remember that often things are mentioned as general principles and not necessarily absolute truths or promises. The Proverbs are guiding principles that will help us to know how to live. Remember though that you can never earn your way into heaven. The only way to be acceptable to God is through accepting Jesus Christ as your Lord and Saviour. Once you are a Christian then good works will follow. The good works and righteous living are a proof that Jesus is your Lord and Saviour; that God has forgiven you; and that you have been given the Holy Spirit who will help you to change.

HOW TO USE THIS BOOK

The ideal situation is that parents and children can sit together every day and spend time talking about the Scripture and how it applies to our daily lives.

Every Week

At the beginning of every week there will be an overview of the big lesson for the week.

Time to Remember

Then you will be given a memory verse for the week on the main theme.

Every Day

Read and Understand
Here you can get your Bible out and find the verses mentioned. Read through those verses in your Bible and then read through the explanation. This will help you to understand what the verse is saying.

Look at Yourself
Then it is time to look at your life and see what you need to do to change and become more like Christ. The Bible says in 2 Timothy 3:16-17 "All Scripture is God-breathed and is useful for teaching, rebuking, correcting and training in righteousness; so that the man of God may be thoroughly equipped for every good work."
So the Bible will TEACH us. This is when we read and understand what the verses are saying. Then it will REBUKE us. This means that it will show us what we are doing wrong. Thankfully it does not stop there, the Bible also CORRECTS us. It shows us what we should be doing. It TRAINS us in RIGHTEOUSNESS, so that we know what God's standards are, and how we should be living so that we can glorify God in everything we do.

Prayer
In everything we do, we need to rely on God. So we must turn to him in prayer. Prayer is our communication with God. It is very important to our spiritual lives. It is just as important as air is for us to breathe and live. So remember not to forget to spend time in prayer with God every day. We must praise him for who He is, thank him for what He has done, ask for His forgiveness, ask for His strength to stop doing wrong and start doing what is right.
I pray that as you use this book you will draw closer to God and become more like the Lord Jesus Christ.

WEEK 1

STUDYING GOD'S WORD

This week we are going to look at why we must study Proverbs. We are going to see how important it is to God, that we learn from His Word. There are also so many benefits to studying from God's Word. We are going to see how good it is to study Proverbs, how much we will be able to learn. We are going to see how we must apply what we learn to our lives.

TIME TO REMEMBER

Proverbs 4:4. "He taught me and said, 'Lay hold of my words with all your heart; keep my commands and you will live.'"

1 January

READ AND UNDERSTAND

Proverbs 1:2a. The Proverbs will give you wisdom.

Proverbs 1:7a. To have knowledge you must first fear the Lord. We must study Proverbs to learn from God, and if we fear and respect God, then we will be able to be wise.

LOOK AT YOURSELF

Do you fear God? If you do you will know that He is holy and that He hates wickedness. If you fear God you will be able to become wise. Do you want to become wise? You must study the Bible and ask God to give you wisdom. As you study the Bible you will learn about God, you will learn about how He wants you to live. Then you will be able to obey him and please him.

PRAYER

Thank you, God. You gave the Bible to us so that we can learn about you and become wise. Dear Jesus, help me to fear and respect you. Help me to obey you so that you may be pleased. Amen.

2 January

READ AND UNDERSTAND

Proverbs 1:2a. The Proverbs will instruct you.

Proverbs 3:28. Never tell your neighbour to wait until tomorrow if you can help him straight away. God commands us to love our neighbours, and if you love them you will help them.

Proverbs 4:5. Get wisdom, get understanding. Don't forget what you have been taught.

LOOK AT YOURSELF

Do you read your Bible? Do you obey the Bible? God commands us in the Bible to love our neighbour; we can do that by doing good things for them. So remember not to get angry with your brother or sister or friend. You must love all people, and you must do something nice even if that person is not nice to you.

PRAYER

Thank you, God, for the Bible. Thank you, Jesus, for dying on the cross and showing what it means to love other people. Dear Jesus, please help me to love all the people that I know and all those who I meet. Help me to do good things for them. Amen.

3 January

READ AND UNDERSTAND

Proverbs 1:2b. The Proverbs will help you to have discernment. They will help you see what is true and false as well as what is good and evil.

Proverbs 21:5. Good planning and hard work will often result in you having plenty. If you are careless and make decisions too quickly and do things without thinking then it could lead to having little. So plan well and work hard.

LOOK AT YOURSELF

Do you always know what is right and what is wrong? You must learn from the Bible and you will learn more about what God sees as good and evil, right and wrong. Do you work hard when you have something to do? Do you always know the right way of doing something? If you learn from the Bible you will be able to know what the best way of doing something is, you will also know that you must work hard, and then what you do will be successful.

PRAYER

Thank you, God. You have given us the Bible and it can teach us about what is right and wrong. Dear Jesus, please help me to know the best way of doing things, the right way, so that I may please you. Help me to do my best and work hard. Amen.

4 January

READ AND UNDERSTAND

Proverbs 1:2b. The Proverbs will give you understanding. So read them and obey them.

Proverbs 16:17. Those who are righteous travel a road that avoids evil. So watch where you are going, it may save your life.

Proverbs 28:5. Evil people don't understand what is right and wrong, but if you want to love and obey God you will be able to understand very well what is right and wrong.

LOOK AT YOURSELF

Do you look at your life to make sure that you are not sinning? Do you try and stay away from evil? The Bible will help you to understand what is right and wrong, to understand what pleases God and what God hates. You must look at your life every day and make sure that you obey God in everything that you do.

PRAYER

Thank you, God, that the Bible helps me to understand what is right and wrong. It will show me what is evil so that I can stay away from it. Dear Jesus, help me to love you and obey you. Help me to live a life that pleases you. Thank you that you died on the cross so that my sins can be forgiven. Help me to stop sinning. Amen.

5 January

READ AND UNDERSTAND

Proverbs 1:4a. The Proverbs are plain and easy and can help anyone to live the way he should.

Proverbs 27:15-16. Having a wife who always wants to fight is as irritating as a hole in your roof when it is raining. The water drips in constantly and gets you irritated. It is so difficult to try and stop her complaining that it is as difficult as stopping the wind or holding oil in your hand. Boys - you must not marry a woman who complains. Girls - you must make sure that you are not someone who complains.

LOOK AT YOURSELF

Do you know that the Bible can teach everyone, even small children who might not know a lot? Everyone can learn from the Bible. Do you complain a lot about things? The Bible says that it is horrible to live with someone who complains all the time. So you must remember that if things don't go the way you want, or you don't get what you want, you must not complain. You must be thankful to God for what you have, don't complain about what you don't have.

PRAYER

Thank you God for the Bible. It can teach everyone how to live a life that pleases you. Thank you that you give me so many things, even my life is a gift from you. Dear Jesus, I know that if I am thankful then you will be pleased. Please help me to be thankful for what I have, help me not to complain about things. Amen.

6 January

READ AND UNDERSTAND

Proverbs 1:4b. The Proverbs will give the young knowledge. So if you want knowledge you must study the proverbs.

Proverbs 2:16a. Wisdom will keep you from an impure relationship. The Bible will tell you about how beautiful and important marriage is.

Proverbs 5:19. Let the love you have in marriage be all that you need.

LOOK AT YOURSELF

Do you study your Bible every day? If you want to have knowledge you must learn from the Bible. Only God can give wisdom, knowledge and understanding. One of the things that the Bible teaches us about is marriage. Do you know how special and important marriage is? It is very important, and God says that you must only have that special relationship if you get married, and then it is only for the person you marry.

PRAYER

Thank you, God, for the Bible. Even if I am young I will be able to get knowledge if I study from your Word. Thank you that you created marriage and that it is very special. Dear Jesus, help me to learn from the Bible every day. Help me to get knowledge. Help me to remember how special and important marriage is, and that having that special relationship with someone is if I get married one day. Thank you that you love me and that you know what is best for me. Amen.

7 January

READ AND UNDERSTAND

Proverbs 1:6. The Proverbs will help you understand difficult things. The more you read them the more you will understand.

Proverbs 8:22. Wisdom existed before the world was created. God is the source of wisdom.

Proverbs 26:12. The most stupid fool is better off than someone who thinks that he knows everything. Don't be proud and think that you are wise; we all need to learn and become even wiser. So be humble and learn from other people.

LOOK AT YOURSELF

Do you understand everything? No one can know and understand everything. If you think you know everything then you are being proud, you think that you are more important than anyone else. Only God knows all things. God is the source of wisdom and so if we want to get wisdom and understand things then we must study the Bible. Remember, you can never know everything. You must be humble. We all need to learn. Keep learning from the Bible your whole life, and remember to learn from other people who are there to teach you.

PRAYER

Thank you, God, for the Bible. Thank you that if I learn from the Bible you will be able to help me understand difficult things. Thank you that you know everything, thank you that we can study the Bible and learn more about you. Dear Jesus, help me to learn from your Word every day. Help me to be humble and to always remember that I need to learn more. Amen.

WEEK 2

THE IMPORTANCE OF WISDOM

This week we are going to learn about wisdom. Wisdom is so important; it will help us with so many things. The most important theme in the book of Proverbs is wisdom. It is mentioned more than any other thing. You will see this week how important wisdom is and how important it is that you listen to what the Bible says so that you can become wise.

TIME TO REMEMBER

Proverbs 2:12. "Wisdom will save you from the ways of wicked men, from men whose words are perverse."

8 January

READ AND UNDERSTAND

Proverbs 1:20-21. Wisdom is available to all people.

Proverbs 20:8. When a king judges, he carefully looks at all the information that is given and will be able to see between what is good and what is evil and between what is true and what is a lie.

LOOK AT YOURSELF

Do you study the Bible so that you can become wise? If wisdom is available to all people then you can also become wise. You must study the Bible and ask God to give you wisdom. Solomon was a king who had a lot of wisdom, he would know what to do in different situation and he would know who was telling a lie and who was telling the truth. Wouldn't it be nice to have that kind of wisdom? God says that we can.

PRAYER

Thank you, God, that you have given us the Bible and that if we ask you for wisdom you will give us wisdom. Thank you that your wisdom will help us to know what is good and evil, what is true and what is a lie. Dear Jesus, help me to study the Bible and become wise, please give me your wisdom. Amen.

9 January

READ AND UNDERSTAND

Proverbs 1:22a. Simple people love simplicity. If you are simple, don't stay simple, become wise.

Proverbs 20:3. Avoiding a fight is the best thing to do; only fools want to quarrel and fight. So don't be foolish, stay out of arguments.

Proverbs 29:11. A fool will get angry quickly, but a wise person will be self-controlled and will not get angry.

LOOK AT YOURSELF

Do you get angry if someone does something horrible to you? Did you know that it is sinful to get angry; it is a foolish thing to do. Even if people are horrible to you the Bible says that a wise person will have self-control and they will not get angry. If you get angry you will just start a fight, so remember that only a fool will start arguments and fight. A wise person will stay away from fights. So if a friend or a brother or sister is mean to you or says something horrible to you, you must remember not to get angry and not to start a fight. The Bible tells us to love people who are horrible to us.

PRAYER

Thank you, God, for the Bible, which tells us what is right and what is wrong. Dear Jesus, please help me to remember that it is wrong to fight and get angry. Thank you, Jesus, that when people were horrible to you, you showed love to them and you asked God to forgive them. Help me to also show love to people who are horrible to me. Amen.

10 January

READ AND UNDERSTAND

Proverbs 1:23. You must want wisdom. If you are a Christian God will give you the Holy Spirit who will help you to understand.

Proverbs 18:24. A person that makes friends with everybody will not benefit from that. You will benefit from choosing friends wisely; a good friend is more loyal than a brother and will support you in difficult times.

LOOK AT YOURSELF

Are you a Christian? Have you asked Jesus to forgive your sins? When you become a Christian you will have the Holy Spirit living inside of you, helping you to do what is right. Are you just friendly with everyone, or do you have some people who are your friends? It is good to have close friends; they will be there to help you when you need it. But remember to choose your friends wisely. You must also make sure that you are a good friend; you must support your friends especially when they have difficult times.

PRAYER

Thank you, God, for the Holy Spirit who lives inside Christians and helps them to understand what is written in the Bible. Thank you that the Holy Spirit helps us to know what makes you happy and what makes you sad. Dear Jesus, please help me to do everything in my life so that you are happy and pleased. Help me to choose friends who love you and who are also people who live a life that makes you happy. Help me to be a good friend, helping my friends whenever I can. Amen.

11 January

READ AND UNDERSTAND

Proverbs 1:24-26. Wisdom is calling you; you are being foolish if you don't want it. Because when you then need wisdom and call for it, wisdom will not answer you. So you must listen and learn, so that when you need wisdom you have it.

Proverbs 8:14a. Wisdom helps people give good advice and make good decisions. So learn from the Bible and become wise so that you can give good advice and make good decisions.

LOOK AT YOURSELF

Do you listen when you are being taught? Do you want to be wise? You must be thankful for all those people who are trying to teach you and help you to become wise. Have you thanked those people who are teaching you? Remember that if you become wise you will be able to help people and you will be able to know what the right thing to do is. So if your parents are teaching you, you must listen carefully, you must not ignore them, they are helping you to become wise.

PRAYER

Thank you, God, for my parents and for all the other people who are helping me to become wise. Thank you for the Bible that can teach us about wisdom. Dear Jesus, please help me to listen carefully when I am being taught. Help me to be wise and be able to make good decisions. Help me to have the wisdom to give the right advice to anyone who needs help. Amen.

12 January

READ AND UNDERSTAND

Proverbs 1:26-28. If you do not want wisdom, when you need it, it will not be there. So listen and learn so that you have wisdom when you need it.

Proverbs 2:1b. Don't forget your parents' commandments. Remember you must honour and obey them.

Proverbs 17:21. There is only sadness and sorrow for parents whose children are fools. There is no joy for them. Don't be a fool, be wise and bring joy to your parents.

LOOK AT YOURSELF

Do you want to be wise? Do you bring joy to your parents by being wise? Do you listen and remember what your parents have taught you? We must learn all that we can and become wise. If you don't want to learn, then one day when you are having a difficult time, and you need wisdom, you will not have it. So listen to your parents, they are helping you to become wise.

PRAYER

Thank you, God, for my parents. Thank you that you will give me wisdom if I want to learn and become wise. Dear Jesus, please help me to bring joy to my parents. Help me to listen when I am taught so that I may become wise. Help me not to be a fool who does not want to learn. Amen.

13 January

READ AND UNDERSTAND

Proverbs 1:33. When you have wisdom, you don't need to fear evil. So become wise.

Proverbs 29:25. If you are scared of people and you don't do what is right, it is like falling into a dangerous trap. You must trust in God and always to what is right, and then you will be safe.

Proverbs 3:25-26. Do not be afraid of the wicked, God is in control of everything and if you are a Christian you can know that things will work together for your good, because God loves you and cares for you.

LOOK AT YOURSELF

Are you afraid of evil? Are you afraid of people? Have you ever done something that you know is wrong, just because someone said you must? It is wrong to do that. You must turn to God and put your trust in Him. God is the most important person in your life. You must obey Him even if somebody will hate you because of it. God will protect the people who love and obey Him.

PRAYER

Thank you, God. You are the most powerful and most important. Thank you that I can trust in you, that you will look after me if I love you and obey you. Dear Jesus, please help me to do what is right all the time. Help me to not be afraid of people. Help me to become wise. Help me to trust in you in everything that happens. Amen.

14 January

READ AND UNDERSTAND

Proverbs 2:2. Listen to what is wise and apply it to your life. Don't just learn things, those things must change how you live.

Proverbs 16:8. It is better to be honest and have only a little, than to lie to get a lot. Honesty is more important than money and things.

Proverbs 10:15b. If you are poor you must look at what you have and be thankful.

LOOK AT YOURSELF

Is it important to you to have a lot of things? Will you steal and cheat to get more stuff? Remember that God hates stealing and cheating, He is pleased with someone who is honest. It is much more important that God is pleased with you, than for you to have a lot of things. You must look after what you have and be thankful to God for it.

PRAYER

Thank you, God, that you have given me so much. Thank you that you provide for me. Dear Jesus, help me to remember that it is terrible to lie and cheat and steal. Help me to be thankful for what I have and to live a life that pleases you. Help me to learn from the Bible. Help me to stop sinning. Help me to change so that I can bring glory to you. Amen.

WEEK 3

GOD BLESSES THE RIGHTEOUS

This week we are going to look at how God blesses the righteous. Righteous people are those who obey God and live a life that pleases Him. God says that if you obey Him and live righteously, He will bless you. He will look after you and protect you; you will have life in heaven with Him. But if you are not righteous, if you are wicked and disobey God, then you will be punished.

TIME TO REMEMBER

Proverbs 10:16. "The wages of the righteous bring them life, but the income of the wicked brings them punishment."

15 January

READ AND UNDERSTAND

Proverbs 10:6. If you are righteous you will receive blessings. With the wicked there is just violence. So don't be wicked, obey God and live a righteous life.

Proverbs 6:14. Wicked people plan evil in their minds. They make trouble everywhere they go. You must be careful of what you think about, never think about evil.

LOOK AT YOURSELF

Are you ever violent? Have you ever hit a friend or a brother or sister? Have you ever thought about a horrible thing to do to someone? These things are all wicked. If you want to receive blessings you must live a righteous life. That means that you must obey God and keep His commandments. You must not think about evil things, you must think about things that are pleasing to God.

PRAYER

Thank you, God, that you bless the righteous. You promise that if we obey you and live a life that is pleasing to you, then you will bless us. Dear Jesus, please help me to never be violent. Help me to think about good things. I want to live a life that is pleasing to you and I want to show love to others just the way you showed love to me. Please help me to obey you. Amen.

16 January

READ AND UNDERSTAND

Proverbs 10:7. Good people are remembered as a blessing, but the wicked are soon forgotten. Don't be wicked, obey God and live a righteous life.

Proverbs 13:15a. If you have understanding you will be respected. So learn from the Bible and get understanding.

Proverbs 31:28-29. A godly wife will be appreciated by her children. She is praised by her husband; he says that she is the best wife in the world. Boys - find a wife who is godly. Girls - be women who are godly.

LOOK AT YOURSELF

Could people think about you as someone who does good things, someone who obeys God? If you do obey God and live a life that is pleasing to Him, then people will think about you as a good person. If you are wise, understanding God's teaching, and living in obedience to that teaching, then people will respect you. They might come and ask you questions about God. Do you get to tell people about Jesus, that HHe died on the cross so that our sins could be forgiven?

PRAYER

Thank you, God, that we can tell people about Jesus. Thank you that we can show them by the way that we live, that you can save people and help them to live a life that is pleasing to you. Dear Jesus, please forgive me for the sins that I have done. Please help me to stop sinning and to live a life that pleases and glorifies you. Help me to be a witness to other people that you are a loving God who can forgive sin. Amen.

17 January

READ AND UNDERSTAND

Proverbs 10:16. The reward for doing good things is life, but sin leads only to more sin and then death. So you must always obey God and do what is right.

Proverbs 23:29-30. Do you know who will be like this? They feel sorry for themselves and are sad, they cause trouble and fighting, they are people who complain about everything, they get into fights and get bruises that could have been avoided and they have red eyes. This is the description of people who get drunk; they spend hours drinking wine and other alcohol. They try out all new drinks and they drink too much. God says that being drunk is sin. It also has terrible consequences, so you must not get drunk.

LOOK AT YOURSELF

Do you want to go to heaven when you die? Do you want to be with Jesus in heaven for ever? The only way to get to heaven is by trusting in Jesus for the forgiveness of sin. If you are not a Christian and you don't obey Jesus, then your sin will lead to death, being without Jesus forever.

PRAYER

Thank you, God, for warning us about how bad it is to get drunk. Thank you for telling us that all sin will lead to death. Dear Jesus, thank you so much for dying on the cross so that my sins can be forgiven. Please help me to live a life that pleases you and brings glory to you. Thank you that we can be with you in heaven one day. Amen.

18 January

READ AND UNDERSTAND

Proverbs 6:15. Wicked people, who plan evil, will be punished. Don't be wicked.

Proverbs 10:24. The righteous will often get what they want but the wicked will get what they are afraid of. So obey God and live a righteous life.

Proverbs 28:17. Someone who has killed another person will try to run away from being punished; you must not help someone like that. God says that if you are a murderer you must be punished.

LOOK AT YOURSELF

If you have done something wrong, do you accept the punishment that you get? Or do you get upset or cross with your parents for punishing you. God says that sin must get punished. So learn from when you are punished for sinning. Then you will remember not to sin again. God promises that there will be good things for those who obey Him and live a righteous life. It is much better to obey God than to be someone who is wicked.

PRAYER

Thank you, God. You warn us in the Bible that if we are wicked and sin, then we will get punished. Thank you, God, you are perfect and without sin. Dear Jesus, please help me to accept punishment when I have sinned. Help me to learn from the punishment not to sin again. Please forgive me for my sin and help me to live a righteous life, a life that pleases you. Amen.

19 January

READ AND UNDERSTAND

Proverbs 10:17. People who listen when they are corrected will live, but those who will not admit that they are wrong are in danger. So listen when you are corrected.

Proverbs 10:25. Storms come (difficult things if life), and the wicked are blown away, but righteous people are always safe. A Christian knows that God is in control of everything and that all things work together for our good. When difficult things come we must trust in God.

Proverbs 12:15. Stupid people always think they are right. Wise people listen to advice. So be wise and listen to advice.

LOOK AT YOURSELF

If something bad happens, do you turn to God? If you do something wrong and someone shows you that you have sinned, do you listen and admit that you are wrong and turn to God for forgiveness? Remember that if you are wicked, and will not admit your sin, then you are in danger. If you want to be safe you must love and obey God, who is able to save and protect us.

PRAYER

Thank you, God. You love us so much that you sent Jesus to die on the cross so that our sins could be forgiven. Thank you that if I love and obey you that I can trust you to protect me. Dear Jesus, please help me to listen when someone shows me my sin. Help me to change and become more like you. Help me to trust in you when there are difficult things happening in my life, I know that you care for me and are there to help me. Amen.

20 January

READ AND UNDERSTAND

Proverbs 6:23. The Bible is a shining light for you; it will show you how you must live. So learn from the Bible and obey it.

Proverbs 10:28. The hopes of the righteous lead to joy, but wicked people can look forward to nothing. So obey God and if you are a Christian you can look forward to the joy of heaven.

Proverbs 13:2. Good people will be rewarded for what they say, but those who are liars only want violence. So don't lie, always tell the truth.

LOOK AT YOURSELF

Have you ever told a lie? God hates lies and tells us that we must always tell the truth. Have you ever been walking somewhere when it was dark? Isn't it so much easier when you have a light showing you where you must go? The Bible is our light, it tells us about what is pleasing to God and what God hates. We must learn from the Bible and if we live a life that is pleasing to God then we will have joy.

PRAYER

Thank you, God. You have given us the Bible to be a light to us, showing us how we must live so that we can please you and glorify you. Thank you that you give joy to those who love you and obey you. Dear Jesus, please help me to always tell the truth. Help me to learn from the Bible about what things we must not do and what things we must do. Help me to obey you. Help me to become more like you. Amen.

21 January

READ AND UNDERSTAND

Proverbs 10:30. Righteous people will always have security, but the wicked will not survive. Obey God and He will protect you. If you are a Christian you can know that God is in control of everything and that He knows what is best for you.

Proverbs 20:13. If you spend your time sleeping when work needs to be done you will be poor. Keep busy and work so that you will have food. Remember to work hard and not to be lazy.

Proverbs 6:9. A lazy person sleeps a lot and does not want to get out of bed. You must not be lazy, work hard.

LOOK AT YOURSELF

Have you ever slept late when you knew that there was something that you had to do? Have you ever sat around doing nothing when you knew that there was something that you should be doing? It is wrong to be lazy; God wants us to do our work when we need to and to do our work well. If we obey God and live the way he says we must, then we will be safe and secure.

PRAYER

Thank you, God. You will protect us if we live a life that pleases you. Dear Jesus, please help me not to be lazy. Help me to work when I know there is work to do. Help me to do my work well. Amen.

WEEK 4

THE IMPORTANCE OF TRUTH

This week we are going to look at how important truth is. God hates lies and so must you. If you have to be a witness, and tell people what you saw, you must always tell the truth. An evil witness, one who tells lies, will be punished.

TIME TO REMEMBER

Proverbs 12:17. "A truthful witness gives honest testimony, but a false witness tells lies."

22 January

READ AND UNDERSTAND

Proverbs 2:15. The wicked are liars. You must not be wicked; you must always tell the truth.

Proverbs 8:7. The wise will speak truth and they will hate wickedness. So you must be wise and always tell the truth.

Proverbs 30:5. Every word of God can be tested and will be proven to be true. We can trust in God, He is like a shield protecting those who trust in him.

LOOK AT YOURSELF

Have you ever told a lie? It is terribly wicked to tell lies. God never lies, He hates lies, and He tells us to be like Him and to always tell the truth. If you have done something wrong, you must not lie about it, you must tell the truth even if that means that you will be punished. Wicked people are liars, so don't be wicked.

PRAYER

Thank you, God, for always telling the truth, all your words can be tested and we will see that they are true. Thank you that we can trust everything that you say. Dear Jesus, please help me to be more like you. Help me to hate lies just like you hate lies. Help me to always tell the truth like you always tell the truth. Please forgive me for telling lies. Amen.

23 January

READ AND UNDERSTAND

Proverbs 12:17. When you tell the truth, justice is done, but telling lies lead to injustice. So always tell the truth.

Proverbs 12:20a. Wicked people are liars in their heart. Don't be wicked, always tell the truth.

Proverbs 28:4. If you don't care about laws and rules, it is like praising wicked people. If you keep the law and obey the rules, then you will be fighting against the wicked. So be someone who obeys, who hates wickedness and loves God.

LOOK AT YOURSELF

Have you ever lied so that you won't get punished? Have you ever done something that you know you should not have done? God hates this, He hates injustice, but He is pleased with truth and obedience. God wants us to stop sinning and live a life that pleases him. You are not pleasing God if you lie and disobey the rules.

PRAYER

Thank you, God. You gave us the Bible which shows us how to live a life in obedience to you. Dear Jesus, please help me to always tell the truth. Help me to obey you and to obey the rules my parents have given. I know that if I obey my parents then I am pleasing you. Thank you that when you lived on earth you showed us how to live, you lived in obedience and you always told the truth. Please help me to be more like you. Amen.

24 January

READ AND UNDERSTAND

Proverbs 12:19. A lie has a short life, but truth lives on for ever. So always tell the truth.

Proverbs 23:17-18. You must not want to do what sinners do, they have no hope, and they will be punished for their sin. If you fear the Lord you will hate sin as He does. Remember that the people who live a life that glorifies God will live forever with him. The hope of heaven is far better than the pleasure of sin.

LOOK AT YOURSELF

Have you ever told a lie so that you could get something that you wanted? It is terrible to lie, it would be better not to have that nice thing and to tell the truth, than to lie and get a lot of nice things. Remember that if we are Christians we must obey God and not sin, we will love God and not want to disobey Him. If we are Christians then we will be in heaven with God forever. That is much better than all the things that you could get on earth.

PRAYER

Thank you, God, Christians will be with you in heaven forever. Dear Jesus, thank you for dying on the cross so that my sins can be forgiven, with my sins forgiven I am able to live with you in heaven forever. Please help me to obey you and to live a life that pleases you. Help me to always tell the truth. Thank you for the hope of heaven, thank you that Christians can look forward to heaven. Amen.

25 January

READ AND UNDERSTAND

Proverbs 13:5. A righteous person hates lies, but the words of wicked people bring embarrassment. Don't be wicked, always tell the truth.

Proverbs 2:16b. The wicked will make an impure relationship sound good, but it is not. Marriage is the most beautiful relationship you can have with someone.

Proverbs 5:17. The marriage relationship is special and must be kept pure.

LOOK AT YOURSELF

Have you ever heard someone say that it is fine for two people to live together as if they were married even though they are not? This is very wrong. It is a lie. God says that marriage is a special relationship for a husband and wife. As a Christian you must remember to hates lies, you must remember that God hates lies, God also hates people who do not see marriage as important as He does.

PRAYER

Thank you, God. You created marriage and it is very good. Help me to remember how important marriage is. Dear Jesus, please help me to remember the truth from the Bible. Help me to hate the lies that people tell. Amen.

26 January

READ AND UNDERSTAND

Proverbs 14:5. A good witness always tells the truth, but a bad witness tells nothing but lies. Be honest and always tell the truth.

Proverbs 1:29. The foolish hate truth and don't fear God. You must fear God and love truth.

Proverbs 2:12b. Wisdom will keep you away from liars. So learn from the Bible and it will help you to know what is true.

LOOK AT YOURSELF

Have you ever told a lie when someone asked you what happened? Have you ever heard someone telling a lie when they were asked what happened? You must be a good witness, telling the truth about what happened. God says that if you are wise and if you fear God, then you will tell the truth, and you will hate lies.

PRAYER

Thank you, God. You will protect me if I fear you and refuse to lie. Thank you that you always tell the truth and that the Bible is always right. Dear Jesus, please help me to be a good witness if I am asked about something. Help me to always tell the truth. Please help me to learn from the Bible and become wise. Amen.

27 January

READ AND UNDERSTAND

Proverbs 14:25. A witness can save lives when he tells the truth, when a witness tells lies, he can hurt people. So you must never lie, always tell the truth.

Proverbs 21:10. Wicked and evil people love to hurt other people; they will have no mercy and will even be horrible to their neighbours. Don't be wicked and evil, love your neighbours and do good things for them.

LOOK AT YOURSELF

Have you ever told a lie so that someone else gets into trouble? Have you ever done something so that someone else will be hurt? It is wicked to do that, God hates lies and He hates people who want to hurt others. God tells us that we must love others; we must do kind things for them and never do evil things, hurting other people.

PRAYER

Thank you, God. You loved me even though I was your enemy. You sent Jesus to die for me even though I did not love you or obey you. Dear Jesus, thank you for dying on the cross so that my sins can be forgiven. Please help me to always tell the truth. Help me to love other people and help me to remember that it is wrong to hurt people. Help me to live a life that pleases you. Amen.

28 January

READ AND UNDERSTAND

Proverbs 17:7. Excellent speech does not suit the character of a fool; neither does lying suit the character of a ruler. You must not be a fool. Remember that lying is a sin and God hates it.

Proverbs 18:7. A fool's mouth will cause his destruction; his lips get him into trouble. Don't be a fool. Be wise and have godly speech.

Proverbs 16:21b. Pleasant words promote instruction.

LOOK AT YOURSELF

Do you know how much God hates lying? Have you learnt in the last week the importance of telling the truth? Today we see how important our speech is. We are told that a fool, who does not have godly speech, will be destroyed by what he says. The things that a fool talks about will get him into trouble. If we are wise, we will think before we speak, we will have speech that pleases God, and we will remember that lies are wrong and God hates them.

PRAYER

Thank you, God. You teach us in the Bible about what will cause trouble and destruction. You tell us how we must live and how we can please you. Dear Jesus, please help me to remember how important my speech is. Help me to remember how wrong it is to lie. Help me to please you in everything that I do and everything that I say. Amen.

WEEK 5

GOD IS HOLY

God is a Holy God and He hates wickedness. You will see this week that God will punish wicked people. You must not be wicked, you must go to God and ask Him to forgive you for your sin and ask Him to help you to live a life that pleases Him.

TIME TO REMEMBER

Proverbs 22:5. "In the paths of the wicked lie thorns and snares, but he who guards his soul stays far from them."

29 January

READ AND UNDERSTAND

Proverbs 2:22. God punishes the wicked. So you must not be wicked, you must obey God.

Proverbs 13:9. The righteous are like a light shining brightly, the wicked are like a lamp going out. Obey God and become more and more like Christ.

Proverbs 14:16. Wise people are careful to stay away from evil, but fools are careless and act too quickly. So be wise, stay away from evil.

LOOK AT YOURSELF

Do you stay away from evil things? Are you careful, do you think about what you are doing and think about if what you are doing is pleasing to God or hated by God? God will punish wicked people, they don't obey God and they don't live a life that is pleasing to him. Righteous people, who love and obey God, want to live a life that is pleasing to God. Righteous people will become more and more like Christ.

PRAYER

Thank you, God. You are holy and pure. You hate evil and you will punish evil. Dear Jesus, thank you for dying on the cross so that my sins can be forgiven. Thank you that I can come to you, washed clean by you, and that I can be forgiven instead of being punished. Please forgive me for all the evil that I have done. Please help me to obey you more and more. Help me to live a life that is pleasing to you. Amen.

30 January

READ AND UNDERSTAND

Proverbs 14:12. Sinners may think they are not doing anything wrong, but sin will only end in death. Obey God and don't sin.

Proverbs 1:10. If sinners want you to sin with them, don't. You must be careful of the friends that you make. Don't make friends with people who love to sin.

Proverbs 16:30. Watch out for people who grin and wink at you, they have thought of something evil.

LOOK AT YOURSELF

Do you have friends who want you to do things with them that you know are wrong? Do people ever ask you to do something that you know is wrong but they tell you that it is not wrong? You must remember what you have been taught; you must remember what is right and what is wrong. Sinning will only get punished, don't think that you can get away with doing wrong. You must also remember how important it is to have friends who love God and want to obey him. It is not nice to have friends who don't care about living a life that is pleasing to God, who don't care about what is right or wrong.

PRAYER

Thank you, God. You gave us the Bible to teach us what is right and what is wrong. Dear Jesus, please help me to always obey you. Help me not to listen to people who want me to do things that I know will not please you. Help me to have friends who love you and want to obey you. Help me to live a life that pleases you. Amen.

31 January

READ AND UNDERSTAND

Proverbs 14:19. Evil people will have to bow down to the righteous. So don't be evil, obey God and live a righteous life.

Proverbs 20:18. You must get good advice and you can succeed; it is foolish to go charging into something without a plan. So be humble and ask advice, be wise and plan ahead.

Proverbs 29:23. If you are proud, you will be brought low, but if you are humble you will be honoured.

LOOK AT YOURSELF

Have you ever struggled with doing something just because you did not ask for help, you wanted to do it on your own, and you didn't want anyone to know that you could not do it? Have you ever done something that has not worked because you did not ask for advice? It is a good thing to be humble and ask advice, it will help you if you ask someone what they thing about your plan. You must also remember that if you can't do something on your own, you must ask for help, you must not be proud. Evil people are proud, they think that they can live without God; they will be humbled by God and punished for their evil.

PRAYER

Thank you, God. You have given me parents and friends who I can go to and ask for help and advice. Dear Jesus, please help me to not be proud. Help me to remember that I need you in my life and I cannot live without you. Please help me to be humble and not proud. Help me to ask for advice and help. Amen.

1 February

READ AND UNDERSTAND

Proverbs 17:13. If you do evil when good has been done to you it shows that your heart is evil and foolish. You will have evil happening to your family and not good. So don't be evil, always do good to others.

Proverbs 15:27. If you try and make money in a way that is not legal, you will only bring trouble on your family. One illegal way is with bribes. Bribes are wrong. If you hate bribes then you will live.

LOOK AT YOURSELF

Have you ever done something horrible to someone? Have you ever hit a child or said something horrible to them, even though they are being nice to you? If you have then you have evil in your heart. You will only bring trouble on yourself and your family.
Have you ever told a friend that you will not get them in trouble if they give you something? This is bribing, it is wrong and it will also only cause trouble for you. You must not just be focused on getting things. If you get things by doing wrong, you will get punished. It would have been better not to have that nice thing.

PRAYER

Thank you, God. You teach us in the Bible about how we must show love to other people. You also teach us about how important it is to tell the truth, be honest and not cheat. Dear Jesus, please help me to never do horrible things to people. Help me to show love just like you showed love by dying on the cross. Please forgive me for all the horrible things that I have done. Help me to live a life that pleases you. Amen.

2 February

READ AND UNDERSTAND

Proverbs 22:5. The wicked will not have an easy life, like having thorns and traps on the path you walk, so the wicked will have difficult things in life. If you are wise, you will be careful and you will stay away from wicked things.

Proverbs 13:25. The righteous have enough to eat, but the wicked are always hungry. So don't be wicked, obey God and live a righteous life.

Proverbs 19:24. Some lazy people are so lazy that they put their hand in a bowl of food, but are too lazy to bring it to their mouth. Don't be lazy. Work hard and always do your best.

LOOK AT YOURSELF

Have you ever had work to do and rather gone and done nothing? This is lazy, we must not be lazy, and we must do the work that we know needs to be done. These verses tell us that there are consequences for what we do, things will happen because of how we live. If we live a life that is wicked, not obedient to God, lazy and just doing our own thing, then we will have a difficult life. But if we live a life of obedience, wanting to please God and do our best, then God will look after us.

PRAYER

Thank you, God. You look after your children. Dear Jesus, please help me to live a life that pleases you. Help me to not be lazy. Help me remember how important it is to obey you. Please help me to stay away from wicked and evil things. Help me to not sin against you. Amen.

3 February

READ AND UNDERSTAND

Proverbs 24:15-16. Wicked people plan to hurt godly people; they want to destroy their homes. But God protects His people and they will cope even if the wicked do bad things to them. The wicked will not cope because God will judge them and they will be punished for their sin. So don't be wicked, obey God and He will protect you.

Proverbs 19:11. If you are wise you will not get angry quickly. When someone wrongs you, it is a good characteristic to be able to ignore it. So be patient and don't get upset or angry.

LOOK AT YOURSELF

Has anyone ever done something horrible to you, trying to hurt you? How did you react? Did you get cross and angry? Or did you go to God and ask him to protect you and help you? God wants us to obey Him; He wants us to show love to people, even if they have been horrible to you. God will punish people who are wicked, so you must not be wicked back, otherwise you will be punished too.

PRAYER

Thank you, God. You will punish people who are horrible to people and hurt people. Thank you that you protect your children. Dear Jesus, please help me to not get angry. Help me to be patient and kind and to show love to people who are horrible to me. Thank you that you showed love even to the people who killed you. You did not hate them. You loved them and died so that our sins could be forgiven. Please forgive me for all my sin. Help me to love you and obey you. Amen.

4 February

READ AND UNDERSTAND

Proverbs 28:10. If wicked people trick an honest person into doing something evil, they will fall into their own trap. But innocent people will be rewarded and will get good things. So don't be wicked, obey God and be innocent.

Proverbs 22:12. God knows all things and He will protect truth, He also knows the plans of the wicked and He will destroy them. Remember that God can see all things; you can't say or think about lies without the Lord knowing. So don't lie, always tell the truth.

LOOK AT YOURSELF

Have you ever tried to trick someone into doing something wrong? Have you ever thought that you can think and do horrible things and that nobody will know? Remember that God knows everything that you think and do. He will punish people who trick others and plan evil things. But God will protect Christians, He will protect the people that love Him and want to live a life that pleases Him.

PRAYER

Thank you, God. You see everything and you know everything. You will punish people who are wicked and you will protect people who obey you. Dear Jesus, please help me to love and obey you. Please forgive my sins and help me to stop sinning and live a life that pleases you. Amen.

WEEK 6

WISDOM AND MONEY

The lesson this week is that you must not put your trust in money. You will not be able to take money with you when you die. What is far more important is that you have a right relationship with God. You must live a godly and righteous life, pleasing Him in everything you do. That is what will count in eternity. The big question is not how much money you have, it is rather, are you a Christian?

TIME TO REMEMBER

Proverbs 11:4. "Wealth is worthless in the day of wrath, but righteousness delivers from death."

5 February

READ AND UNDERSTAND

Proverbs 10:15a. A rich person may think that their money will protect them. It won't. Only God can protect you.

Proverbs 28:16. If a leader is horrible to people, and only wants to get things for himself even if he has to cheat, he is being foolish. A good and wise leader will hate cheating and will be honest, and then he will be able to lead the people for a long time. So you must always be honest and hate cheating.

LOOK AT YOURSELF

Do you like having lots of things? Do you think it is important to have a lot of money? These verses say that if you have a lot of money and things you might trust in them instead of trusting in God. You also might do things that are wrong like cheating and stealing so that you will get more. You must not be selfish and want a lot of things for yourself. It is much better to be honest and to be thankful for what you have.

PRAYER

Thank you, God. You have given me so much: the house that I stay in, the food that I get every day, the clothes that I have. Dear Jesus, please help me to be more thankful for what I have. Help me not to want to have a lot of things. Please help me to trust in you and to always obey you. Amen.

6 February

READ AND UNDERSTAND

Proverbs 10:22. It is the Lord's blessing that makes people rich. And the Lord does not add sadness to your riches. Don't rely on money; rely on God who will provide the money that you need.

Proverbs 13:12a. If you have been hoping for something for a long time and it does not happen, it makes you very sad. So you must not expect lots of things in this life. Be happy with what you have.

LOOK AT YOURSELF

Do you thank God for everything that you get? God is the one who provides for us. We must work hard but we must trust in God to provide, we must not trust in money.

Have you ever wanted something very much and not gotten it? It is sad when we are disappointed and don't get what we wanted. But we must remember that God knows what is best and we must thank Him for what we do have.

PRAYER

Thank you, God. You have given me so much, everything that I have is a gift from you. Dear Jesus, please help me to be more thankful. Please help me to not want a lot of things but to be thankful and grateful for all the things that I already have. Thank you for providing for me. Help me to trust in you. Amen.

7 February

READ AND UNDERSTAND

Proverbs 11:4. Riches will do you no good on the day you face death, but honesty can save your life. Never try and get money by lying or cheating, always be honest.

Proverbs 19:1. It is better to be poor and honest than to be a fool that lies. Remember to always tell the truth. God hates lies.

Proverbs 31:30. Remember that charm and beauty do not last, but a woman who fears God will be praised. Boys - you must find a wife who is godly. Girls - you must be women who are godly.

LOOK AT YOURSELF

Have you ever lied to get money? Have you ever thought that money will protect you? You must remember that when we die, it is not our money that will get us into heaven. The only way to get to heaven is by trusting in Jesus as your saviour and Lord, having all your sins forgiven and living a life that is pleasing to God. We need to fear God and remember how much He hates lies.

PRAYER

Thank you, God. You have made a way for us to go to heaven. Thank you that Jesus died on the cross to pay for my sins. Thank you for your forgiveness. Dear Jesus, please help me to always obey you. Help me to never lie or cheat or steal. Thank you that you died on the cross for me. Amen.

8 February

READ AND UNDERSTAND

Proverbs 11:7. When a wicked person dies, their hope dies with them. Trusting in money will not help at all. Trust in God.

Proverbs 11:18. Wicked people do not really get anything, but if you do what is right, you will be rewarded. Obey God and do what is right.

Proverbs 14:32. Wicked people will be destroyed by their evil, but the righteous are protected by God. So don't be wicked, obey God and live a righteous life.

LOOK AT YOURSELF

Have you ever done something that you know is wrong just so that you could get something that you really wanted? It is never good to sin, even if you get something that you think is nice, that won't last forever. But if we are Christians and we love God and desire to obey him, if we confess our sins and try to stop sinning and live a life that pleases God, then we will have hope forever. Only Christians can go to heaven, and nothing in this life is as good as that.

PRAYER

Thank you, God, for heaven. Thank you that all Christians will be with you in heaven forever. Dear Jesus, please help me to never be wicked and evil. Please help me to obey you and live a life that pleases you. Amen.

9 February

READ AND UNDERSTAND

Proverbs 11:28. If you depend on money you will fall like the leaves in autumn, but if you are righteous you will do well like the green leaves in summer. Don't trust in money; trust in God.

Proverbs 5:10. Impure relationships will result in strangers taking your wealth and what you have worked hard for will belong to someone else. Marriage was created by God and it is good.

LOOK AT YOURSELF

Have you ever heard someone say that marriage is not important? That is very wrong. A righteous person, someone who lives a life that pleases God, knows that marriage is important and will only give their special love to the person that they marry. The righteous people will do well, but those who are not, those who depend on money and don't obey God, will lose what they have. It is better to obey God and live a life that pleases him.

PRAYER

Thank you, God. You protect those who trust in you. Thank you that you created marriage and it is a good and special relationship. Dear Jesus, please help me to depend on you and not on money or things. Help me to obey you and to remember what you have taught me. Amen.

10 February

READ AND UNDERSTAND

Proverbs 13:8. A rich man has to use his money to save his life, but no one threatens a poor man. Money is not the most important thing in life.

Proverbs 27:13. Anyone who is foolish enough to promise to pay what a stranger owes will probably never pay the money back. So you would have to take his own property to make sure that he pays. It is foolish to promise to pay what someone else owes.

LOOK AT YOURSELF

Have you ever heard of someone being kidnapped? The family have to pay a lot of money to get the person back. This is just an example of how having a lot of money can sometimes not be a nice thing. You must not think that having a lot of money will make everything fine. You need to remember that the most important thing in life is your relationship with God. Are you a Christian? Have you asked God to forgive your sins, have you made a commitment to Jesus that you will love him and obey Him. That is the most important thing, not money.

PRAYER

Thank you, God, for salvation through Jesus. Thank you that I can have a relationship with you, that you are my heavenly Father and I can trust in you. Dear Jesus, please help me to stop sinning. Please help me to obey you and to live a life that pleases you. Amen.

11 February

READ AND UNDERSTAND

Proverbs 18:11. Rich people may think that their money can protect them. They could think it is like a high wall around them, protecting them. But they are wrong, only God can protect us. Remember to place your trust in God alone.

Proverbs 16:20b. Blessed is he who trusts in the Lord.

Proverbs 13:14. The teachings of the Bible are a fountain of life; they will help you escape when your life is in danger. So learn from the Bible and it will help you in life.

LOOK AT YOURSELF

Have you ever seen a house with very high walls around it? Do you think that such a big wall could really protect you? This week we have seen that money and things cannot protect us. Only God can protect us and we must trust in Him. If we need to escape from danger then we need to learn from the Bible and we need to trust in God.

PRAYER

Thank you, God. You are a powerful and mighty God who can protect me. Thank you that you bless those who trust in you. Dear Jesus, please help me to trust in you only. Help me never to trust in money or things but to remember that you are the only one who can protect me. Amen.

WEEK 7

THE IMPORTANCE OF WISDOM

Again this week we will look at the importance of wisdom. We will look through Proverbs 2:3-10 and learn more about the wisdom that we can get from the Bible and how important it is for us. You will see how important it is that you want to be wise and also that wisdom comes from God.

TIME TO REMEMBER

Proverbs 2:6. "For the Lord gives wisdom, and from his mouth come knowledge and understanding."

12 February

READ AND UNDERSTAND

Proverbs 2:3. Beg for knowledge and understanding. If they are important to you, you will be able to get knowledge and understanding.

Proverbs 2:6. God gives wisdom, knowledge and understanding. You can only get these things from God, so learn what the Bible teaches.

Proverbs 16:16. Wisdom is better than gold and understanding is better than silver.

LOOK AT YOURSELF

Do you enjoy learning? Do you enjoy being taught? Having knowledge and understanding must be important to us; we should enjoy learning and being taught. God teaches us in the Bible and He is the only one who can give you wisdom. So you must listen when you are taught and you must ask God to help you understand.

PRAYER

Thank you, God. You know and understand everything. Thank you that I can come and ask you to give me wisdom. Dear Jesus, please help me to remember how important wisdom is. Please help me to listen when I am taught, and help me to understand. Amen.

13 February

READ AND UNDERSTAND

Proverbs 2:4. You must look for wisdom as you would for silver or hidden treasures. If it is important to you, you will find it.

Proverbs 12:1. Anyone who loves knowledge wants to be told when he is wrong. It is stupid to hate being corrected. Listen when you are corrected.

Proverbs 15:5. If you refuse to learn from your parents, you are foolish. It is wise to accept correction. Remember the command to honour and obey your parents.

LOOK AT YOURSELF

Have you ever been on a treasure hunt? Can you think how hard you would look if you knew you could find something very expensive and valuable like silver or gold? That is how hard you need to look for wisdom; God says that if you look hard, you will find it. Remember that if you want to find wisdom and understanding, then you must listen when people correct and discipline you. The only way you can learn is if you listen to other people, especially your parents, when they tell you that you are doing something wrong. Then you will be able to stop doing that, and do what is right and what is pleasing to God.

PRAYER

Thank you, God. You gave me parents and other people who can help me to see what I am doing wrong. Dear Jesus, please help me to listen when I am told I am wrong. Help me to change and become more like you. Amen.

14 February

READ AND UNDERSTAND

Proverbs 2:5b. If you look for wisdom and it is important to you, you will succeed in learning about God.

Proverbs 21:3. Outward acts of worship, like going to church or reading our Bible, are things that God wants, but He hates those things if you are wicked. Your righteousness is more important to God. So remember to be a person that glorifies God in your heart, worship God in your heart and live in the right way so that you will please him.

LOOK AT YOURSELF

Do you want to know what pleases God? Do you want to know more about who God is? The way to find out is by studying the Bible and asking God to teach you. Then you will be able to know what pleases God and what He hates. You will know how important it is to God that you live a righteous life, where you are learning more and more about how you can be like Jesus.

PRAYER

Thank you, God. You show us in the Bible how important it is that we love you with all our heart. You know everything, and you know my thoughts and my desires. Dear Jesus, help me to love you and worship you in everything that I do as well as in everything that I think and want. Thank you that you showed us what it is to live a righteous life, a life without sin. Amen.

15 February

READ AND UNDERSTAND

Proverbs 2:7a. God gives wisdom to the righteous. So you must live a righteous life.

Proverbs 2:13. The wicked don't live a righteous life; they live in the darkness of sin. Don't be like the wicked, obey God and do not sin.

Proverbs 4:23. Be careful how you think, your life is shaped by your thoughts. If you think evil things you will end up doing evil things, you must think godly thoughts and then you will do godly things.

LOOK AT YOURSELF

Have you ever thought about doing something horrible to someone? Have you ever thought about doing something you know is wrong? Remember that the way you think will affect the way you live. God wants you to live a righteous life, obeying Him and doing everything so that He would be pleased. If you live a righteous life, then God will give you wisdom.

PRAYER

Thank you, God, the Bible warns us to be careful about what we think. Dear Jesus, please help me to live a life that pleases you. Please help me to be careful about what I think about. Help me to have thoughts that are pleasing to you so that I can live a life that is pleasing to you. Thank you that you will give wisdom to those people who love and obey you. Please help me to love and obey you more. Amen.

16 February

READ AND UNDERSTAND

Proverbs 2:9a. If you are wise you will know what is right and just. So learn from the Bible and become wise.

Proverbs 25:11-12. It is very valuable and attractive to be able to say the right thing at the right time. Sometimes the right word is a rebuke, telling someone when he or she is wrong. But even that, if it is done with wisdom, at the right time and with the right words, will be something more valuable than gold to the listener. Think before you speak, and listen when someone rebukes you.

LOOK AT YOURSELF

Can you think of a time when someone told you that what you were doing was wrong? How did you react? Did you appreciate the rebuke, or did you get cross and proud and not want to listen? God wants us to listen when people correct and rebuke us. That is one of the ways that He helps us to learn.

Have you ever told someone that what they were doing was wrong? Did you think carefully about what you were going to say? Did you say it at the right time? You need wisdom to know the right thing to say and the right time to say it.

PRAYER

Thank you, God, the Bible can teach me how to be wise, how to know what is right and what is pleasing to you. Dear Jesus, please help me to listen when people correct and rebuke me. Please help me to see what I am doing wrong and help me to change. Amen.

17 February

READ AND UNDERSTAND

Proverbs 2:9b. If you are wise you will know what is fair and good. So learn from the Bible and become wise.

Proverbs 24:11-12. You must help people who are treated unfairly and who are sentenced to death if they are innocent, don't stand back and let them die. If you say that you did not know, God knows if you are lying. God can see what you are thinking and why you do things. Help people when you know they need help.

LOOK AT YOURSELF

If you were in a room with your brother and an expensive vase got knocked off a table, by a curtain blowing in the wind, what would you do? Would you tell your mother that it was not your brother? Or would you keep quiet and let your brother get punished for something that he did not do?

If you are wise, you will tell the truth, and help your brother not to get punished if he did not deserve it. You must remember that God sees everything; He knows if you saw what happened, and if you keep quiet and don't tell the truth, then God will know that you are lying.

PRAYER

Thank you, God. You know everything. You know about everything that I do and everything that I think about. Dear Jesus, please help me to always think and do everything in a way that pleases you. Help me to be honest and to remember how important it is to help people who I know need help. Amen.

18 February

READ AND UNDERSTAND

Proverbs 2:10. When you are wise, knowledge is pleasing to you. So if you are wise, you will enjoy learning.

Proverbs 10:5. If you are wise you will work when you need to. You must not sleep when there is work to be done.

Proverbs 13:18. Someone who will not learn will be poor and will not be respected. If you listen to correction you will be respected. So be humble and listen when you are corrected.

LOOK AT YOURSELF

Do you enjoy learning? Do you want to have knowledge? People who do not want to learn will be poor; they will not learn how important it is to work when there is work to be done. Have you ever slept when you knew there was work that you needed to get done? The Bible says that it is foolish to do that, you must not be foolish; you must learn from the Bible and become wise.

PRAYER

Thank you, God. You gave us the Bible and it teaches us about what is pleasing to you. Thank you that we can learn from the Bible and become wise. Dear Jesus, please help me to become wise. Help me to love learning. Please help me to work when I have work to do. Forgive me for the times when I have been lazy and foolish. Thank you that I can receive forgiveness for all the things that I have done that have not pleased you. Please help me to learn from the Bible and become wise; knowing what pleases you and how you want me to live. Amen.

WEEK 8

DON'T BE LAZY - DO YOUR BEST

This week you will see how important it is that you do your work properly and that you work hard. It is foolish to be lazy; you must rather be wise and work hard, you must always do the best job that you can.

TIME TO REMEMBER

Proverbs 12:24. "Diligent hands will rule, but laziness ends in slave labour."

19 February

READ AND UNDERSTAND

Proverbs 6:6. Lazy people should learn a lesson from the way the ants live. They work hard.

Proverbs 20:21. The more easily you get money the less good will be done with it. If you work for your money you will be wise with it and you will look after it, then it will be a blessing to have. Don't think that getting lots of money will be the best thing, thank God for what you have.

LOOK AT YOURSELF

Have you ever been given money? How quickly did you spend it? Did you think about what you really wanted to buy, or did you just buy the first thing that you saw that was nice? If you work for your money, then you will think about how to spend it, you will remember that you must be wise and that once it is spent it is gone.

PRAYER

Thank you, God. You have given me so much, I have a house to live in, clothes to wear and food to eat. Please help me to be more thankful for what you have already given me. Dear Jesus, please help me to work hard when I have work to do. Help me to remember that if I am lazy I am not pleasing you. Amen.

20 February

READ AND UNDERSTAND

Proverbs 9:1. If you are wise you are hard working. So don't be lazy, work hard.

Proverbs 16:3. In prayer you must give your plans to God, and then you will be able to do what you plan. Always pray to God and ask him to guide you so that you can please Him.

Proverbs 4:26. Plan to do things in a wise way, and whatever you do will turn out right. Learn from the Bible how to do what is right.

LOOK AT YOURSELF

If you were going to go on holiday, would you think about things and plan things before you left? Can you imagine what it would be like if you just left home, did not think about what clothes you would need to bring with you, did not organise to have a place to stay on holiday, did not have any money to put petrol in your car? I don't think it would be a nice holiday. It is better to plan ahead, that is the wise thing to do.

PRAYER

Thank you, God, we can give our plans to you and ask you to help us to know what the right thing to do is. Dear Jesus, please help me to not be lazy. Help me to think about things before I start. Help me to plan and to ask you to guide me. Thank you that I can pray to you and ask you to help me so that I can do things in a way that pleases you. Amen.

21 February

READ AND UNDERSTAND

Proverbs 9:2. If you are wise you will do your work properly. So don't be lazy, work hard and work well.

Proverbs 25:13. It is very nice to have snow or cold water to drink when it is the middle of summer and you are very, very hot. It is just as nice to have someone working for you who is faithful and trustworthy. So make sure you are someone who can be trusted.

Proverbs 2:5a. If you look for wisdom and it is important to you, you will know what it means to fear the Lord.

LOOK AT YOURSELF

Have you ever been asked to do a job for someone? Did you do the best that you could? Did you work hard and work well? Could you be trusted to do your work? If you want to please God, then you will remember how important it is to Him that you are faithful and trustworthy, that you are a hard worker and not lazy.

PRAYER

Thank you, God. You are always faithful. You can always be trusted. Dear Jesus, please help me to be a person who can be trusted. Please help me to do my work well and to do the best that I can. Please help me to live a life that pleases you. Amen.

22 February

READ AND UNDERSTAND

Proverbs 6:10. Lazy people rest when they should be working. You must not be lazy, work when there is work to be done.

Proverbs 26:16. A lazy person will think that he is cleverer than lots of other people who give wise advice and council. He does not listen to what they say; he thinks he knows it all. Don't be a lazy fool, listen to others and remember that you need to learn.

Proverbs 5:7. Listen to what the scripture teaches and don't forget what you learn. Study the Bible and obey what it says.

LOOK AT YOURSELF

Have you ever gone and had a sleep just because you had work to do and you did not want to do it? This is being lazy; a wise person will work when there is work to be done. A lazy person will not listen when he is taught and instructed, he will think that he knows enough and does not need to listen. So when he is told that it is foolish to sleep when there is work to do, a lazy person will not listen, he will just go and sleep and ignore what he has been told.

PRAYER

Thank you, God. You have given us the Bible so that we can learn about what is wise and what is foolish. Dear Jesus, please help me to not be lazy. Help me to do my work when I have work to do. Please forgive me for the times when I have been lazy. Please help me to change. Amen.

23 February

READ AND UNDERSTAND

Proverbs 12:11. A hard-working farmer has lots to eat, but a stupid person will waste time doing things that are useless. So work hard.

Proverbs 23: 33-35. It is terrible to get drunk, a drunk will think that he see things that are not there and his mind thinks up strange things that are not real. He feels dizzy and sick, like someone who is on a ship in the ocean and is sea-sick from all the swaying of strong seas. He will not even know that someone hit him; he will not even feel it. But as soon as he feels the pain of being hit, then he wants another drink so that he won't feel it again. This is foolishness; getting drunk is a dangerous sin.

LOOK AT YOURSELF

Have you ever been on a farm? If you ask a farmer how important it is to do his work at the right time, he will tell you that it is very important. If a farmer does not look after the fields, if he does not do what he is supposed to throughout the year, he will not make any money, he will have nothing to eat. One way that some people waste time when they should be working, is by getting drunk. We are told how foolish and sinful it is to get drunk. You must remember that God is not pleased if you get drunk, it will also waste your time.

PRAYER

Thank you, God. You warn us about how sinful it is to get drunk. Thank you for reminding us about how important it is to do our work when it needs to be done. Dear Jesus, please help me to not waste my time. Please help me to live a life that pleases you. Amen.

24 February

READ AND UNDERSTAND

Proverbs 12:24. Hard work can give you power, being lazy can make you a slave. So don't be lazy, work hard.

Proverbs 18:21. The greatest good and the greatest harm are in the power of the tongue. You must remember that your words will have consequences. Remember to think before you speak. Let your speech bring glory to God.

Proverbs 10:31. Righteous people speak wisdom, but the tongue of the wicked will be cut out. So think before you speak.

LOOK AT YOURSELF

Have you ever thought about being a boss of a company or having your own company? The only way that you will be able to be important in a company is if you work hard. If you want to do well in anything you must work hard. You must also remember that what you say will affect how well you do, if you want to do well you must make sure that what you say is pleasing to God. Someone who is horrible in what he says to people will not be liked; he will not be put in an important position.

PRAYER

Thank you, God. You have told us to be careful of what we say. You have warned us to think before we speak so that we can have speech that is pleasing to you. Dear Jesus, please help me to remember how important it is to think about what I am going to say. Please also help me to not be lazy. Please help me to do my work well. Amen.

71

25 February

READ AND UNDERSTAND

Proverbs 18:9. Being lazy is as bad as destroying things. A bad or unfinished job is similar to something that has been destroyed; both are useless. Don't be lazy, work hard and do your work well.

Proverbs 26:6. Trusting a fool to deliver a message is foolish, it is like cutting off your feet, you are asking for trouble.

LOOK AT YOURSELF

Have you ever started making something and then not finished it? That is being lazy; the things that you have used are now useless. You must finish what you start, then you will be able to use what you have made and you will not be wasting things. Imagine how frustrating it would be if you gave a message to someone and that person was lazy and did not deliver your message. It is always important to do the job properly.

PRAYER

Thank you, God. You are never lazy. You created the world and you made everything so perfectly and wonderfully. Dear Jesus, please help me to learn from you. Help me to always do my best and finish the work that I start. Please help me to do my work for your glory, that you can be pleased. Amen.

WEEK 9

BEING HONEST CAN SAVE YOUR LIFE

The lesson for this week is that being honest can save your life, and being dishonest will destroy you. Truth is very important to God. It is important to God that you do not lie. You must always be honest.

TIME TO REMEMBER

Proverbs 10:9. "The man of integrity walks securely, but he who takes crooked paths will be found out."

26 February

READ AND UNDERSTAND

Proverbs 10:2b. Honesty can save your life. So always be honest.

Proverbs 25:19. Trusting someone who is not trustworthy is like having toothache or a damaged foot. It can bring you trouble and make things difficult for you. So make friends with people who can be trusted, people who love God and hate lies.

LOOK AT YOURSELF

Have you ever asked someone to keep a secret and then they told someone else anyway? It is horrible to have a friend who can't be trusted. You must make sure your friends are people who can be trusted. You must make sure that you are a good friend, and that your friends can trust you.

PRAYER

Thank you, God. You can always be trusted. You never lie. Thank you for warning me about how bad it is to have a friend who can't be trusted. Dear Jesus, please help me to be an honest person. Help me to be someone who can be trusted. Please forgive me for all the times that I have not told the truth; when I have not been honest and trustworthy. Please help me to become more like you. Amen.

27 February

READ AND UNDERSTAND

Proverbs 10:9. Honest people are safe and secure, but the dishonest will be caught. Always obey God and be honest.

Proverbs 22:14. Getting involved in an impure relationship is a trap; it is like falling into a hole that you can't get out of. If you listen to the lies that having a relationship outside of marriage is good, you will be punished. God hates impure relationships, He created marriage and it is good.

LOOK AT YOURSELF

Have you ever heard someone say that marriage is not important? They are lying; God says that the marriage relationship is very special and that it must be kept pure and clean. If a person is dishonest and pretends to be married to someone when he is not, then he will be caught, just like something caught in a trap. Always be honest and live a life that is pleasing to God, and then He will protect you and keep you safe.

PRAYER

Thank you, God. You created marriage and it is good. Thank you that you will protect me and keep me safe if I am honest and live a life that pleases you. Dear Jesus, please help me to always be honest. Help me to please you in everything that I do. Amen.

28 February

READ AND UNDERSTAND

Proverbs 10:29. The Lord protects honest people, but He destroys those who do wrong. So obey God and always be honest.

Proverbs 15:10. If you do what is wrong, you will be punished. You will die if you do not let yourself be corrected. So rather be corrected when you are wrong.

Proverbs 30:33. Just like beating cream makes butter, and hitting someone's nose will make it bleed, so if you make people angry you will cause trouble and fighting. So don't cause people to get angry, you are only asking for trouble.

LOOK AT YOURSELF

Have you ever gotten angry with someone? Did you start fighting and arguing with them because you were cross with them? You need to make sure that you don't get angry with people. It will only cause trouble. God hates anger and fighting. Remember that God will punish people who do not live a life that pleases Him. If you want to please God you must learn when you are corrected and you must always be honest.

PRAYER

Thank you, God. You protect honest people, people who desire to live in a way that pleases you. Dear Jesus, please help me to be someone who is always honest. Please help me to not disobey you. Help me to remember that it is wrong to get angry. Please help me to learn from the way you lived, that I can always be honest, kind, and obedient to the Bible. Amen.

1 March

READ AND UNDERSTAND

Proverbs 11:3. If you are good, you are guided by honesty. People who can't be trusted are destroyed by their own dishonesty. Obey God and always be honest.

Proverbs 12:7. The wicked will be destroyed and will not be remembered, but the families of righteous people will be big and they will be people who are known by others. So obey God and live a righteous life.

LOOK AT YOURSELF

Do you know of a family who are known by a lot of people? Who are liked by people? The only way to have a family like that is by living lives that please God, living righteous lives. People who are not righteous, who are wicked, will be destroyed, their families will not be remembered, they are destroyed by their own wickedness.

PRAYER

Thank you, God. You guide those who are honest. You bless people who live righteous lives. Dear Jesus, please help me to be an honest person. Please help me to live a righteous life, a life that pleases you. Thank you, Jesus, for dying on the cross so that my sins can be forgiven and I can be with you in heaven one day. Amen.

2 March

READ AND UNDERSTAND

Proverbs 11:5. Honesty makes a good person's life easier, but a wicked person will cause their own downfall. Always be honest.

Proverbs 12:14. Your reward depends on what you say and what you do. You will get what you deserve. So obey God and live a righteous life.

Proverbs 31:31. A godly wife will get rewarded for all the work that she does. Boys - you must find a wife who is godly. Girls - you must be women who are godly.

LOOK AT YOURSELF

Have you ever disobeyed a rule and because you disobeyed you had a difficult time? Have you ever lied and because you lied you got into more trouble? It is better to be honest and obedient. Then things will be easier and you will get rewarded in a good way, rather than being rewarded with punishment.

PRAYER

Thank you, God. You reward those who do good and you punish those who don't. Dear Jesus, please help me to be an honest and obedient person. Help me to be careful of what I say and of what I do, so that I can live a life that pleases you, obeying you in everything that I do. Amen.

3 March

READ AND UNDERSTAND

Proverbs 11:6. Righteousness rescues the honest person, but someone who can't be trusted is trapped by their own greed. Always be honest.

Proverbs 18:5. It is wrong to show partiality and say that the guilty person is innocent because he is important, or to say that an innocent person is guilty just because he is poor. Don't show partiality to people, it is a sin and God hates it.

LOOK AT YOURSELF

Have you ever had to choose someone to be in your team and you chose someone because of what you could get? Choosing someone who is rich so that he will maybe give you something or buy you something? God hates it when people show favour to a person just because he is rich, people who are horrible to poor people just because they are poor. Remember that God is always fair and we must learn to be like God.

PRAYER

Thank you, God. You don't show favouritism to people. You give love to people who don't deserve it or earn it. Thank you that you are always fair and honest. Dear Jesus, please help me to be more like you. Please help me to be honest and fair. Please forgive me for the times that I have not lived in the way that I should. Please help me to change. Amen.

4 March

READ AND UNDERSTAND

Proverbs 28:18. Honest people are safe and secure, God will rescue them from harm, but dishonest people will be caught. Always obey God and be honest.

Proverbs 26:24. Some people have hate in their heart and they lie but will talk with nice words to the people that they hate. They are liars; don't believe them. Don't be someone who has hate in your heart.

Proverbs 23:23. The truth is so important that you must use whatever you have to get it, your time, energy and money. You must get wisdom, instruction and understanding.

LOOK AT YOURSELF

This whole week we have looked at honesty. Have you tried to be honest this week? Have you remembered how important truth is? God hates lies and He hates people who have hate in their heart. Today you must think about if there is someone that you hate. God does not want you to hate. You must have love for that person.

PRAYER

Thank you, God. You showed us so much love by sending your son to die for me. Thank you that you are always honest. You cannot lie. Dear Jesus, please forgive me for all my sins. Please help me to stop sinning. Please help me to be more like you. Help me to be an honest person. Amen.

WEEK 10

PURITY AND MARRIAGE

This week we will look at Proverbs 6:24-31, a passage that talks about the foolishness of having impure relationships. It teaches about how ungodly relationships outside marriage are sinful and destructive. The marriage relationship was created by God and it is very good, it must be kept pure.

TIME TO REMEMBER

This verse reminds us that there are consequences to sin. We cannot get away from the consequences. Proverbs 6:28. "Can a man walk on hot coals without his feet being scorched?"

5 March

READ AND UNDERSTAND

Proverbs 6:24. The Bible will help you stay away from bad relationships. The Bible will teach you about marriage, it is a good relationship.

Proverbs 1:4b. The Proverbs will help the young to have discernment. They show you the difference between what is true and false as well as what is good and evil.

LOOK AT YOURSELF

People who get involved with bad and impure relationships will talk about it as such a nice thing. You must not believe them. The Bible will help you to understand how important marriage is and how horrible it is to live with someone and act as if you are married when you are not. God hates it, He has created the marriage relationship and it must be kept pure.

PRAYER

Thank you, God. You created marriage and it is good. Thank you that the Bible can teach me to understand what is good and what is evil. Dear Jesus, please help me to remember what you have taught me. Please help me to understand what is good and what is evil. Amen.

6 March

READ AND UNDERSTAND

Proverbs 6:25. You must have eyes for your marriage partner only. Don't be tempted by other people.

Proverbs 15:11. Since God sees the dead in their graves, surely He can see living people's hearts. God knows all your thoughts and desires; you cannot hide anything from Him.

Proverbs 4:15. Turn away from wickedness and evil; avoid the temptations to do evil. You must always obey God and not sin.

LOOK AT YOURSELF

Have you ever though about doing something even though you knew it was wrong? God knows what you are thinking. You must not think about evil things, you must try and stay as far away from evil as possible. In your life you will be tempted to sin, you will see things or think about things that seem nice, but you must remember how much God hates sin. Even if sin looks nice, you must remember that sin will get punished.

PRAYER

Thank you, God. You remind me how important it is to stay away from sin. You know everything and you know what I am thinking. Dear Jesus, please help me to have thoughts that are pleasing to you. Please help me to remember how important it is to stay away from sin. Please help me to stop sinning and to live a life that pleases you. Amen.

7 March

READ AND UNDERSTAND

Proverbs 6:26. Relationships outside of marriage will destroy you. The marriage relationship is important and you must keep it pure.

Proverbs 30:32. If you have been foolish by being proud or planning evil, don't brag about it, cover your mouth with your hand and stop. So don't be proud or plan to do evil things.

Proverbs 14:3. The speech of a proud fool will result in punishment. Wise people's words protect them. Don't be proud; speak with humility.

LOOK AT YOURSELF

Do you know how much God hates sin? Do you know that there are consequences if you sin? God hates sin so much, He is a holy God and He cannot be in the presence of sin. God will punish sin. One way people are punished for their sin is through the consequences. Sometimes things will happen to you because of your sin. The consequences of having relationships outside of marriage are terrible; those kinds of relationships will destroy you. Remember that it is never good to sin; it will always bring consequences and punishment.

PRAYER

Thank you, God. You show us in the Bible how holy you are. You are pure and perfect and you cannot be in the presence of sin. Dear Jesus, please help me to remember how bad it is to sin against you. Please help me to live a life that pleases you. Amen.

8 March

READ AND UNDERSTAND

Proverbs 6:27. You can't get away with sin. It is like holding fire against you; it will burn your clothes. Sin will always have consequences, don't think it won't.

Proverbs 4:3-4a. Remember your parents teaching. Honour and obey your parents.

Proverbs 25:3. Leaders will not tell the people everything; there are things that the leader thinks that nobody knows. Remember that God knows everything, even the leader's heart.

LOOK AT YOURSELF

Have you ever done something wrong and thought that no one knew about it, that no one would find out? Remember that God knows everything. You cannot hide your sin from God. Sin will have consequences .Things will happen because of your sin. Listen to your parents teaching, they will help you to understand what sin is, they will help you to stay away from sin.

PRAYER

Thank you, God. You gave me parents, help me to listen when they teach me, help me to honour and obey them. Thank you that you know everything, it is good that I cannot hide sin. Dear Jesus, please help me to remember that you know if I sin. Help me to hate sin and to stop sinning. Help me to live a life that pleases you. Amen.

9 March

READ AND UNDERSTAND

Proverbs 6:28. You can't get away with sin. It is like walking on hot coals, you will burn your feet. Sin will always have consequences, don't think it won't.

Proverbs 1:12. The wicked say they will hide their sin, so it is safe to join them. Don't believe them. You can never hide your sin from God.

Proverbs 2:12a. Wisdom will stop you from doing the wrong thing. So learn from the Bible and it will help you to do what is right.

LOOK AT YOURSELF

Has anyone ever asked you to do something with them that was wrong? Did they tell you that you would not get caught, that it is safe to sin? Never believe that lie. God knows everything and you can't hide your sin from Him. Sin will have consequences, you will not be able to get away from them. So remember not to sin. Study the Bible and ask God to give you wisdom so that you can know what sin is and so that you can stop sinning.

PRAYER

Thank you, God. You gave us the Bible so that we can become wise and know what pleases you and what you hate. Dear Jesus, please help me to stop sinning. Please help me to remember that there are consequences to sin and I cannot hide my sin. Thank you that you died on the cross so that my sins can be forgiven. Amen.

10 March

READ AND UNDERSTAND

Proverbs 6:29. If you have a relationship outside of marriage it will bring punishment. The marriage relationship is special and must be kept pure.

Proverbs 22:3. Wise people are careful to stay away from evil and sin, when they see evil they go the other way and hide from it. But fools are careless and don't try to avoid evil or stop sinning, they will be punished for that. So be wise, stay away from evil and all sinful things.

LOOK AT YOURSELF

Again today we see that sin will be punished. If you are wise you will stay away from sin. You will stay away from relationships outside of marriage. You must remember how important marriage is between a man and a woman. Nobody must break that marriage up. Marriage is special and it is for that man and woman for the rest of their lives.

PRAYER

Thank you, God. You warn me to stay away from sin. Thank you for teaching me in the Bible about sin so that I can stop sinning, so that I can stay away from sin. Dear Jesus, please help me to remember how important marriage is. Help me to remember how important it is to stay away from sin. Please help me to stop sinning. Please help me to live a life that pleases you. Amen.

11 March

READ AND UNDERSTAND

Proverbs 6:30-31. People might feel sorry for a thief who steals for food, but if he is caught he must repay what he has stolen. People will not feel sorry for someone who steals someone else's marriage partner. The punishment will be great.

Proverbs 11:29a. The person who brings trouble on their family will have nothing in the end. God commands us to love our neighbour, which means love everyone.

LOOK AT YOURSELF

We have seen this week how sin will have consequences and sin will be punished. Remember that there are consequences for all sin, but the consequences for breaking up a marriage are much worse. It is terrible to destroy marriage. If you love other people then you will know how important their marriage is and if you are married you will know how important your marriage is.

PRAYER

Thank you, God, for teaching me about how important marriage is. Dear Jesus, please help me to remember what I have learnt this week. Please help me to live a life that pleases you and help me to remember that I cannot hide my sin. Amen.

WEEK 11

GOD BLESSES THE RIGHTEOUS

This week we will learn about the righteous. Righteous people are those who live lives that are pleasing to God. Righteous people will get life while wicked people will get death. This week we will see all that the righteous will get, how secure they are (like a strong tree).

TIME TO REMEMBER

Proverbs 11:19. "The truly righteous man attains life; but he who pursues evil goes to his death."

12 March

READ AND UNDERSTAND

Proverbs 11:19. If you want to do what is right you will live, but anyone who wants to do what is wrong will die. Obey God and do what is right.

Proverbs 25:24. It is better to live in a small and cramped corner, where there is peace and quiet, than to live in a big house with a wife who wants to argue and fight. Women should not be quarrelsome; you must not look for things to fight about.

LOOK AT YOURSELF

Do you complain and moan about things? Do you make comments to people, looking for something to fight with them about? It is a sin to be a quarrelsome and argumentative person. God wants you to be a person who has speech that is godly; speech that is pleasing to God and kind to others. You must think about your speech. You must make sure that you are not someone who likes to fight and argue.

PRAYER

Thank you, God. You sent Jesus to die for my sins. Thank you that I can be forgiven for the times that I have argued and fought. Dear Jesus, please help me to live a life that pleases you. Please help me to have speech that is pleasing to you. Help me not to fight and argue. Thank you that my sins can be forgiven and that Christians can live with you in heaven one day. Amen.

13 March

READ AND UNDERSTAND

Proverbs 11:30. The fruit of the righteous is a tree of life; they will attract others to righteousness. So obey God and be an example to other people.

Proverbs 27:23-24. Most of the Israelites were farmers. Their flocks were very important. God wants us to look after what we have, to know that He has given them to us. When you farm with animals, if you look after them and care for them, they will have babies and you will get more and more animals. It is not the same with money. Once you spend money it is gone. So be careful to look after what you have.

LOOK AT YOURSELF

Do you look after the toys and books and clothes that you have? God has given everything you have to you and He wants you to look after it. If you are given money, do you spend it all very quickly? Or do you take time to think about what to do with it? Are you wise with your money? God wants you to look after what you have.

PRAYER

Thank you, God, for everything that you have given to me. I have so much and I know that I must look after it. Dear Jesus, please help me to be more thankful for everything that I have. Please help me to look after what you have given to me, including any money that I get. Please help me to be wise with the money I get; help me to please you in what I do with it. Help me to please you in everything that I do. Amen.

14 March

READ AND UNDERSTAND

Proverbs 12:3. Wickedness does not give security. If you are righteous you are like a tree with a strong root, it cannot be moved. So obey God and live a righteous life.

Proverbs 16:32b. It is better to win control over yourself than over whole cities.

Proverbs 26:8. If you were going to throw a stone with a sling, you would not tie the stone into the sling; if you did it might hurt you. It is the same with a fool, you must not praise a fool; it could damage your reputation.

LOOK AT YOURSELF

Have you ever gotten cross or said something horrible to someone and you knew that it was wrong? If you have self-control you will be able to stop yourself doing something that is wrong. Having self-control means that you will think before you say something; you will make sure that it is the best and right thing to say. It means that you will not get angry and upset if someone is horrible to you; but you will pray to God and ask Him to help you to show love to others and not evil. Having self-control will help you to stop sinning in so many ways.

PRAYER

Thank you, God. You give security to Christians, you will look after your children. Dear Jesus, please help me to not be wicked. Please help me to be self-controlled. Help me to live a life that pleases you and to stop sinning. Please forgive me for all the times that I have not had self-control. Please help me to change. Amen.

15 March

READ AND UNDERSTAND

Proverbs 12:12b. The righteous are like a plant with a strong root that causes it to grow and bear fruit. Obey God and you will live a righteous life.

Proverbs 20:24. God has determined the road we will walk and the steps we will take. We do not know what will happen in our lives, so we must live by faith, trusting in God to direct us.

LOOK AT YOURSELF

Do you ever worry about things? God says that we must not worry, we must trust in Him. God is in control of all things and He will look after the righteous. You must ask God to forgive you of your sin and ask Him to help you to live a life that pleases Him. If you are a Christian then God will look after you. You don't have to worry about anything.

PRAYER

Thank you, God. You help Christians to become more righteous. You can help me to live a life that pleases you. Dear Jesus, please help me to stop sinning. Please help me to trust in you and not worry about things. Thank you that you are in control of everything and that I can trust in you. Amen.

16 March

READ AND UNDERSTAND

Proverbs 12:28. Righteousness is the road to life; wickedness is the road to death. So obey God and live a righteous life.

Proverbs 14:33. Wise people will not show off their wisdom, but the fool talks about the little knowledge that he has. Don't be proud and talk about everything that you know.

LOOK AT YOURSELF

Do you ever want to tell people how much you know so that they will say nice things about you? You must remember that all the wisdom and understanding that you can have is given to you by God. You must not be proud and want people to say nice things about you. You must be humble and make sure that the nice things are said about God. He is the one who gives wisdom and understanding; we must thank Him for what He has given to us.

PRAYER

Thank you, God. You are the source of wisdom and you will give me wisdom if I ask for it and if I study the Bible and obey what it says. Dear Jesus, please help me not to be proud. Help me to remember that everything that I have is from you and that all the nice things that can be said must be said about you. Help me to obey you and to live a life that pleases you. Amen.

17 March

READ AND UNDERSTAND

Proverbs 16:31. Long life is the reward of the righteous, grey hair is a glorious crown.

Proverbs 15:2. When wise people speak, they make knowledge attractive, but fools only speak about foolish things. Think about what you say.

Proverbs 22:10. If a person who mocks other people is thrown out, then there will be no more arguments, quarrelling, or calling of names. By getting rid of a troublemaker, the trouble will stop. So don't mock other people, that only causes fighting and trouble.

LOOK AT YOURSELF

Someone who has been a Christian for a long time has learnt a lot and can be able to show you how attractive wisdom is. We must be thankful for the people who are godly; who can teach us about God and about how to live in a way that pleases Him. You must learn how to have speech that is pleasing to God. If you are wise and godly you will have wise speech; you will not be someone who argues and fights and says horrible things about other people. Horrible speech only causes trouble.

PRAYER

Thank you, God, for all the older people in my life who can teach me more about you and about becoming a person who lives a life that is pleasing to you. Dear Jesus, please help me to have speech that is wise. Please help me not to be someone who fights and argues and says horrible things. Please help me to have speech that is kind and gentle and tells people about you. Amen.

18 March

READ AND UNDERSTAND

Proverbs 21:21. If you try to live a godly life, being kind to others, then God will give you life, godliness and respect. If we trust in God and desire to glorify and please him, He will give us the Holy Spirit who will help us to become godly.

Proverbs 20:29. The young are admired for their physical strength; the older are admired for their wisdom, shown by their grey hair. Remember that whatever age we must use what we have to serve God and bring glory to Him.

LOOK AT YOURSELF

Do you try and live a life that glorifies and pleases God? Do you want to serve God, even if you are young? Everyone is called to glorify God and to serve Him. It is the most important thing you can do. Whatever you do, you must do it for God. If you are a Christian you have the Holy Spirit in you who will help you to live a godly life. He will help you to know what is sin and then He can give you the strength to stop sinning.

PRAYER

Thank you, God, that you give the Holy Spirit to Christians to help us live lives that are pleasing to you. Thank you that Christians will be with you in heaven one day. Dear Jesus, please help me to obey you in everything that I do. Please help me to live a life that glorifies you. Please forgive me for the times that I have not obeyed you, please help me to change. Amen.

WEEK 12
WISDOM AND FAMILY LIFE

This week we are going to look at how important it is for you to listen to your parents and to learn from them. Also how important it is that you obey what they teach you.

TIME TO REMEMBER

Proverbs 6:20. "My son, keep your father's commands and do not forsake your mother's teaching."

19 March

READ AND UNDERSTAND

Proverbs 1:3a. To receive instruction is wise behaviour. You must listen when you are taught and obey those who teach you.

Proverbs 25:16-17. These verses are teaching us that there can be too much of a good thing. Just like eating too much honey can make you sick, so if you visit your friends too often, they might get tired of you and even hate you.

LOOK AT YOURSELF

Do you have a friend who you like visiting? Have you ever asked to go and visit and your parents have said no. You must listen to your parents. They will help you to make sure you do not visit too often. You don't want your friend to get tired of having you over. Remember to obey your parents.

PRAYER

Thank you, God. You gave me parents to instruct me and help me. Dear Jesus, please help me to listen to my parents, help me to always honour and obey them. Please forgive me for times that I have not listened and obeyed. Please help me to change. Amen.

20 March

READ AND UNDERSTAND

Proverbs 2:1a. Listen to the instruction of your parents. Remember you must honour and obey them.

Proverbs 22:15. Children are all foolish and will sin if they are not corrected and disciplines. Children will speak and act foolishly, not obeying God's commands and sinning against Him. If parents correct their children and discipline them, they will be teaching the child how to live and not to sin. It will take the foolishness away and make them wise.

LOOK AT YOURSELF

Have your parents ever given you a hiding? Did you get cross with them for that? God says that it is good if parents discipline their children. It will help you to become wise. Your parents can teach you and help you to live a life that pleases God. It pleases God if you honour and obey your parents.

PRAYER

Thank you, God, for my parents. Dear Jesus, please help me to learn when I am disciplined. Help me to obey my parents and to please you in the way that I live. Thank you that you died on the cross so that my sins can be forgiven. Please help me to stop sinning. Amen.

21 March

READ AND UNDERSTAND

Proverbs 4:1. Listen to the instruction of your father, pay attention so that you can understand. Remember the command to honour and obey your parents.

Proverbs 22:1. Having a good reputation because you have a good character is much more important than having lots of money and things. Having God pleased with you is far more important than having silver or gold.

LOOK AT YOURSELF

Is money important to you? Is it important to you that you have a lot of things? God says that the most important thing to have is a good character. You must be someone who lives a righteous life, pleasing God in everything that you do. You must listen when your parents teach you, they will help you to know how to live, and they will help you to know what is pleasing to God. It is pleasing to God when you listen to your parents and obey them.

PRAYER

Thank you, God, for my parents. Thank you that I can learn from my parents how to have a good character. Dear Jesus, please help me to listen and obey my parents. Help me to become more like you. Help me to remember what is important to you, that I live a life that pleases you. Amen.

22 March

READ AND UNDERSTAND

Proverbs 4:20. Listen and pay attention to your parents teaching. Remember the command to honour and obey your parents.

Proverbs 4:24. Never say anything that isn't true. Have nothing to do with lies. Always tell the truth.

Proverbs 16:11. God wants people to be honest and fair. So you must not cheat and lie.

LOOK AT YOURSELF

Have you ever had to share something out, like sweets or biscuits? Did you share evenly and give everyone the same, or did you give yourself an extra one or two? God hates it when people cheat. God wants you to always be honest and fair. You must remember how important it is to God. God also wants you to be a child who listens to your parents. You must pay attention when your parents teach you.

PRAYER

Thank you, God. You are always honest and you are always fair. Thank you for my parents, please help me to listen and obey them. Dear Jesus, please forgive me for all the times I have not listened and obeyed, for the times when I have not been honest or fair. Please help me to change. Amen.

23 March

READ AND UNDERSTAND

Proverbs 6:20. Listen and remember the commandments and laws that your father and mother give you. Remember the command to honour and obey your parents.

Proverbs 24:21-22. You must fear the Lord and you must respect the leaders that He has placed above you. You must have nothing to do with people who rebel against God and leaders. Those people will have a sudden disaster. Who knows what punishment they will have from God and the leaders? So you must not be a rebel, you must submit to God and your leaders.

LOOK AT YOURSELF

Who are the leaders in your life? Your parents are the first leaders that God has put over you. You must remember to listen to them when they teach you, you must respect them and you must obey them. God has made your parents your leaders and He wants you to honour them, you must never rebel against your parents.

PRAYER

Thank you, God, for my parents. Thank you that they are my leaders and that they teach me. Dear Jesus, please help me to listen when my parents talk to me, help me to remember what they say. Please help me to show respect to them and to honour and obey them. Amen.

24 March

READ AND UNDERSTAND

Proverbs 23:22. You must listen to the instruction that your parents have given you, they gave you life. Be wise and respect your parents when they are old. Remember that God commands you to honour and obey your parents.

Proverbs 28:24. People who steal from their parents and then say that there is nothing wrong with it are sinning in a terrible way. It is wicked to steal from your parents; you must honour and respect them.

LOOK AT YOURSELF

Have you ever taken something from your parents without asking? Have you ever seen some of their money fall out of their pocket and taken it for yourself? It is a terrible thing to steal from your parents. You must respect them; you must remember that they gave you life. Another way you can show them respect is when they teach and instruct you, you must listen to what they say, you must remember what they have taught you and you must obey them.

PRAYER

Thank you, God, for my parents. Dear Jesus, please help me to respect my parents. Help me to honour and obey them and to listen when they teach me. Please help me to remember how horrible it is to steal from my parents and help me to always be honest. Amen.

25 March

READ AND UNDERSTAND

Proverbs 23:26. You must think about what your parents teach you, you must listen and obey their instruction so that you will be able to live a life that glorifies God. When you see someone who is living a godly life, you must want to be like them.

Proverbs 17:11. A rebellious person only looks for evil; he will be punished for his sin. So don't be rebellious, stay away from evil.

Proverbs 4:2. Listen to true and good teaching, do not forget instruction. If you do this you will become wise.

LOOK AT YOURSELF

This week you have seen how important it is to listen and obey your parents. If you are not obedient and are rebellious, you will be punished. So listen to what the Bible has taught you, listen to what your parents teach you, and do not forget what you have learnt.

PRAYER

Thank you, God. You have taught me about how important it is to honour and obey my parents. How important it is for me to listen to them and remember what they have taught me. Dear Jesus, please help me to remember. Help me to live a life that pleases you. Amen.

WEEK 13

THE IMPORTANCE OF WISDOM

This week we are going to study through Proverbs 3:13-18. These verses are about the importance of wisdom. Wisdom is mentioned often in Proverbs because it is so important.

TIME TO REMEMBER

Proverbs 3:13. "Blessed is the man who finds wisdom, the man who gains understanding."

26 March

READ AND UNDERSTAND

Proverbs 3:13. It is a blessing to have wisdom and understanding. So learn what the Bible teaches and become wise.

Proverbs 30:24-28. There are four animals that are small but wise. Ants, they are small and weak, but they store up their food in the summer so they have food in the winter. Rock-badgers are like rabbits, they are too weak to protect themselves but they make their homes in caves up on rocky cliffs. Locusts, which don't seem to have a king are organised and fly together like a strong army. Insects like spiders or lizards, which are so small that you could catch them in your hands, are able to make their homes in a king's palace. So you must learn from these animals, work hard, be organized and plan, wisdom can do much more than just being strong.

LOOK AT YOURSELF

Do you work hard? Do you organise and plan what you need to do? Do you always know what to do? If you study the Bible, you will be able to become wise. If you are wise you will be able to do a lot, even if you are not very big or strong. So ask God to give you wisdom.

PRAYER

Thank you, God, for giving us the Bible and teaching us about how important wisdom is. Dear Jesus, please help me to become wise. Please help me to study from the Bible so that I can learn about you and learn about what pleases you. Amen.

27 March

READ AND UNDERSTAND

Proverbs 3:14. Wisdom is more precious than silver or gold. So you must learn from the Bible and become wise.

Proverbs 20:15. Speech that is wise, with knowledge and said at the right time is more precious and important than gold or expensive jewels. Remember to think before you speak. Your speech must bring glory to God.

LOOK AT YOURSELF

Do you know someone who has expensive jewellery? Do you think people like having expensive things? The most important, precious and expensive thing to have is wisdom. Wisdom will help you in knowing what to say and when to say it. You must think before you speak and ask God to give you the wisdom to know what to say.

PRAYER

Thank you, God. You have given us the most important thing, the wisdom that we can learn from you in the Bible. Dear Jesus, please help me to learn from the Bible and become wise. Help me to have wise speech. Help me to think before I speak so that I can have speech that is pleasing to you. Amen.

28 March

READ AND UNDERSTAND

Proverbs 3:15. Wisdom is more precious than jewels, nothing you could want can compare with it. So you must learn from the Bible and become wise.

Proverbs 10:23. It is foolish to enjoy doing wrong. Wise people enjoy understanding. So don't be foolish, always obey God and do what is right.

Proverbs 12:20b. Joy comes to those who desire and work for other people's peace. God commands us to love our neighbour; if we obey we will have joy.

LOOK AT YOURSELF

Have you ever enjoyed doing something that you knew was wrong? It is very foolish to do that. If you are wise you will enjoy doing things for other people, you will want to be wise and know how to live a life that pleases God. Nothing can compare to being wise, it is the best thing to have.

PRAYER

Thank you, God. You have given us the Bible so that we can learn and become wise. Dear Jesus, please help me to be wise. Help me to only want to do what is right and pleasing to you. Help me to love other people and do good things for them. Please forgive me for all the times that I have done what is wrong and sinned against you. Help me to stop sinning and live a righteous life. Amen.

29 March

READ AND UNDERSTAND

Proverbs 3:16. Wisdom brings long life, riches and honour. So learn from the Bible and become wise.

Proverbs 2:18-19. An impure relationship leads to death. It destroys what God created marriage for.

Proverbs 1:5a. The Proverbs will help a wise man to become wiser. So even if you know the Proverbs, you must keep reading them and they will teach you more.

LOOK AT YOURSELF

Do you think that you know the Bible? Nobody can ever know everything that the Bible has to teach. You will always be able to become wiser the more you study the Bible. The benefits of having wisdom are so good; you should remember how good it is to be wise. You must also remember how bad it is to have relationships outside of marriage. They are not good at all; they will only lead to death.

PRAYER

Thank you, God. You gave us the Bible and we can always learn more from it. Thank you that you know everything and that you never need to learn. Thank you that we can learn from you. Dear Jesus, please help me to always want to learn more and become wiser. Please help me to become wise. Please also help me to live a life that pleases you. Amen.

30 March

READ AND UNDERSTAND

Proverbs 3:17. Wisdom can make your life pleasant and it will bring peace. So learn from the Bible and become wise.

Proverbs 12:16. When foolish people get upset, they quickly let it be known. Wise people will ignore an insult. Don't get upset, even if someone is horrible to you. Just ignore it.

Proverbs 14:29. If you stay calm, you are wise. If you get angry quickly, you show how foolish you are. So don't get angry, stay calm.

LOOK AT YOURSELF

Have you ever gotten upset when someone said something to you, or did something to you? It is very foolish to get upset and angry. If you are wise, you will stay calm and then you won't get into so many fights, you will be able to enjoy peace with other people. You must show love to others, you must always be kind and gently, not angry and upset.

PRAYER

Thank you, God. You show us how foolish it is to get angry and upset. Dear Jesus, please help me to be wise. Help me to remember to stay calm and not get upset. Please forgive me for the times that I have gotten upset and angry, please help me to change. Please help me to live a life that pleases you. Amen.

31 March

READ AND UNDERSTAND

Proverbs 3:18. Wisdom brings life and happiness. So learn from the Bible and become wise.

Proverbs 28:25. Someone who is selfish and who thinks that he is the most important person will fight with other people and will cause trouble to get what they want. It is much better to trust in the Lord, and then you will do well and have all that you need. So don't be greedy for things, don't think that you are so important. Trust in God and do what is right.

LOOK AT YOURSELF

Have you ever fought with your brother or sister so that you could get what you wanted? It is very selfish to do that. God wants you to show love to others, He wants you to think of other people as more important than you. You must not be selfish and think that you deserve everything. You must trust in God and ask God for the things that you want, but you must remember how much He has already given you. Having things is not most important; it is much better to be wise and loving and to live a life that pleases God.

PRAYER

Thank you, God, for all the things that you have given me. Thank you that I have so much. Dear Jesus, please help me to not be selfish. Help me to not always want things for myself. Please help me to not fight with anyone so that I can get what I want. Help me to remember that it is not pleasing to you if I do that. Help me to have wisdom and to live a life that pleases you. Amen.

1 April

READ AND UNDERSTAND

Proverbs 2:11. Wisdom and understanding will watch over you. So learn from the Bible so that you have wisdom and understanding.

Proverbs 3:19. With wisdom and understanding, God created the heavens and the earth. God is the source of wisdom and understanding and we must go to Him to get them.

LOOK AT YOURSELF

Have you ever looked into the sky on a clear night and looked at how many stars there are? Have you ever looked around you at all the plants and animals that God has made; how perfectly every little flower is formed? God created everything, when we look around us we see how wonderful and wise God is. If we learn from the Bible and ask God to give us wisdom, we will be able to get wisdom. We will never be able to be as wise as God though. God is all wise, but we will always need to learn.

PRAYER

Thank you, God. You are so wise; I can see how wonderfully you made the heavens and the earth. Thank you that you will give me wisdom if I ask for it and if I study the Bible that you have given to me to learn from. Dear Jesus, please give me wisdom as I read and study the Bible. Help me to learn more about you so that I can praise you more and know more about how wonderful you are. Amen.

WEEK 14

DON'T BE FOOLISH

This week we are going to see how foolish people hate wisdom. They hate knowledge and refuse to learn.

TIME TO REMEMBER

Proverbs 17:16. "Of what use is money in the hand of a fool, since he has no desire to get wisdom?"

2 April

READ AND UNDERSTAND

Proverbs 1:7b. Fools think wisdom is not needed and refuse to learn. They are stupid because everyone needs to learn.

Proverbs 15:14. The mind of wise people looks for knowledge. They will get knowledge. Fools don't care about their mind; they only want to enjoy feelings. All they will get is foolishness.

LOOK AT YOURSELF

Have you ever thought that you did not have to learn? That you were wise enough and did not need to get any more wisdom? That is being a fool. A fool does not enjoy learning, but someone who is wise will love to learn more about God and what pleases Him. Don't think that your mind is not important, it is very important.

PRAYER

Thank you, God. You have told me that it is foolish to hate knowledge and wisdom. You have warned me that I must not be a fool but that I must be wise. Dear Jesus, please help me to remember how important it is to learn. Please help me to not be a fool. Amen.

3 April

READ AND UNDERSTAND

Proverbs 1:22c. Fools hate knowledge. So you must not be foolish, learn as much as you can.

Proverbs 21:20. A wise person stores up food and is prepared for winter. But a foolish person eats all he has; when winter comes he has nothing. Plan ahead and don't spend or use all that you have.

Proverbs 31:27. A godly wife looks after her family and she does not waste time. Boys - find a godly wife. Girls - be women who are godly.

LOOK AT YOURSELF

Have you ever gone on a long trip where your parents gave you sweets and cool drink for the trip? Did you eat and drink everything up at the start of the trip and then had nothing left for the rest of the long trip? Or did you eat and drink just a little and keep some for later when you were hungry and thirsty? God says that we should not be foolish and eat everything up when we have it, just to enjoy it now. We should instead be wise. We should plan ahead and keep some for later. Another way that you can plan ahead is by using your time properly; it is foolish to waste time.

PRAYER

Thank you, God. You tell me how important it is to plan ahead and be wise. Dear Jesus, please help me to plan ahead and save things for later. Please also help me to not waste time. Help me to use my time well and to please you in everything that I do. Amen.

4 April

READ AND UNDERSTAND

Proverbs 5:13. The fool will not listen to teachers and does not pay attention when instructed. Don't be foolish, pay attention when you are being taught.

Proverbs 4:21. Remember your parents teaching and obey it. Remember the command to honour and obey your parents.

Proverbs 28:9. If you don't listen to God's rules and you refuse to obey God, then if you pray to God He will not answer your prayer, He hates your prayer because you hate His law. So listen to God's word and obey Him.

LOOK AT YOURSELF

Have you ever not wanted to listen to your parents? Did you concentrate and pay attention to what they were saying or did you think that it was not important and that you did not have to listen? God says that it is foolish not to listen and pay attention when you are taught. It is terrible to be a fool. You should want God to listen to your prayers, and if you do then you will obey God and you will listen when you are taught. Your parents can help you to know what pleases God and they can help you to obey God.

PRAYER

Thank you, God, for my parents. Thank you that they can teach me about you and help me to live a life that pleases you. Dear Jesus, please help me to listen carefully when I am taught. Please help me to listen and obey my parents. Please forgive me for the times that I have not obeyed you. Please help me to change. Amen.

5 April

READ AND UNDERSTAND

Proverbs 9:16. If you don't understand things, you must not be foolish, get wisdom. Learn form the Bible and become wise.

Proverbs 27:25-27. Most Israelites were farmers and their flocks were very important. God provided for them in nature. The flocks would eat the grass on the fields and then the Lord would cause more grass to grow. If their animals were fed, it meant that they had clothing from the wool of the sheep. They had money if they sold any of their animals, they would also have enough milk from the goats for their whole family. So God provided for them, but He also told them to look after what He had given them. We must also look after all that God has given us.

LOOK AT YOURSELF

Have you ever had something that you did not look after and so it got broken and you could not use it anymore? It is important that you look after what you have. God has given you so many things and you need to remember that He wants you to look after what He has given you. You must not be foolish and think that it is not important. You must learn from the Bible and you must obey what you read. You can ask God to give you wisdom as you read and He will help you to understand.

PRAYER

Thank you, God, for the Bible. Thank you that it teaches me about how I must live and that I must look after what I have. Thank you so much for all the things that you have given me. Dear Jesus, please help me to remember to be wise and to look after what you have given to me. Amen.

6 April

READ AND UNDERSTAND

Proverbs 17:16. It is a waste of money to try and educate a fool because he does not want to learn and become wise. Don't be a fool. Love wisdom and understanding.

Proverbs 10:14. The wise get all the knowledge they can. When a fool talks you know that trouble is coming. So be wise and think before you speak.

Proverbs 9:5. People without wisdom must get wisdom and get all the good things that wisdom brings. They must learn from the Bible and become wise.

LOOK AT YOURSELF

Have your parents spent money buying things for you to help you to learn? Maybe they have bought you books and maybe they pay for you to go to school or they pay for you to do school work at home? Do you appreciate all the time and money that they have spent? Do you learn as much as you can? You must not be a fool and waste your parent's time and money. You must love wisdom; you must learn and become wise so that you can live a life that pleases God.

PRAYER

Thank you, God, for my parents; they have spent time and money in helping me to become wise. Dear Jesus, please help me to love learning. Help me to not be a fool. Please help me to learn more about you every day so that I can please you in everything that I do. Amen.

7 April

READ AND UNDERSTAND

Proverbs 26:9. If a drunk man got something sharp in his hand he could hurt himself and those around him, he would not be able to control it or know what to do with it. It is the same when a fool talks about the Proverbs. The fool does not know what to do with them, he does not obey them and so if a fool talks about the Proverbs, he is bringing more judgement on himself if he does not obey them. He will also be a bad example to others.

LOOK AT YOURSELF

Do you obey what you read in the Bible? You must read the Bible and obey what you learn. You are a fool if you do not listen and obey what you learn. You must be a good example to other people. You should show people how they should live by being a good example of a person who obeys God and lives a life that pleases Him.

PRAYER

Thank you, God, for the Bible. Dear Jesus, please help me to obey what I learn; I don't want to be a fool. Help me to be a good example to people. Help me to live a life that pleases you. Thank you that you died on the cross so that I can be forgiven for the times that I have not obeyed you. Please forgive me and help me to change. Amen.

8 April

READ AND UNDERSTAND

Proverbs 29:9. If a wise person is trying to talk to a fool and discuss something with him, the fool will either get angry or he will laugh at the wise person. They will not be able to agree.

Proverbs 28:15. A wicked leader is as dangerous to poor people as a lion or bear who attacks them. Don't be horrible to poor people, God commands us to be kind and show love.

Proverbs 16:10. God gives rulers authority, so they must not be unrighteous.

LOOK AT YOURSELF

Have you ever had to be a leader of a group? God has a high standard for leaders. He gives leaders their authority and they are accountable to God, they must rule in a fair and just way, they must be righteous, living a life that pleases Him. Everything that a leader does must be the way God wants. This week we have seen how important it is to be wise and not foolish. Leaders must especially make sure they are not foolish but are wise in everything that they do.

PRAYER

Thank you, God. You have given me the Bible so that I can learn about how to become wise and not be foolish. Dear Jesus, please help me to remember how important it is to learn and become wise. Please will you give me wisdom, I want to know more about you and I want to know more about what pleases you. Amen.

WEEK 15

MARRIAGE AND PURITY

This week we are going to study Proverbs 31:10-16. These verses tell us about a godly wife. Now all the girls must learn this week about what kind of women they must be. But the boys must also pay attention, they must learn about what a godly wife is like so that they will know what kind of a woman they must marry.

TIME TO REMEMBER

Proverbs 31:10. "A wife of noble character who can find? She is worth far more than rubies."

9 April

READ AND UNDERSTAND

Proverbs 31:10. It is hard to find an excellent wife; she is a lot more valuable than expensive jewels. Boys - you must find a wife who is godly. Girls - you must be women who are godly.

Proverbs 27:12. Wise people are careful to stay away from evil and sin, when they see evil they go the other way and hide from it. But fools are careless and don't try to avoid evil or stop sinning, they will be punished for that. So be wise, stay away from evil and all sinful things.

LOOK AT YOURSELF

Do you know what it means to be godly? It means that you live in a way that God would, you live a life that pleases Him, obeying Him in everything that He has said in the Bible. If you want to be godly and please God, then you must remember to stay far away from sin. When you see sin in your life, you must stop sinning and do what is right.

PRAYER

Thank you, God. You have told me in the Bible how to be godly. Dear Jesus, please help me to obey the Bible and live a life that pleases you. Help me to run away from evil and sin. Please forgive me for the times that I have sinned. Please help me to change. Amen.

10 April

READ AND UNDERSTAND

Proverbs 31:11. A husband can trust a godly wife; she will add to his wealth and not take from it. Boys - you must find a wife who is godly. Girls - you must be women who are godly.

Proverbs 18:6. A fool's lips will start an argument, his mouth will cause a fight and he will get hit for what he says. Don't be a fool. Don't start arguments.

Proverbs 10:32. Righteous people know the kind thing to say, but the wicked are always saying things that hurt. Be kind to others in what you say.

LOOK AT YOURSELF

Have you ever said something that hurt someone else? Have you ever said something to start a fight and argument with someone else? If you want to live a godly life, a life that is pleasing to God, you must remember how important it is to have speech that is kind. You must think before you speak, you must have speech that is pleasing to God.

PRAYER

Thank you, God. You have told me how important it is to think before I speak, you have told me how foolish it is to start an argument. Dear Jesus, please help me to have speech that is pleasing to you. Help me to have speech that is kind and gentle. Please help me be godly. Help me to live a life that is pleasing to you. Amen.

11 April

READ AND UNDERSTAND

Proverbs 31:12. A godly wife will help her husband; she will support him and encourage him. Boys - you must find a wife who is godly. Girls - you must be women who are godly.

Proverbs 27:9. Can you think how nice it is to smell sweet perfume, or how nice it is to smell good food cooking? It is just as nice for you to get wise counsel from a friend. Remember to listen when people give you advice, it is good for you and it shows that the person cares for you.

LOOK AT YOURSELF

Have you ever needed some help with something? It is so nice to have a friend come and help you. You must remember how important friends are. You must also be a good friend; you must give advice and help to your friends when they need it. In marriage the husband and wife help each other. It is wonderful to have a close friend showing care for you when you need it.

PRAYER

Thank you, God, for my friends. Thank you that I can be helped by other people, people who care for me and want to help me. Dear Jesus, please help me to listen when someone gives me help and advice. Help me to learn from them and help me to change when I need to. Thank you that you give me so much advice and help in the Bible. Help me to learn from the Bible and know what is pleasing to you. Amen.

12 April

READ AND UNDERSTAND

Proverbs 31:13. A godly wife will love making clothes for her family; she enjoys working with her hands. Boys - you must find a wife who is godly. Girls - you must be women who are godly.

Proverbs 27:5. If someone really loves you they will correct you when you are wrong. It is a proof of their love and concern for you if they are open and tell you what you have done wrong. So listen when you are corrected.

LOOK AT YOURSELF

Has someone ever come to you and told you that you are doing something that is not pleasing to God? Did you listen to what they said? Did you think about how much that person cares for you? If you care for someone you will tell them when they are sinning. You will want them to live a life that pleases God, and so you will help them. If someone comes and speaks to you, you must listen and learn. If you have to speak to someone about their sin, you must remember to be gentle and kind. We are all sinners and we all need help to change.

PRAYER

Thank you, God. You have given me friends and family who can help me to become more like you. Dear Jesus, please help me to learn when I am corrected. Please help me to change when I am shown my sin. Thank you that you died on the cross so that my sins can be forgiven. Thank you that you will help me to change. Amen.

13 April

READ AND UNDERSTAND

Proverbs 31:14. A godly wife will bring the best food for her family even if it is from far places. Boys - find a godly wife. Girls - be women who are godly.

Proverbs 19:22. It is better to be a poor person who shows love and is kind and loyal than to be a rich person who lies and never does the kind things he says he will. Always show love and never lie about what you will do.

Proverbs 10:10a. If you plan to do something bad you will only cause trouble for you and others. Never plan bad things, always obey God.

LOOK AT YOURSELF

It is a sin to plan to do something that is wrong. If you pretend that you are going to do something good just to get something, that is wrong too. You should only plan to do good things, and you must always do the good things that you say you will. God hates lies and He hates evil and wicked plans. You must obey God and live a life that pleases Him, showing love to the people who are around you.

PRAYER

Thank you, God. You showed love to me and planned to send your son so that I can be forgiven. Thank you that Jesus died on the cross so that my sins can be forgiven. Thank you that you have shown me what love is. Dear Jesus, please help me to never lie or plan evil. Please help me to show love to people and to do good things for the people around me. Please forgive me for the times that I have not obeyed you. Please help me to change. Amen.

14 April

READ AND UNDERSTAND

Proverbs 31:15. A godly wife will get up early in the morning to organise everything for the day, she makes sure there is food ready for everyone and she delegates work to the people that work for her.

Proverbs 6:8. Learn from the ants, they plan ahead and store up their food during the summer so that they are ready for the winter. So plan ahead and work hard.

Proverbs 1:16. The wicked always want to do something bad. Don't be like them and don't be friends with them either.

LOOK AT YOURSELF

Have you ever gotten up early so that you could plan for a busy day? Do you get up early enough every day to get the things ready for that day? Or are you always running late in the morning, needing to rush to get things ready? If you are wise you will learn to plan and work hard at organising things. Sometimes that might mean that you have to get up earlier so that you can get things ready. Maybe you can get things ready the night before. If you are wise you will plan ahead.

PRAYER

Thank you, God, we can even learn from the ants that you made. They plan ahead and they work hard. Dear Jesus, please help me to be someone who plans ahead. Help me to work hard and to do my best. Please forgive me for the times that I have been lazy, please help me to change. Amen.

15 April

READ AND UNDERSTAND

Proverbs 31:16. A godly wife will save money and use her money to make more money, she is wise and knows how to do business and she works hard.

Proverbs 17:23. Only wicked judges will accepts bribes, they are not just but wicked. God hates bribes and injustice.

Proverbs 6:5. Do not promise to pay what someone else owes. It is a trap and you must not get caught.

LOOK AT YOURSELF

Have you had your own money, or do you have some money now that is your own? Do you look after you money? If you are wise you will learn from the Bible about how to be wise with your money. The Bible teaches us a lot about how to look after the money that God has given us. We must save, we must use it well, we must never use it to bribe someone, and we must never promise to pay what someone else owes.

PRAYER

Thank you, God. You teach me in the Bible about what I should do with the money that you have given me. Dear Jesus, please help me to remember what I have learned. Please help me to be wise with my money, help me to use it in a way that pleases you. Amen.

WEEK 16

OUR WONDERFUL GOD

This week we are going to study Proverbs 8:23-29 and learn about how God is the source of wisdom. Wisdom is talking to us and telling us how wisdom was there before the world was created. You will also see that it could also be Christ talking; who was also there when God created the world.

TIME TO REMEMBER

Proverbs 8:27. "I was there when he set the heavens in place, when he marked out the horizon on the face of the deep."

16 April

READ AND UNDERSTAND

Proverbs 8:23. Wisdom existed before the earth was created. God is the source of wisdom.

Proverbs 14:8. Why does a wise person have understanding? Because he knows what to do. Why is a fool foolish? Because he thinks he knows everything. Be wise and not a fool; learn as much as you can.

LOOK AT YOURSELF

Have you ever not listened when someone was teaching you because you thought that you did not need to learn anything? That is being foolish. A wise person will listen and learn whenever they can. If you are wise you will want to learn as much as you can. God is the source of wisdom so you must learn from the Bible and ask God to give you wisdom.

PRAYER

Thank you, God. You are the source of wisdom. You know everything and you don't have to learn anything more. Dear Jesus, please help me to remember that I will always need to learn more. Please help me not to be a fool and think that I know everything. Please will you give me wisdom? Amen.

17 April

READ AND UNDERSTAND

Proverbs 8:24. Wisdom existed before the oceans and rivers were created. God is the source of wisdom.

Proverbs 11:2. Proud people will be embarrassed, while the humble have wisdom. Don't' be proud, be humble.

Proverbs 15:33. The fear of the Lord is not only the beginning of knowledge, it also teaches wisdom. The humility that comes when you fear the Lord must come before you get the respect for being wise.

LOOK AT YOURSELF

Are you proud? Do you think that you know everything? Only God knows everything. You must be humble and ask God to teach you so that you can become wiser. You must fear God and know that only He can give wisdom.

PRAYER

Thank you, God. You know everything. Thank you that I can come to you and learn from your word, thank you for the Bible. Dear Jesus, please help me to be humble. Help me to remember how wonderful and powerful and wise you are. Help me to remember how much I have to learn. Thank you that I can pray to you and ask you for wisdom. Please help me to get wisdom. Help me to know how I must live so that you will be pleased. Amen.

18 April

READ AND UNDERSTAND

Proverbs 8:25. Wisdom existed before the mountains and hills were created. God is the source of wisdom.

Proverbs 30:6. You must not think that you know something that God does not, God has told us things in the Bible and we must not add our own thoughts to them. We must not say that God said something that is not in the Bible. God says that it is wrong; it is lying.

LOOK AT YOURSELF

Did you know that everything that we need to know about God is written in the Bible? All that we need to understand about God, He has told us in the Bible. Don't you think that is great? If you ever need to know what to do, if you ever need help, you can go to the Bible and read about what God has said. You must then pray to God and ask Him to give you wisdom. God is the source of wisdom and we must always remember that.

PRAYER

Thank you, God. You have given me the Bible so that I can learn more about you and so that I can become wise. Thank you that you know everything. Dear Jesus, please help me to remember how important the Bible is. Help me to read it every day so that I can learn more about you and how you want me to live. Please help me to live a life that pleases you. Amen.

19 April

READ AND UNDERSTAND

Proverbs 8:26. Wisdom existed before land and soil were created. God is the source of wisdom.

Proverbs 29:13. There is something that is the same between poor people and rich people who are horrible to the poor. The Lord created them both and gives them life. God has given the truth in the Bible and both the poor and the rich can read the truth and God calls them both to obey and love Him.

LOOK AT YOURSELF

Have you ever thought that God would rather save someone else than you? God saves anyone that He wants to. God has shown His wonder and majesty to everyone. You will see that if you look around at the word that He created, how wonderful and amazing it is. Everyone is responsible to repent and turn to God. But it is God who opens the eyes of those who will be saved. He has chosen the people who will be Christians and He will help them to understand what is written in the Bible. You must pray to God and ask Him to help you understand, you must pray that He would save you.

PRAYER

Thank you, God. You save whoever you choose to save, and you forgive all the sins of those who are saved. Dear Jesus, please forgive me of my sins. Please help me to understand the truth that is in the Bible. Please help me to live a life that pleases you. Amen.

20 April

READ AND UNDERSTAND

Proverbs 8:27. Wisdom existed before the sky was created. God is the source of wisdom.

Proverbs 14:14. The wicked will get what they deserve, punishment. The righteous will be rewarded. So don't be wicked, obey God and live a righteous life.

Proverbs 29:3. A wise son will make his father very happy. But if the son gets involved in impure relationships then he will waste all of his father's money and his father will not be happy at all. So be wise, remember that impure relationships are sin and that they only destroy your life.

LOOK AT YOURSELF

Do you think it would be better to be punished or to have happy parents? I am sure everyone would prefer to have happy parents. If you want to make your parents happy you must become wise. Then you will know how foolish it is to get involved in a relationship outside of marriage. You will remember that disobeying God will bring punishment. So remember how important marriage is, remember to be wise and not a fool.

PRAYER

Thank you, God, that you know everything. Thank you that you have warned me in the Bible that relationships outside of marriage are sinful and that they will be punished. Dear Jesus, please help me to remember how important marriage is. Help me to remember to be wise and not a fool. Please forgive me for the times that I have not obeyed you. Help me to obey you and live a life that pleases you. Amen.

21 April

READ AND UNDERSTAND

Proverbs 8:28. Wisdom existed before clouds were created. God is the source of wisdom.

Proverbs 20:1. Drinking too much makes you loud and foolish. If you get drunk you are not being wise, you are being stupid. So remember that getting drunk is sin.

Proverbs 3:30. Don't look for argument. You must try as much as you can to be at peace with everyone.

LOOK AT YOURSELF

Have you ever seen someone who was drunk? People who are drunk normally get very loud and they will start arguments with anyone. This is foolish and sinful behaviour. If you are wise you will never get drunk, you will know that it is foolish and that it can get you into a lot of trouble. You must also remember how foolish it is to start arguments. You must not look for something to fight about.

PRAYER

Thank you, God, for warning me about the foolishness of getting drunk. Thank you that you have given me the Bible so that I can learn about what is pleasing to you and what you hate. Dear Jesus, please help me to not start arguments, please help me to remember that it is foolish to fight with other people and that it is not pleasing to you. Please forgive me for all the times that I have argued, please help me to change. Amen.

22 April

READ AND UNDERSTAND

Proverbs 8:29. Wisdom existed before the land and sea were given their places. God is the source of wisdom.

Proverbs 26:10. If a boss needs someone to do work, he must not get a fool to do the work, he must also not just get someone who is walking past to do the work. If he did it would be as dangerous as an archer shooting arrows without aiming, the arrows will go anywhere and hurt people. So he should be careful to get someone he knows who is wise to do work for him.

LOOK AT YOURSELF

Have your parents ever had to hire someone to help them with something? Did they take time to find someone who they knew could do the job, someone that they could trust? It is wise to take time and find the right person. If you get someone who you don't know, it could cause trouble for you.

PRAYER

Thank you, God. You know everything. Thank you that I can come to you and ask you for wisdom. Dear Jesus, please help me to remember all that I learn in the Bible. Help me to be wise and to live a life that pleases you. Thank you that you died on the cross so that I can be forgiven. Please forgive me for all my sins. Help me to change and to live a life that pleases you. Amen.

WEEK 17

GOSSIP IS UNGODLY

This week we are going to look at how horrible gossip is. Gossip is talking about other people in a bad way. Making up stories that are not true about someone is gossip. Telling a person about what someone did that was wrong is gossip. Telling people about how someone made a mistake or could not do something is gossip. Gossip is anything that will make the person look bad or make people think badly about them. Gossip is sin and we will see this week how bad it is.

TIME TO REMEMBER

Proverbs 26:20. "Without wood a fire goes out; without gossip a quarrel dies down."

23 April

READ AND UNDERSTAND

Proverbs 10:18. A man who hides his hatred is a liar. Anyone who speaks badly about others is a fool. Never speak badly about other people.

Proverbs 26:25. A person who has many wicked thoughts in his head might use nice words and sound gracious, but you must not believe him. There is only wickedness in his heart. Don't be wicked, and be careful of wicked people.

LOOK AT YOURSELF

Have you ever said something bad about someone? Have you ever said something nice but you were thinking about how much you don't like that person? Both are wrong and sinful. If you are wise you will have godly speech, speech that is pleasing to God and speech that will not hurt other people. If you are godly you will not be wicked, you will not even have wicked thoughts.

PRAYER

Thank you, God. You never lie and you are never wicked. Dear Jesus, please help me to become more like you. Please help me to never say anything horrible about anyone. Help me not to have wicked and evil thoughts. Please forgive me for the times that I have done those things, the times that I have not pleased you. Please help me to change and to live a life that pleases you. Amen.

24 April

READ AND UNDERSTAND

Proverbs 16:28. Gossip is spread by wicked people; they stir up trouble and break up friendships.

Proverbs 15:18. People who get angry will only cause arguments. You must not get angry; you must be a peace-maker, not wanting to argue.

Proverbs 11:9. You can be ruined by the talk of godless people, but the wisdom of the right words can save you. Choose your friends wisely.

LOOK AT YOURSELF

Have you ever gotten angry and started a fight because you were cross? Have you ever been upset with a friend because of what someone else said? You must be very careful of getting angry, you must also make sure you don't gossip or listen to gossip. Gossip will only cause trouble, it can get people cross and upset with each other and it can break up a friendship. God wants you to love other people; He wants you to have speech that is godly, speech that is pleasing to Him and kind to others.

PRAYER

Thank you, God, for giving me friends. Thank you that you tell me in the Bible about what good friends are. Dear Jesus, please help me to be a good friend, not fighting or gossiping. Help me to have speech that is pleasing to you. Please forgive me for the times that I have gotten angry, for the times that I have spoken about other people when I should not have. Please help me to change. Amen.

25 April

READ AND UNDERSTAND

Proverbs 18:8. Listening to gossip is like eating tasty things, we gobble them in but don't realise that they will sink deep into our minds and that they will cause suspicion and distrust. It is wrong to listen to gossip; it is like poison in our stomach.

Proverbs 15:26. The Lord hates evil thoughts and words, but He is pleased with pure thoughts and words. Remember that your thoughts are known to God as well as your words.

LOOK AT YOURSELF

Have you ever heard someone saying bad things about someone else? Did you tell the person not to gossip or did you listen and enjoy hearing? Everyone will be tempted to listen to the stories about other people, but you must make sure that you remember that it is wrong. God is only pleased with words that are pure and true. God hates lies and stories that hurt people. God knows our thoughts as well as our words and we must make sure that we don't listen or talk badly about other people and we must also make sure we don't think badly about them either.

PRAYER

Thank you, God, that you know everything. Thank you that I cannot hide my sin. That helps me to stop sinning and live a life that pleases you. Dear Jesus, please help me to not listen to gossip, please help me never to gossip. Please help me to have words and thoughts that are pure and godly. Please forgive me for the times that I have sinned against you, please help me to change. Amen.

26 April

READ AND UNDERSTAND

Proverbs 25:23. The Israelite farmers knew that if the wind blew from the North it would rain. It is just as certain that someone who gossips will bring anger. So don't gossip, it will only make people cross, it is sin and God hates it.

Proverbs 17:1. It is better to eat a small bit of dry bread were there is peace, than to have a big meal were there is quarrelling and fighting going on. So remember to be at peace with people, don't argue.

LOOK AT YOURSELF

If you gossip or listen to gossip, you can be sure that it will cause anger and fighting. It is terrible to have fighting and quarrelling going on. You must rather try to be at peace with people, having a good relationship were you are good friends. Gossip can break friendships up, so make sure you don't gossip and make sure you don't listen to gossip.

PRAYER

Thank you, God, that you tell us how to stay away from sin. Thank you that you have shown me that one way to stay away from fighting is to not gossip and to not listen to gossip. Dear Jesus, please help me to not gossip; help me not to listen to gossip. Please help me to not be someone who fights and quarrels with others. Help me to be a good friend. Amen.

27 April

READ AND UNDERSTAND

Proverbs 26:20. Now you must think about a fire. If you don't put wood or coal on a fire, the fire will go out. In the same way if there is no gossiping then the fighting will stop. So don't gossip, don't fight.

Proverbs 19:13b. A wife that quarrels is like a leak in the roof that drips and drips. It is irritating and is does not stop. Women should not be quarrelsome; you must not look for things to fight about.

Proverbs 9:15. Even if you are living a righteous life, you must make sure you are not tempted to be foolish. Foolishness will "call" and tempt everyone.

LOOK AT YOURSELF

Do you look for something to fight and argue about? Do you like having an argument with someone? The Bible tells us that fighting and arguing are sin. We also see that fighting sometimes starts because people gossip. So you must not be a person who gossips and you must not be a person who fights and argues. Sometimes people will say things that make you want to fight, but you must remember not to sin. Don't let sin tempt you. Rather obey God and do what is right.

PRAYER

Thank you, God, for warning me that sin is going to tempt me. I will be tempted to act foolishly and to gossip or fight or argue. Dear Jesus, please help me to not be foolish. Help me not to gossip and fight. Please help me to live a life that pleases you. Please forgive me for the times that I have been foolish, all the times that I have sinned against you. Please help me to change. Amen.

28 April

READ AND UNDERSTAND

Proverbs 26:21. Think about a fire again. If you put wood and coal on a fire it will make the fire stronger and hotter. In the same way if you gossip you will cause more fighting. So don't gossip, don't fight.

Proverbs 30:11. There are people who say bad things about their parents and do not appreciate what their parents have done for them. This is sin and God hates it. God commands children to honour their parents.

LOOK AT YOURSELF

Have you ever said something bad about your parents? That is also gossip and it is very bad. You must always appreciate your parents; you must thank God for them. You must remember that God commands children to honour and obey their parents. So that means that you must obey your parents and you must also respect them; you must never talk badly about them or to them.

PRAYER

Thank you, God, for my parents. Thank you for all the things that they do for me. Dear Jesus, please help me to be more thankful for my parents. Help me to obey them and to show respect and love to them. Please help me to remember that it is sin to gossip and say bad things about people. Please help me to be a person who says nice things and not bad. Amen.

29 April

READ AND UNDERSTAND

Proverbs 26:22. Listening to gossip is like eating tasty things, we gobble them in but don't realise that they will sink deep into our minds and that they will cause suspicion and distrust. It is wrong to listen to gossip; it is like poison in our stomach.

Proverbs 16:23. Wise people think before they speak. It is then easier to learn from them.

Proverbs 10:10b. If you are not wise when you talk, you will get into trouble. So think before you speak.

LOOK AT YOURSELF

Have you ever said something and then realised that it was the wrong thing to say? It is much better to think about what to say before you say it. Then you will be able to be wise in what you say and not foolish. You will also be able to make sure that you are not gossiping. So remember to think before you speak. Remember that gossip is sin and God hates it. Remember how much anger and fighting gossip will bring. Rather have speech that is wise, speech that is pleasing to God.

PRAYER

Thank you, God, for the Bible. Thank you that I can learn about how bad gossip is and how much trouble it can cause. Dear Jesus, please help me to think before I speak. Please help me to have speech that is pleasing to you. Please help me to be wise and remember everything that I have learnt this week. Amen.

WEEK 18

THE IMPORTANCE OF WISDOM

This week we will study Proverbs 3:20-25b and learn again about wisdom and how important it is. Our memory verse is about sin and how important it is that we confess our sin and turn to God for forgiveness.

TIME TO REMEMBER

Proverbs 28:13. "He who conceals his sins does not prosper, but whoever confesses and renounces them finds mercy."

30 April

READ AND UNDERSTAND

Proverbs 3:20. With knowledge God created the seas, rivers, dams and clouds. God is the source of knowledge and we must go to him to get knowledge.

Proverbs 3:21. Hold onto wisdom and insight; never let them get away from you. You will always need wisdom.

Proverbs 1:5b. The Proverbs will guide the man of understanding. They will show you how to live if you want to learn how.

LOOK AT YOURSELF

Do you want to live a life that is pleasing to God? Do you want to know what God loves and what He hates? Then you need to study the Bible and become wise. Then you will be able to know how to live.

PRAYER

Thank you, God, for the Bible. Thank you that I can learn more about you. Thank you that I can learn about what is pleasing to you and what is not. Dear Jesus, please forgive me for all the times that I have sinned against you and not lived in a way that is pleasing to you. Please help me to change and to live a life that glorifies you. Amen.

1 May

READ AND UNDERSTAND

Proverbs 3:22. Wisdom will give you a pleasant and happy life. So learn from the Bible and become wise.

Proverbs 29:2. When good people are in charge they do well and everyone is glad. But if a wicked person is in charge, people groan and are unhappy.

LOOK AT YOURSELF

Do you want to have a happy and pleasant life? The only way that you can have that is if you live a life that is pleasing to God. The only way to know how to live is by learning from the Bible and becoming wise. So remember to study the Bible, and what you learn must change the way you live.

PRAYER

Thank you, God, I can learn from the Bible about you and what is pleasing to you. Dear Jesus, please help me to live a life that pleases you and brings glory to you. Thank you that you died on the cross so that my sins can be forgiven. Please forgive me for my sins and help me to change. Amen.

2 May

READ AND UNDERSTAND

Proverbs 3:23. With wisdom you will walk safely and not stumble. So learn from the Bible and become wise.

Proverbs 31:4-5. It is wrong for rulers to drink wine and strong drink, if they get drunk they will forget their duties and they will ignore the rights of people in need. As rulers they need to be able to think clearly and make judgments that are right and fair. So remember that it is sin to get drunk.

LOOK AT YOURSELF

Have you ever seen someone who was drunk? People who are drunk do not know what they are doing. They do not have self-control and they might do things that afterwards they wish they had not. So remember how wrong it is to get drunk. If you want to be safe and not get into trouble then you will be wise and remember what the Bible teaches about getting drunk.

PRAYER

Thank you, God. You have warned me in the Bible about how bad it is to get drunk. Thank you that you know everything and that I can learn from you. Thank you that you will keep me safe if I learn from the Bible and become wise. Dear Jesus, please help me to be wise. Help me to remember what I learn from the Bible so that I can live a life that pleases you. Amen.

3 May

READ AND UNDERSTAND

Proverbs 3:24. Wisdom will help you not be afraid when you go to bed, and you will sleep soundly through the night. So learn from the Bible and become wise.

Proverbs 24:24-25. If a judge says to a wicked and guilty person "you are innocent" that judge will be hated by many people. But if a judge punished the guilty person, the judge will be respected and appreciated. So remember that truth is important, you must not show partiality.

LOOK AT YOURSELF

Have you ever lied so that you could get something? Have you ever lied and caused someone else to get punished when they should not have? If you are godly and live a life that pleases God, then you will know how important truth is to God. You must never lie. If you are wise and live a righteous life, then you will be able to have peace and not fear. You will know that God is pleased with you and will not punish you.

PRAYER

Thank you, God. You give Christians peace. Thank you that I can trust in you and I don't need to be afraid of anything. Dear Jesus, please help me to learn more about you. Please help me to become wise. Please forgive me for the times that I have lied, please help me to change and to always tell the truth. Amen.

4 May

READ AND UNDERSTAND

Proverbs 3:25a. The wise don't need to be afraid of the future. So learn from the Bible and become wise.

Proverbs 28:13. If you try and hide your sin you will never do well. But if you confess your sin and you stop doing it, then God will show you mercy and He will forgive you. Trust in Christ for the forgiveness of sin, stop sinning and obey him.

LOOK AT YOURSELF

Have you gone to God and asked him to forgive you of your sins? Have you asked Christ to save you and to help you to stop sinning and live a life that pleases Him? If you are a Christian you don't have to be afraid of the future. God will protect his children and He will forgive those who are His. He will forgive sin and help you to change.

PRAYER

Thank you, God. You protect Christians and I don't need to be afraid of the future if I love you and obey you. Dear Jesus, please forgive me for the sin that I have done against you. Please help me to stop sinning and to live a life that pleases you. Amen.

5 May

READ AND UNDERSTAND

Proverbs 3:25b. The wise don't need to be afraid of the wicked. So learn from the Bible and become wise.

Proverbs 23:10-11. You must not steal. In Israel's time they marked the border of their farms with big stones; some people would move the stones and take some of their neighbors land as their own. Some farmers would go and use the land that belonged to orphans, who could not defend it. God says that this is stealing. It is sin, just like any other stealing and so you must never take something that belongs to someone else, especially when they can't defend themselves. Remember that God looks after the orphans and He is very strong.

LOOK AT YOURSELF

Have you ever felt alone and weak? Have you ever felt that people would hurt you? If you know God and are a Christian you don't have to be afraid of people. Even if wicked people try and hurt you, God is all powerful and He will protect His children. You don't have to be afraid of anyone if you are protected by God.

PRAYER

Thank you, God. You are so powerful and so caring. Thank you that you promise to look after those people who are in need. Thank you that I don't need to be afraid of wicked people. Thank you that I can trust in you. Dear Jesus, please help me to trust in you more. Help me to study from the Bible and learn more about how wonderful and loving you are. Amen.

6 May

READ AND UNDERSTAND

Proverbs 3:25b. The wise will not get punished like the wicked. So learn form the Bible and become wise.

Proverbs 19:5. If you tell lies in court, you will be punished. If you are a liar you will not be able to escape punishment. So remember to always tell the truth. God hates lies.

LOOK AT YOURSELF

Have you ever told a lie and nobody found out? You must remember that God knows everything and even if your parents don't find out, God always knows. You must always tell the truth. God hates lies and people who lie will get punished. If you are wise and live a life that pleases God, you will not get punished like the wicked. So remember what you have learnt and obey it.

PRAYER

Thank you, God. You are a God of truth and you always tell the truth. Thank you that you know everything and that I cannot hide my sin from you. That will help me to remember not to lie, you will know and it will not please you. Dear Jesus, please help me to always tell the truth. Please forgive me for the times that I have lied and please help me to change. Amen.

WEEK 19

CHOOSING RIGHT FRIENDS

This week we are going to see how foolish it is to get involved with or to copy wicked people. Wicked people are only trapped by their sin; they will be punished. If you are wise you will not be wicked and sinful, you will stay away from wicked and evil people and you will not want to be like them.

TIME TO REMEMBER

Proverbs 5:22. "The evil deeds of a wicked man ensnare him; the cords of his sin hold him fast."

7 May

READ AND UNDERSTAND

Proverbs 1:14. The wicked will promise to share what they steal with you. Don't listen to them. There is no happiness in having things that belong to someone else.

Proverbs 9:17. It is foolish to think that you can hide your sin. Foolish people like to try and get away with doing the wrong thing; they think that it is fun to be able to hide what you are doing. Remember that God knows everything; you can't hide from Him.

LOOK AT YOURSELF

Has anyone ever asked you to do something that you knew was wrong? Did they promise you that it would be fun, that you would not get caught, that you would get things out of it? You must not believe the lie that sin will not be found out, that sin will not be punished. God knows everything and every sin is displeasing to Him. You must remember that God knows everything. You must live a life that is pleasing to Him, knowing that He sees everything.

PRAYER

Thank you, God. You know all things and I cannot hide my sin from you. I know that it can help me to stop sinning if I know that my sin displeases you. Dear Jesus, please forgive me for the times that I have sinned and thought that no one knew. Please help me to remember that all my sin is known by you, it is all displeasing to you. Please help me to live a life that is pleasing to you. Amen.

8 May

READ AND UNDERSTAND

Proverbs 1:17-18. Birds are clever enough to stay away from a trap they see set up. But the wicked are more stupid than birds; they see the trap because they set it up themselves. They are caught in their own trap. The wicked will not get away from punishment.

Proverbs 23:27-28. Getting involved in an impure relationship is a trap; it is like falling into a hole that you can't get out of. Ungodly women hide and wait like a robber, looking for another victim who will be unfaithful to his wife. God hates impure relationships, He created marriage and it is good.

LOOK AT YOURSELF

Doesn't it sound foolish to be caught in a trap that you set up yourself? That is how foolish it is to be a wicked person. That is how foolish it is to have a relationship outside of marriage. You must remember what God has said about marriage; how important and special it is and how a marriage between a man and his wife must be kept pure.

PRAYER

Thank you, God, for creating marriage. Thank you that it is a special relationship that you created for a man and a woman. Dear Jesus, please help me not to be foolish. Help me to remember how important marriage is. Please help me not to be a wicked person. Thank you that you died on the cross so that my sins can be forgiven. Please forgive me for all my sin and please help me to change. Amen.

9 May

READ AND UNDERSTAND

Proverbs 3:31. Don't be jealous of violent people, and do not copy them. We must copy Christ and become like him.

Proverbs 14:24. Wise people are often rewarded with riches, but fools will only get more foolish. So learn from the Bible and become wise.

Proverbs 15:24. Wise people walk the road that leads to life, not the road that leads to death. To walk the road to life you must fear the Lord and be righteous.

LOOK AT YOURSELF

Have you ever seen people who are violent and disobedient but that get what they want because of it? Did you wish that you could also get what you want? You must not be jealous of people who disobey God and who are violent and ungodly. Even if they get what they want, they will also get punishment for their sin and disobedience. So remember that it is far better to be a wise person, someone who knows how God wants you to live and who lives in a way that pleases God. Wise and godly people will be rewarded with riches and life.

PRAYER

Thank you, God. You will give eternal life to all Christians. Dear Jesus, please help me to remember that obeying you is a lot more important than having things on earth. It is much better to be a Christian and know that I am going to be with you in heaven one day, than disobeying you and having things on earth. Please help me to not be violent and help me not to be jealous of people who are. Please help me to live a life that pleases you. Amen.

10 May

READ AND UNDERSTAND

Proverbs 4:14. Do not go where evil men go. Do not follow the example of the wicked. Follow Christ who is our example of how to live.

Proverbs 6:12. Worthless, wicked people go around telling lies. Don't be wicked, always tell the truth.

Proverbs 15:17. It is nicer to have simple food with people you love than eat a feast of the best and fanciest foods were there is hatred between people. Love is more important than things.

LOOK AT YOURSELF

Have you ever been at a party where there were lots of nice things to eat but people were not happy, people where upset with each other? If that happens you won't even enjoy the nice food. If is important that you are not upset and angry with people. You must forgive people if they do something horrible to you and you must show love to all people. Then even the simplest food will be nice. Remember that one way that gets people upset is if others tell lies about them. Remember not to tell lies, it is displeasing to God and it can hurt other people. So don't be wicked. Rather obey God and try to live a life the way Jesus lived. Show love to everyone and never disobey God's law.

PRAYER

Thank you, God; that Jesus came to earth and showed us how we are to live. Thank you that he died on the cross so that my sins can be forgiven. Dear Jesus, please help me to live a life that pleases you. Please help me to become more like you every day. Please help me to always tell the truth and to always show love to other people. Amen.

11 May

READ AND UNDERSTAND

Proverbs 5:22. The sins of the wicked are a trap. The wicked will get caught in the net of their own sin. Don't fall into that trap, obey God and don't be wicked.

Proverbs 25:6-7. It would be embarrassing if you sat in the best seat because you thought you were the most important, and then when someone more important came you had to move to a less important seat. It is better to be humble and take the least important seat and then they might ask you to move to a better seat. Don't be proud and think that you are so important, be humble instead.

LOOK AT YOURSELF

Have you ever done something you thought was so good? Did you find out that there were others who were better than you? You must not be proud about what you can do or how much you know. Everything that you can do is because God has given you the ability to do it. Everything that you know is from God who is the source of wisdom. So do not be proud. Thank God for what you can do and always try to do your best. If you disobey God it will only be a trap and cause problems for you. Obey God and be a humble person.

PRAYER

Thank you, God, for all the things that you have given me the ability to do. Thank you that everything I know is from you because you gave me the ability to learn and you are the source of wisdom. Dear Jesus, please help me to be a humble person. Please help me to thank you for what I can do rather than being proud. Please help me to remember that disobeying you is a foolish thing to do, it is like a trap and will only cause trouble. Please help me to obey. Amen.

12 May

READ AND UNDERSTAND

Proverbs 29:6. Evil people are trapped in their own sins, but godly people are happy. So don't be evil, being evil will only cause trouble for you. Rather be righteous and you will be happy.

Proverbs 14:11. A good person's house will still be standing after the evil person's house has been destroyed. So don't be evil, obey God and live a righteous life.

Proverbs 12:4. A godly wife is like a crown for her husband, but an ungodly wife is like sickness to his body. God wants wives to be godly.

LOOK AT YOURSELF

Have you ever disobeyed your parents and because you disobeyed, things did not go well? You must remember that all sin will lead to trouble and problems. But if you are a godly person, someone who obeys God and obeys your parents, then you will have a happy life. Godly people will have success and will be protected by God. If you are wicked and do not care about what is pleasing to God, if you disobey Him, then you will have trouble and you will not succeed.

PRAYER

Thank you, God, that godly people will not be destroyed. Thank you that Jesus died so that my sins can be forgiven. Dear Jesus, please help me to remember how important it is to obey you in everything. Please help me to live a life that pleases you. Amen.

13 May

READ AND UNDERSTAND

Proverbs 29:24. If you help someone steal something you are only causing problems for yourself. If you go to court and tell the truth, then you will get into trouble for stealing. If you lie in court to protect yourself, then you will be punished for lying. So remember that if you steal it will only bring problems. Never steal; it is sin.

Proverbs 2:20. God wants us to be good people, who are obedient to him. So you must obey God.

LOOK AT YOURSELF

Have you ever stolen anything? Even taken something small like a pencil or a sweet? You must remember that stealing is a sin and God hates it. You must also remember that if you help someone to steal, you are also sinning. If you are a righteous person, someone who wants to live a life that pleases God, you must obey Him in everything. One thing that God commands is that you don't steal.

PRAYER

Thank you, God. You have given us the Bible and told us what is pleasing to you and what is sin. Dear Jesus, please help me to obey you in everything that I do. Please help me to remember how bad it is to steal. Please forgive me for the times that I have sinned and disobeyed you. Please help me to change. Amen.

WEEK 20

GODLY AND UNGODLY PEOPLE

This week we are going to see the comparison between godly, righteous people and people who are wicked and evil. Righteous people are those who obey God and desire to live a life that pleases Him. We will see how the righteous are given life and blessing while the wicked will be given punishment and death.

TIME TO REMEMBER

Proverbs 15:9. "The Lord detests the way of the wicked but He loves those who pursue righteousness."

14 May

READ AND UNDERSTAND

Proverbs 11:21. You can be sure that evil people will be punished, but righteous people will be saved. Obey God and live a righteous life.

Proverbs 30:17. Someone who makes fun of their parents and who does not show them respect and honour, should be eaten by wild birds, he should have his eyes picked out by the wild ravens. God commands children to honour and obey their parents, if you don't you will be punished.

LOOK AT YOURSELF

Do you respect your parents? Do you always speak to them in a kind and respectful way? Have you ever said something bad about your parents? God wants you to honour and obey your parents. If you do not obey God by obeying them you will be punished. So remember to think about how you speak to your parents. Make sure that you have speech that is godly. Also remember that God wants you to obey them.

PRAYER

Thank you, God, for my parents. Dear Jesus, please help me to always have godly speech and especially when I speak to my parents. Help me to show respect to them and never say bad things about them. Thank you that you died on the cross so that my sins can be forgiven. Thank you that I will not be punished but will have eternal life with you. Amen.

15 May

READ AND UNDERSTAND

Proverbs 11:23. What righteous people want always result in good, but the wicked must only expect punishment. So obey God and live a righteous life.

Proverbs 27:22. Have you seen a pestle and mortar? It is normally a stone bowl with a thick stone rod, they would put grain into the bowl and use the rod to crush and pound it. Can you think how that heavy peace of stone hits the grain against the hard bowl? This proverb says that if you had to punish a foolish person as hard as you crush that grain, the fool will still not repent and stop doing his foolish things. So don't be a fool.

LOOK AT YOURSELF

I am sure you would not like to be crushed in a pestle and mortar. You must remember what the Bible teaches and you must not be a fool. Study from the Bible and become wise. If you are wise and know what is pleasing to God; if you are a righteous person and desire to obey God in everything; then you will be blessed. If you are wicked you will be punished. So obey God and life a righteous life.

PRAYER

Thank you, God. You have given us the Bible so that we can study and become wise. Thank you that Jesus died on the cross so that we can be forgiven. Thank you that you help me to live a righteous life. Dear Jesus, please help me to stop sinning. Please help me to not be foolish but to rather repent and obey you. Please forgive me for all my sins and help me to change. Amen.

16 May

READ AND UNDERSTAND

Proverbs 11:27. If your goals are good, you will be respected. If you want to be evil, evil will come on you. Obey God and always want to do what is right.

Proverbs 11:20. The Lord hates evil-minded people, but He loves those people who do what is right. Make sure that you do not think about evil things, think about good things so that you will do good things.

Proverbs 16:12. God hates leaders who are wicked. Leadership is based on righteousness.

LOOK AT YOURSELF

Have you ever thought about evil things? Have you ever thought about doing something that you knew was wrong? You must remember that God knows your thoughts. You cannot hide anything from God. So make sure you have godly thoughts, thoughts that are pleasing to God and not evil. Remember that if you think and do evil things, evil will happen to you. So obey God and live a godly life, pleasing Him in everything that you do and think.

PRAYER

Thank you, God, that you know everything. Thank you that you know who are evil and you will punish them. Dear Jesus, pleas help me to live a life that pleases you. Please help me to always have good thoughts, thoughts that please you. Please forgive me for all my bad and evil thoughts. Please help me to change and to become more like you. Amen.

17 May

READ AND UNDERSTAND

Proverbs 12:2. The Lord is pleased with good people, but He punishes those who plan evil. Obey God and live a righteous life.

Proverbs 10:13. If you are wise, you will speak with understanding. If you don't have understanding you will be punished. So think before you speak.

Proverbs 14:15. A fool will believe anything, but people with wisdom will think before they do something. So think before you do something.

LOOK AT YOURSELF

Do you think before you speak? Do you think before you do something? If you are wise you will think before you speak and you will check if what you are going to say is wise and kind and godly. If you are wise you will think before you do something whether it is pleasing to God or disobeying Him. You must always look at your life and see if you are obeying God and living a righteous life. Remember that God will punish wicked and evil people; people who do not care about what is right and wrong.

PRAYER

Thank you, God, for your forgiveness. Thank you that I can come to you. Thank you that I can ask you to help me to change. Dear Jesus, please forgive me for all the times that I have said things and done things without thinking. Forgive me for all the times that I have disobeyed you and not pleased you in my speech and in my actions. Please help me to change and to please you in everything that I think, say and do. Amen.

18 May

READ AND UNDERSTAND

Proverbs 13:6. Righteousness protects the innocent; wickedness is the downfall of sinners. So obey God and live a righteous life.

Proverbs 19:19. A person who gets angry quickly will get into trouble over and over again. If you help him once, you will have to do it again. Hot-tempered people don't learn. So don't get angry, have self-control and patience.

LOOK AT YOURSELF

Do you get angry quickly? Do you get upset and cross? You must remember that anger is a sin. You must not get angry; you must have self-control and stop yourself from getting upset. You must remember what Jesus did when people were horrible to Him. Jesus showed love even to the people who killed Him. Before He died He asked God the Father to forgive them. He did not get angry and upset. He trusted in God the Father and prayed to Him. Remember to not get angry when people are horrible to you, you must rather forgive them and show love to them.

PRAYER

Thank you, God, that you will help me to have love for other people, even those people who are horrible to me. Dear Jesus, please help me to become more like you. Help me to show love to people. Help me to not get angry and upset. Please forgive me for the times that I have gotten angry, please help me to change. Amen.

19 May

READ AND UNDERSTAND

Proverbs 15:9. The Lord hates the way that evil people live, but He loves people who want to do what is right. You must obey God and live a righteous life.

Proverbs 20:22. If someone does something bad to you, you must not do something bad back to them. God will punish everyone for their bad behaviour, you must trust in God to look after you.

Proverbs 11:25. Be generous with your money and you will be blessed. Help others and you will be helped. So share what you have.

LOOK AT YOURSELF

Has anyone ever done something horrible to you? Did you do something horrible back to them? God says that we must not be horrible to people even if they are horrible to us. Remember that God wants us to show love and kindness, even to those who are horrible to us. One way that you can show love is by helping people who are in need and sharing what you have. If you see someone who does not have lunch with them, and you do, you should share your food with them. If you show love to other people, God will look after you when you are in need. So remember to be generous and share what you have.

PRAYER

Thank you, God. You will look after me and you will punish everyone for the evil that they do. Dear Jesus, please help me to always show love. Help me to be generous with what I have and to share with other people. Help me not to be selfish but to think about other people's needs. Thank you that you care so much for me and have given me so much. Amen.

20 May

READ AND UNDERSTAND

Proverbs 19:16. If we obey God and keep His commandments, God will save our souls. If we ignore the Bible and do what we want to in life, we will die. Turn to God for salvation, obey him and trust in Jesus Christ for salvation.

Proverbs 23:9. Don't try and teach someone who is a fool, he will only despise your wisest advice. So remember that you must not be a fool, listen when people teach you so that you can become wiser.

LOOK AT YOURSELF

Jesus died on the cross so that you can have your sins forgiven. If you are not a Christian you will be punished for all you sins. But if you trust in the Lord Jesus Christ your sins will be forgiven and you will not be punished. If you are a Christian you must read your Bible and learn about how God wants you to live. If you are a Christian you will want to obey God and you will want to live a life that pleases him. So turn to God and ask him to forgive your sins.

PRAYER

Thank you, God, I can come to you and ask for forgiveness. Dear Jesus, thank you for dying on the cross for my sins. Please forgive me for all my sins and help me to live a life that pleases you. Amen.

WEEK 21

SHOWING LOVE AND BEING KIND

This week we are going to look at showing love. We will look at how we can show love by being kind to the poor and helping them.

TIME TO REMEMBER

Proverbs 21:13. "If a man shuts his ears to the cry of the poor, he too will cry out and not be answered."

21 May

READ AND UNDERSTAND

Proverbs 20:6. Many people will talk about how much love they have for others, how kind, generous and giving they are, but there are not many people who will actually do the good things that they talk about. Remember to do good things for others; don't just talk about doing good.

Proverbs 25:14. People who promise things that they never give will disappoint people. Just like farmers are disappointed if there is no rain, when they think the clouds and the wind are bringing rain. So don't make promises that you will not keep.

LOOK AT YOURSELF

Have you ever promised to do something for someone and then you never did it? Have you ever told people that you are kind to the poor and give to them but you never have? You must never lie and if you promise to do something you must do it. You must show love to people and one way to do that is by being kind, generous and giving.

PRAYER

Thank you, God. You have given me so much. Dear Jesus, please help me to share what I have with people who are in need. Please help me to always do what I say I will do. Please help me to become more like you. Amen.

22 May

READ AND UNDERSTAND

Proverbs 11:16. A kind-hearted woman will get respect. Violent men might get rich, but they don't get respect. So don't' be violent, be kind.

Proverbs 16:29. Violent people deceive their friends and lead them into a way that is not good.

Proverbs 18:3. Wicked people will only get shame and disgrace. Don't be wicked, obey the Bible and do not sin.

LOOK AT YOURSELF

Have you ever hit anyone? Have you ever been violent so that you can get what you want? Remember that violent people will not be respected and liked, they will get shame and disgrace and they are not nice friends to have. So remember to have self-control and don't get angry. Also remember that even if you get things by being violent, you will be punished for it. Rather show love and be kind and godly.

PRAYER

Thank you, God. You have given me the Bible so that I can learn about what is pleasing to you. Dear Jesus, please help me to remember that violence is wrong and that it is not pleasing to you. Please help me to show love and kindness and not violence and anger. Please forgive me for the times that I have not been kind. Please help me to change. Amen.

23 May

READ AND UNDERSTAND

Proverbs 21:13. If you don't listen to the cry of the poor when they need help, you will also be ignored when you are crying for help. So love others and do good to the poor and needy.

Proverbs 11:24. If you are generous with your money and are willing to help others, God will bless you. If you don't want to help others with your money and keep it all for yourself, you will become poor. So share what you have.

LOOK AT YOURSELF

Do you share what you have? Do you help people who are in need? If you know that someone needs something and you can help them but you don't, then you will also be in need and nobody will help you. God wants you to show love and kindness to other people. If you do He will always look after you.

PRAYER

Thank you, God. You look after people who are generous and kind. Dear Jesus, please help me to show love to others and to help people who are in need. Please forgive me for the times that I have been selfish and not wanted to share what I have. Please help me to think of others and share what I have. Please help me to change. Amen.

24 May

READ AND UNDERSTAND

Proverbs 11:17. You do yourself a favour when you are kind. If you are cruel, you only hurt yourself. So don't be cruel, always show kindness. God commands us to love our neighbour.

Proverbs 31:26. A godly wife is wise and teaches others, she is also kind and her speech shows her kindness. Boys - you must find a wife who is godly. Girls - you must be women who are godly.

Proverbs 1:3b. The Proverbs will teach you to do what is just and fair towards your neighbour. God tells us how to love our neighbour and we must obey.

LOOK AT YOURSELF

Are you a kind person? Do you have speech that is kind and gentle? Do you show love to the people around you? Those are all things that God wants from you. He wants you to be a kind person, showing love to others and also telling others about Him and His kindness. You must tell other people about God and salvation through Christ.

PRAYER

Thank you, God. You teach us in the Bible about how you want us to live. Dear Jesus, please help me to remember what I learn in the Bible. Help me to live a life that pleases you. Please help me to show love to others and to have speech that is kind and gentle. Please forgive me for the times that I have not obeyed you. Please help me to change. Amen.

25 May

READ AND UNDERSTAND

Proverbs 22:9. God blesses those people who are generous, they see people who need food and they give some of their own food to them. Be generous and help people who are in need.

Proverbs 25:2. God knows all things, and there are things that He does not explain to us because we are only human. This is something that is wonderful about God, that there is nothing that He does not know, nothing that He needs to find out. But with people and even kings, it is a good thing for them to get more wisdom and understanding. People do not know everything and it is a very good thing for people to want to learn more. To want to find out what God wants them to do.

LOOK AT YOURSELF

Have you ever given some of your food to someone who did not have any? God wants you to be generous with what you have and help others who are in need. If you read the Bible and learn about what God wants, you will see that God wants you to love Him and He wants you to love others. You must always remember how important it is to learn from the Bible. The more you learn the more you will know how to show love to God and others.

PRAYER

Thank you, God. You know everything and there is nothing that you don't know. Thank you that I can learn from you in the Bible. Dear Jesus, please help me to show love to others and to share what I have. Please also help me to show more love to you by obeying you. Please forgive me for the times that I have disobeyed. Please help me to change. Amen.

GOD'S BOOK OF WISDOM

26 May

READ AND UNDERSTAND

Proverbs 28:27. If you give to the poor, God will look after you and you will always have what you need. But if you try to ignore the poor and to look away when you see someone who is in need, then those needy people will hate you. So do good to the poor and God will look after you.

Proverbs 16:21a. If you are wise you will know the difference between what is true and false as well as what is good and evil.

LOOK AT YOURSELF

Do you trust that God will look after you? God cares for His children and He will always provide for their needs. You must trust in God to provide. Often God will use the kindness of other Christians to provide for those who are in need. So remember how important it is that you share what you have and help those people who are struggling. Christians must show love to other people and a way you can do that is by helping the poor.

PRAYER

Thank you, God. You look after your children. Thank you that I can trust in you. Dear Jesus, please help me to be a generous person. Please help me to show love to others and especially those who are in need. Please forgive me for the times that I have been selfish and have not wanted to share. Please help me to change and become more like you. Amen.

27 May

READ AND UNDERSTAND

Proverbs 29:7. A godly person shows love and concern for poor people just like God does. A wicked person shows that he does not love God because he does not care about the poor, he does not care if they are treated badly. So don't be wicked, show love for the poor.

Proverbs 20:5. A person's thoughts are like water in a deep well, difficult to get too, but a person with understanding and wisdom will be able to draw them out and understand them.

Proverbs 3:12a. God disciplines those He loves. He wants you to obey him and become more like Christ.

LOOK AT YOURSELF

Do you want to become more like Christ? God cares so much for the poor. If you are a Christian you must also care for those in need. If you don't obey God and don't desire to be like Him, He might discipline you so that you learn to obey Him. God cares for you and He wants you to stop sinning.

PRAYER

Thank you, God. You care for the poor and for those who are in need. Dear Jesus, please help me to become more like you. Please help me to have more love for those who are in need. Help me to show love to them and help me to know what I can do for them. Please forgive me for the times that I have not obeyed you and have not lived a life that pleases you. Please help me to change and become more like you. Amen.

WEEK 22

CHOOSING THE RIGHT FRIENDS

This week we will look at what kind of friends we should have. We will see that gossip can separate friends and we will see how your friends can influence the type of person you become.

TIME TO REMEMBER

Proverbs 13:20. "He who walks with the wise grows wise, but a companion of fools suffers harm."

28 May

READ AND UNDERSTAND

Proverbs 1:15. Do not be friends with the wicked. Stay far away from them and don't copy them. Be careful who your friends are.

Proverbs 29:27. Godly people hate wicked people and wicked people hate the godly. God hates wickedness, so we must hate wickedness as well. Wicked people don't want to do what is right, so they hate anyone who does obey God.

LOOK AT YOURSELF

Do your friends love God and desire to live a life that pleases Him? Or do you have friends who are wicked, who do not love God and do not obey Him? You must be careful who your friends are. If you are a Christian you should not be able to be best friends with wicked people, you should hate their wickedness just like the Lord does. So make sure your friends are also Christians.

PRAYER

Thank you, God. You have warned me to stay away from wicked people. Dear Jesus, please help me to choose my friends wisely. Help me to find friends who love you and want to live lives that please you. Please help me to live a life that pleases you. Please help me to hate wickedness just like you hate it. Please help me to become more like you. Amen.

29 May

READ AND UNDERSTAND

Proverbs 12:26. Righteous people are a guide to their friends, but the path of the wicked will get you lost. So make sure you choose your friends wisely.

Proverbs 16:19. It is better to be humble with the poor than to be rich with the proud.

Proverbs 24:5-6. A wise person is strong; someone who has knowledge will get stronger. That person is strong because he asks for wise advice, he knows that the more good advice he gets, the more likely he is to do well. So be wise and ask for advice.

LOOK AT YOURSELF

Do you have wise friends who you can ask advice from? Your friends should be Christians and then they can help guide you and help you to become more like Christ. You must also be a good friend and guide and help your friends to become more like Christ. Friends are important and you must make sure that your friends love God and want to please Him.

PRAYER

Thank you, God, for wise friends and family. They give me advice and help me to do the right thing. Dear Jesus, please help me to be a good friend, a friend who will help and guide. Please help me to find Christian friends who can help guide me to becoming more like you. Please forgive me for the times that I have not obeyed you. Please help me to change. Amen.

30 May

READ AND UNDERSTAND

Proverbs 13:20. If you keep company with the wise you will become wise. If you make friends with fools, you will be harmed. So choose your friends wisely.

Proverbs 17:8. Some people use bribery to get what they want. If they have a lot of money they may think that they can do anything, and sometimes they can. But remember that giving a bribe is sin. God hates it and even if it looks like they are getting what they want, God will punish their sin.

LOOK AT YOURSELF

Do you know someone who has a lot of money? Do you want to be their friend just because they have money? That is wrong. You should have a godly and wise friend, that is what is important, not money. Do you have a lot of money? Do you use your money to get friends or things that you want? You must remember that bribery is sin. What is important is that you live a life that pleases God and you get friends who love God and will help you to love Him more.

PRAYER

Thank you, God, for wise friends who will help me to become wise. Dear Jesus, please help me to have wise and godly friends. Please help me to have friends who will help me to love you more. Please help me to remember that money is not the most important thing. The most important thing is to love you and to love others. Please help me to become more like you. Amen.

31 May

READ AND UNDERSTAND

Proverbs 17:9. The way to keep peace among friends is to forgive when you are sinned against. If you tell others about someone's sin you will be gossiping and you will break up friendships.

Proverbs 10:12. Hate will cause trouble. Love will forgive others. God commands us to love our neighbours.

Proverbs 2:17. You must keep your marriage vows, which say that you will love each other for the rest of your life.

LOOK AT YOURSELF

Have you ever told a lie about someone? Have you ever told another person about something that someone did that was wrong? Remember that gossip is sinful. If you gossip you could break up friendships. Gossip can even cause trouble between a man and his wife, the closest friendship that there is. So remember that friendships are important and you must forgive your friend if they did something wrong. You must not tell other people about it. God has forgiven you of so many sins. You must be prepared to forgive your friend.

PRAYER

Thank you, God, for forgiving all my sins because Jesus died on the cross for me. Dear Jesus, please help me to forgive my friends if they do something wrong. Please help me to be a good friend and to never tell lies or gossip about my friends. Thank you that you forgive me, help me to become more like you. Amen.

1 June

READ AND UNDERSTAND

Proverbs 20:19. Someone who gossips can't keep a secret, so stay away from people who like to talk about others. It is wrong to say bad things about people.

Proverbs 30:10. You must never speak badly to a boss about someone who works for him. If you lie about the person, the boss will call you a liar and you will deserve it. So remember not to say bad things about other people.

LOOK AT YOURSELF

It is important to have friends you can trust. Make sure that your friends are not gossips. Gossips will only cause trouble and hurt between people. So remember that you must also never gossip. Gossip can be lying and it can also be telling the truth about what happened when you should not have spoken about it at all. You must not talk about things that will make other people look bad, even if it is true. You would not like someone to tell everyone when you did something wrong. So make sure you don't do that to others.

PRAYER

Thank you, God, the Bible can help me to learn what kind of a friend I need to be and it can help me to know what kind of friends I should have. Dear Jesus, please help me to have friends who love you and who live lives that please you. Help me to have friends who don't gossip and help me to be a person who does not gossip. Please forgive me for the times that I have said things about people that have not been pleasing you. Please help me to change. Amen.

2 June

READ AND UNDERSTAND

Proverbs 22:24-25. Don't be friends with a person who gets angry or is easily upset and gets violent. If you are friends with someone like that you will learn to be like them, and you may not be able to change.

Proverbs 17:14. Starting a quarrel is like making a small crack in a dam wall. The crack will grow until the wall breaks and there is a flood. So stop a quarrel before it goes any further.

Proverbs 15:21. Foolish people are happy with their foolishness, but the wise will do what is right. Always do what is right.

LOOK AT YOURSELF

Do you know someone who likes to fight and argue? Do you know someone who gets angry quickly? You must not be friends with people like that because you don't want to be like that. If you are wise you will love God and want to obey Him. If you obey God you won't get angry and you won't start fights and arguments. You must rather show love to other people. If someone has done something bad to you, you must forgive them and not get angry. If someone is trying to start a fight or argument, you must try and stop the fight. You must not get involved and make it worse.

PRAYER

Thank you, God for giving me the Bible so that I can know what is right and what is wrong. Dear Jesus, please help me to live a life that is pleasing to you. Please forgive me for the times that I have started fights and gotten angry. Please help me to change and become more like you. Amen.

3 June

READ AND UNDERSTAND

Proverbs 27:17. *If you rub two pieces of iron together they will shape each other and sharpen each other. In the same way your friends will affect the type of person you are. You must make sure your friends are people who love God and want to glorify Him, and then you will be able to help each other become more like Christ.*

Proverbs 5:9. *If you get involved in impure relationships you will not be known as a good person, you will waste your life. You must rather get married.*

LOOK AT YOURSELF

This week we have seen how important friends are. You must choose friends who love God and want to please Him. Then you will be able to help each other become more like Christ. A very important friendship is when you get married. You must make sure that the person that you marry is a Christian and loves God. Then you will be able to help each other grow for the rest of your lives.

PRAYER

Thank you, God for giving me friendships with other Christians who can help me to grow and to become more like you. Dear Jesus, please help me to choose my friends wisely and help me to stay away from people who are wicked and who do not love you. Please help me to live a life that pleases you. Amen.

WEEK 23

WISDOM AND MONEY

This week we are going to look at money and how bad it is to get money by cheating, lying, stealing or any dishonest way. Money is not the most important thing. The most important thing is that we obey God and live lives that are pleasing to Him. If you have to disobey God to get money it is sinful and very displeasing to God.

TIME TO REMEMBER

Proverbs 13:11. "Dishonest money dwindles away, but he who gathers money little by little makes it grow."

4 June

READ AND UNDERSTAND

Proverbs 1:13. The wicked will sin in order to get rich. Don't copy them. You must work hard to earn money.

Proverbs 31:24. A godly wife will take care of the family and will have time to do extra things to make some money; this lady makes clothes and sashes to be sold.

LOOK AT YOURSELF

Do you think that having a lot of money is very important? Do you think that having a lot of things is important? What is important is that you are a godly person and that you live a life that is pleasing to God. You must work hard and save little by little to buy things that you would like. Then you will appreciate the money that you have and the things that you can buy. Remember that if you are wicked you will be punished. Even if you got rich from being wicked, your punishment will show you how unimportant money is.

PRAYER

Thank you, God. You have given me so many things. Dear Jesus, please help me to be more thankful for what I have. Please help me to remember that money is not the most important thing. Please help me to live a life that pleases you and help me to remember how much you hate sin. Please help me to change. Amen.

5 June

READ AND UNDERSTAND

Proverbs 10:2a. Getting money by lying and cheating is wrong. You must work for your money.

Proverbs 30:7-9. The writer of these proverbs asks for two things from God, to never be a liar and to always trust God for his needs. He does not want to be rich, in case he trusts in riches rather than God. He does not want to be poor in case he disobeys God and steals. So remember that you must always be honest and you must trust in God for all things.

LOOK AT YOURSELF

There are two warnings today. Do you have a lot of money? Then you must make sure that you don't trust in your money. Only God can look after you and provide for you. Don't think that your money will keep you safe. Are you poor? Then you must make sure that you never sin to get what you need. God promises to provide for His children and He will not let you go hungry. You must then pray to God and ask Him to provide for you. You must also remember to look at what you do have and be thankful for that.

PRAYER

Thank you, God, for everything that you have given me. Thank you that I have the Bible and that I can learn more about you and about your promises. Thank you that you will look after me and only you can protect and care for me. Dear Jesus, please help me to trust in you more. Please help me to be more thankful. Please forgive me for the times that I have sinned against you and disobeyed you. Please help me to change. Amen.

6 June

READ AND UNDERSTAND

Proverbs 13:11. If you cheat to get money you will soon lose it. If you work hard to earn your money, you will get more. So work hard and don't cheat.

Proverbs 13:19. How good it is to get what we want. Fools only want to do evil, so they will never have happiness. Don't be foolish, hate evil and do good.

Proverbs 17:24. A wise person finds wisdom and understanding easily, but a fool looks everywhere and he does not find wisdom. Don't be a fool, study the Bible and become wise.

LOOK AT YOURSELF

Have you ever cheated in a game so that you could win? Have you ever cheated so that you could get something? Remember that cheating is a sin; God hates it and you must never cheat. Only fools will not want to obey God; all they want is evil and they will never be happy. So remember to study the Bible and become wise. If you want to learn more about God and what is pleasing to Him, you will be able to become wise and you will know how to live.

PRAYER

Thank you God for the Bible. Thank you that I can learn more about you and how you want me to live. Dear Jesus, please help me not to be foolish. Please help me to never what evil things. Please help me to never do something evil to get things. Please forgive me for the times that I have disobeyed you. Please help me to change and become more like you. Amen.

7 June

READ AND UNDERSTAND

Proverbs 21:6. If you get riches by lying, those riches will soon disappear. Being dishonest is a deadly trap. Remember to be honest and work hard to earn your money.

Proverbs 12:5. The thoughts of the righteous are good; the words of the wicked are lies. Our words will be like our thoughts, so make sure your thoughts are good.

Proverbs 8:13c. If you fear the Lord you will hate lies. God hates lies and so must you. You must always tell the truth.

LOOK AT YOURSELF

Have you ever told a lie? Have you ever told a lie so that you could get something? You must remember that lying is sinful. God hates it and if you are a Christian then you will hate lies too. If you love God and want to obey Him then you will have godly thoughts, godly words and godly actions. Your whole life must be pleasing to Him.

PRAYER

Thank you, God that you always tell the truth. Thank you that you are Holy and that you can never lie. Dear Jesus, please help me to become more like you. Please forgive me for the times when I have lied. Please help me to remember to obey you and to tell the truth. Please help me to change. Amen.

8 June

READ AND UNDERSTAND

Proverbs 22:16. If you get rich by bribing rich people or being horrible to poor people you will become poor yourself. God hates bribes and He hates people who are mean to poor people, both are sin.

Proverbs 28:21. It is wrong to show partiality and say that the guilty person is innocent because he has given you something, or to say that an innocent person is guilty. Don't take bribes and show partiality to people, it is a sin and God hates it.

LOOK AT YOURSELF

Have you ever wanted to be friends with someone just because they had a lot of money and so you thought you could get things from them? Remember that showing partiality, choosing someone just because of what they have, is sinful. It is also sinful to bribe. If you were fighting with your sister in the house and you broke a vase, it would be bribing and sinful if you told her that you would give her money if she told Mum that it was the dog that knocked it down and not you. If you ever give someone something so that you don't get into trouble, it's bribing and it is wrong.

PRAYER

Thank you, God that you don't show partiality. Thank you that you love me even though I am nothing. Dear Jesus, please help me to never show partiality and never to bribe. Please help me to remember that living a life that is pleasing to you is much more important than having money. Amen.

9 June

READ AND UNDERSTAND

Proverbs 28:8. The Israelites were not allowed to charge another Jew interest if he lent him money, so if they charged interest it was sin. It is also sin to charge so much interest that the person will never be able to pay. If someone gets rich because he sins in those things, God will take his money away and give it to someone who is kind to the poor. So be kind and love others as God has commanded.

Proverbs 3:33b. God blesses the house of the obedient. So learn from the Bible what God wants you to do, and obey Him.

LOOK AT YOURSELF

You must never take advantage of the poor. God wants you to show love and kindness to poor people. You must remember that everything that you have is given to you by God. You must remember to use what you have to glorify God and please Him. If you live a life that pleases God, if you obey Him, then He will bless you. So learn from the Bible about what God commands and obey what you learn.

PRAYER

Thank you, God, that you care for the poor. Thank you that you have given me so much. Dear Jesus, please help me to become more like you. Help me to show love to the poor and to help them whenever I can. Please help me to obey you in everything that I do. Please forgive me for the times when I have not obeyed you. Please help me to change. Amen.

10 June

READ AND UNDERSTAND

Proverbs 28:22. Selfish people want to get rich quickly and money is all that is important to them, but they don't realise that they could become poor at any time. Don't focus on money and things. It only leads to becoming poor.

Proverbs 23:20-21. Do not get drunk or be somebody who eats too much, both are sinful. You must not be friends with people who are like that. If you do these thinks they will make you poor. You will sleep too much, become lazy and by not working you will become poor.

LOOK AT YOURSELF

What is more important to you? Is it money or is it obedience to God? You must not be selfish and always think about how much money you can have or would like to have. Rather you must spend your time thinking about God. If all that is important to you is money, the money will disappear. God wants you to focus on living a life that pleases Him.

PRAYER

Thank you, God for warning me about the sinfulness of getting drunk. Please help me to remember how bad it is. Dear Jesus, please help me to not be selfish and always think about having money. Please help me to be thankful for what you have given to me. Please help me to remember how important it is for me to live a life that is pleasing to you. Please help me to change. Amen.

WEEK 24

THE IMPORTANCE OF WISDOM

This week we are going to study Proverbs 4:6-13. Again we are going to look at wisdom and how important it is to have, also how much it helps you. Wisdom is spoken of as a lady, how she will protect you and save you.

TIME TO REMEMBER

Proverbs 4:6. "Do not forsake wisdom, and she will protect you; love her, and she will watch over you."

11 June

READ AND UNDERSTAND

Proverbs 4:6. Wisdom will guard you. Love wisdom and it will watch over you. Learn from the Bible and you will become wise.

Proverbs 25:15. If you are patient and you don't get angry and shout, but stay calm and use soft words, you can do difficult things; you can get rulers to listen to what you are saying. So don't be someone who gets angry and shouts, remember to be patient and to have kind and gentle words.

LOOK AT YOURSELF

Have you ever gotten angry and shouted at someone? If you are wise you will be patient and calm, you will use soft and gentle words rather than shouting. So remember that wisdom will protect you, but if you are foolish and you become angry quickly, then you will probably get fighting and trouble. So obey the Bible and become a patient person.

PRAYER

Thank you, God for being so patient with me when I sin. Thank you for forgiving me when I sin against you. Dear Jesus, please help me to be a patient person. Please help me not to get angry and shout. Please forgive me for the times that I have disobeyed you. Please help me to change. Amen.

12 June

READ AND UNDERSTAND

Proverbs 4:7. Getting wisdom is the most important thing you can do. Whatever else you get, get understanding. So learn from the Bible and get wisdom and understanding.

Proverbs 6:33. If you have an impure relationship you will be punished. God created marriage and it is good.

Proverbs 21:4. Wicked people look down on others and think that they are better than others. Their actions are sinful. So don't be proud, be humble and love others.

LOOK AT YOURSELF

Do you think that you are better than others? Have you ever told someone that you could do something better than they could? This is to be proud. God wants you to be humble and not proud. If you are able to do things well you must thank God for it. Do not show off. Everything that you are able to do is because God has given you the ability. So be thankful to God and don't be proud. If you are wise you will know that you will always need to learn more. The most important thing is to get wisdom and understanding.

PRAYER

Thank you, God for giving me so much. Thank you for all the things that you have allowed me to be able to do. Dear Jesus, please help me not to be proud. Please help me to show love to others and think about others as more important than myself. Thank you that you died on the cross so that my sins can be forgiven. Please help me to change. Amen.

13 June

READ AND UNDERSTAND

Proverbs 4:8. Wisdom must be very important to you. Learn from the Bible and become wise.

Proverbs 14:13. Laughter may hide sadness. When the laughing stops there is only sadness left.

Proverbs 30:12. There are people, who say that they are pure and holy, but they are not, they are sinners and are dirty before God because of their sin. Go to God and confess your sins, God will forgive you and clean you. He will make you pure.

LOOK AT YOURSELF

Do you think that you never sin? Do you think that you live a life that is pleasing to God in everything that you do? If you think that then you are wrong. Everyone is sinful and everyone needs to go to God and confess their sins. You must learn from the Bible about what is pleasing to God and what He hates. Then you will be able to see were you are sinning, and then you must confess your sins and you must try to change.

PRAYER

Thank you, God for giving me the Bible so that I can learn about how I must live. Thank you that if I confess my sins, you will forgive me and cleanse me. Dear Jesus, please help me to live a life that pleases you. Please help me to stop sinning. Thank you that you died on the cross so that my sins can be forgiven. Amen.

14 June

READ AND UNDERSTAND

Proverbs 4:9. If wisdom is important to you, you will have a good life. So learn from the Bible and become wise.

Proverbs 4:10. Listen to your parent's instruction and you will have a long life. Remember that command to honour and obey your parents.

Proverbs 8:13b. If you fear the Lord you will hate pride and evil. God hates pride and evil and so must you.

LOOK AT YOURSELF

Do you listen carefully when your parents speak to you and instruct you? Is it important to you to learn and become wise? You must remember how important wisdom is and you must remember that God has told your parents that it is their job to instruct you and teach you. So if you want to obey God and learn more about Him and how to please Him, then you will listen to your parents and you will want to become wise.

PRAYER

Thank you, God for my parents. Thank you that they can teach me about you and help me to know more about you. Dear Jesus, please help me to hate pride and evil. Please help me to know what is pleasing to you and how I must live. Please forgive me for the times when I have not listened to my parents. Please help me to always listen and remember how important wisdom is. Amen.

15 June

READ AND UNDERSTAND

Proverbs 4:11. The Scriptures will teach you wisdom and they will lead you in the right way to live. So you must study the Bible and obey it.

Proverbs 4:12. Nothing will stand in your way if you walk wisely, and you will not stumble when you run. So learn from the Bible and become wise.

Proverbs 16:9. We might make plans, but God is in control of what happens.

LOOK AT YOURSELF

Do you know that nothing will happen that is out of God's control? Don't you think it is wonderful to know that God is in control of all things? If you are wise and walk in a way that pleases God, God will look after you and He will protect you. So if you want to please God, you must learn from the Bible about what is right and what is wrong. Then you must do your best to obey God and live a life that glories Him and pleases Him.

PRAYER

Thank you, God that you know everything and you are in control of everything. Thank you that I can trust in you to look after me. Dear Jesus, please help me to learn from the Bible and become wise. Help me to know how I must live. Please forgive me for the times when I have done things that are not pleasing to you. Please help me to change. Amen.

16 June

READ AND UNDERSTAND

Proverbs 4:13. Always remember what you have learnt. Your education is your life - guard it well.

Proverbs 26:11. If a fool goes back and does the same foolish thing over and over, it is like a dog that has gotten sick because of what he had eaten, but then is so foolish to go and eat the vomit. This is how horrible it is for a person to go back to sin that they know is wrong. So don't be foolish, learn and stay away from sin.

LOOK AT YOURSELF

Do you know of something that you do that is sinful? Do you keep doing that sinful thing even though you know it is disobeying God and displeasing to him? It is very foolish to keep sinning when you know that it is wrong. You must want to stop that sin and you must ask God to help you to stop. God wants you to live a godly life. He wants you to become more like Christ. So remember how important it is to live a life that is pleasing to God, and try as hard as you can to change.

PRAYER

Thank you, God for forgiving me for all the times that I have sinned against you. Dear Jesus, please help me to stop sinning. Please help me to live a godly life, doing everything in the way you would do it. Please help me to remember what I have learnt from the Bible about what is pleasing to you. Please help me to change and become more like you. Amen.

17 June

READ AND UNDERSTAND

Proverbs 4:25. Focus your eyes on the wise path and don't be distracted from it. Learn from the Bible and become wise.

Proverbs 26:4-5. Sometimes if a fool asks a silly question or he wants to start a foolish argument, you must not answer him, so that you don't act like he is acting. But there are also times when a fool needs to be answered so that he knows that he is being foolish and that he is not wise. So remember not to speak as a fool and get into arguments but also remember to give the truth when you can.

LOOK AT YOURSELF

Have you ever heard someone say something about God that was not true? You must tell them that they are wrong and you must tell them what the Bible says. But remember to be careful of getting into arguments with people who are foolish and don't want to know the truth. If they are saying things just to get into a fight you must be careful. You must pray to God and ask Him to give you wisdom so that you can know if you should say something and what to say if you should.

PRAYER

Thank you, God that you have given us the Bible so that we can learn about who you are. Thank you that the Bible is true and I can trust what it says. Dear Jesus, please help me to have wisdom to know what to say when people say things that are not true. Please help me to learn from the Bible so that I know what is true. Please help me to be wise and to live a life that is pleasing to you. Amen.

WEEK 25

DON'T BE LAZY - DO YOUR BEST

This week we are going to see the difference between someone who works hard and someone who is lazy. Most of the time people who work hard will get rewarded and will succeed. But if you are lazy it can end in poverty. Remember again this week that Proverbs are general principles and not promises. Sometimes people are poor and it is not because they are lazy, other times lazy people can get a lot of money. But remember that it pleases the Lord if we work hard.

TIME TO REMEMBER

Proverbs 13:4. "The sluggard craves and gets nothing, but the desires of the diligent are fully satisfied."

18 June

READ AND UNDERSTAND

Proverbs 12:27. If you are lazy you will never get what you want, but if you work hard you will appreciate what you work for. So work hard.

Proverbs 13:23. If the poor only have a little, it can be enough if they look after it. If you don't look after what you have, it might be taken away from you. Be thankful for what you have and look after it.

LOOK AT YOURSELF

Have you ever wished that you had more; that your family had more money; or that you had more things? Remember to be thankful to God for what you do have. There are people who have less that what you have got. Also remember that if you want to have money you need to work hard. If you are a lazy person you will never have what you want and you won't appreciate what you do get.

PRAYER

Thank you, God, for everything that you have given to me. Thank you that I have a place to sleep, clothes to wear and food to eat. You have blessed me with so much. Dear Jesus, please help me to not be a lazy person. Please help me to be thankful for what I have and work hard when I have something to do. Please forgive me for the times that I have not been thankful. Please help me to realise how much I have. Amen.

19 June

READ AND UNDERSTAND

Proverbs 13:4. No matter how much lazy people may want something, they will never get it. If you are a hard worker you will get everything you need. So work hard.

Proverbs 15:22. Get all the advice you can, and you will succeed. Without advice you will fail. Don't be proud and think that you know everything.

Proverbs 5:12. The fool will never learn and never let anyone correct him. Don't be foolish. Learn when you are corrected.

LOOK AT YOURSELF

Have you ever been proud and not asked people to give you advice and help? It is wise to ask for advice, to learn when someone corrects you. So don't be a fool. Remember that you will never know everything; you will always need to learn more. What you can learn from the Bible is how to be someone who works hard and does the best job that you can. If you work hard the Lord will provide for you.

PRAYER

Thank you, God, for giving me people in my life who I can go to and ask for advice. Thank you for the people who can correct me and help me to live a life that pleases you. Dear Jesus, please forgive me for the times when I have been proud and not asked for advice and help. Please forgive me for the times when I have not wanted to listen when someone corrected me. Please help me to change and become more like you. Amen.

20 June

READ AND UNDERSTAND

Proverbs 11:12. It is foolish to say bad things about others. If you have understanding you will keep quiet. Never say bad things about other people.

Proverbs 14:23. Work hard and you will get what you need. If all you do is sit around talking, you will become poor. So work hard.

Proverbs 19:13a. Foolish children can bring their parents to ruin. So remember to honour and obey your parents and don't be foolish.

LOOK AT YOURSELF

Have you ever sat around talking and not doing the work you should have been doing? Have you ever spoken horribly about other people? Remember that it is foolish and sinful to gossip and talk about people in a horrible way. You must not say hurtful things about others; you must not lie about them or say things that would make people not like them. Talking too much can get you in to trouble, especially if you have work to do. So be wise and think before you speak. Make sure you do your work before you spend a lot of time talking with your friends.

PRAYER

Thank you, God, for my parents, please help me to honour and obey them. Dear Jesus, please forgive me for the times when I have sinned against you and not lived in a way that is pleasing to you. Please help me to think before I speak and to remember to do my work when it needs to be done. Thank you that you died on the cross so that my sins can be forgiven. Please help me to stop sinning and to live a life that pleases you. Amen.

21 June

READ AND UNDERSTAND

Proverbs 21:26. Lazy people are always asking for more, but a godly person has enough for themselves and for others. Don't be lazy, work and you will have enough to show kindness to others.

Proverbs 13:22. Most of the time good people will have money to leave for their children and grandchildren, but often the money of sinners will go to the righteous. So obey God and live a righteous life.

Proverbs 3:27. Whenever you possibly can, do good to those who need it. God commands us to love our neighbour.

LOOK AT YOURSELF

Are you ever selfish and only worried about what you want? Or do you care about other people and think about what you can do for others? Lazy people do not care about anyone but themselves. If you love God and want to obey Him you will work hard and also enjoy showing kindness to others. Remember that God wants you to show kindness to people whenever you can.

PRAYER

Thank you, God, for all the kindness and love that you show to me. Thank you for everything that you have given me. Dear Jesus, please help me to show love to others. Please help me to not be lazy but to do my work as well as I can. Please help me to live a life that pleases you. Thank you for loving me so much that you died on the cross for me. Please forgive me for my sins and help me to live a righteous life. Amen.

22 June

READ AND UNDERSTAND

Proverbs 22:29. People who work hard and do a good job will often work for important people and not just ordinary people. If a king heard about a good worker, he would want that person to work for him. So remember to work hard and do a good job. This is pleasing to our King, who is God.

Proverbs 5:21. The Lord sees everything you do. Wherever you go, He is watching. Don't think you can hide from Him, because you can't. Obey God always.

LOOK AT YOURSELF

Have you ever done a bad job because you thought nobody would know? Remember that God sees everything and knows everything. Even if nobody is sitting making sure you do your work, God can always see. So remember to always do your work for God. Work well and do the best job that you can so that God can be pleased with you.

PRAYER

Thank you, God, that you can see everything and that you know everything. You are the King of the universe and the King of me. Dear Jesus, please help me to always do the best job that I can so that I can please you. Please forgive me for the times when I have been lazy and not done the best job that I can, please help me to change and to always live a life that is pleasing to you. Amen.

23 June

READ AND UNDERSTAND

Proverbs 27:18. If you do your work well and you work hard and do the best job that you can, things will go well for you. Just like a farmer who looks after a fig tree will be able to eat the figs that grow on the tree, so if you work hard you will be rewarded. So always do your best.

Proverbs 24:3-4. If you want to be successful with building a house or with building a family, what you need is wisdom, understanding and knowledge. So learn from the Bible and get those things.

LOOK AT YOURSELF

What do you think is more important? To have lots of money and things or to have wisdom, understanding and knowledge? God says that money is not as important. You must rather spend time learning about God and about how you should live. Then if you live a life that is pleasing to God, if you are not lazy but do the best job that you can, God will look after you. That does not always mean that you will have a lot of stuff. But God will always provide what you need.

PRAYER

Thank you, God. You provide food for me to eat, clothes for me to wear and a place for me to sleep. Thank you for everything that you have given to me. Dear Jesus, please help me to remember how important it is to learn from the Bible and become wise. Help me to learn about you and about how I must live so that I can please you. Amen.

24 June

READ AND UNDERSTAND

Proverbs 28:20. If you are a good worker and are honest and committed to your work, you will be rewarded for that, you will be blessed. But if you want to get rich and will do anything to get rich, then you will get punished. So be a good worker and be honest.

Proverbs 26:27. If you set a trap for others, you will get caught in it yourself. If you roll a boulder down to hurt others, it will roll back and crush you. Remember that there are consequences for the evil that you do and want to do. God will judge and you will be punished. So don't be evil, you must obey God and love others.

LOOK AT YOURSELF

Have you ever lied or cheated so that you could get something that you wanted? God hates dishonesty and lies; you must remember how important it is that you are always honest. All sin must be punished, but remember that is why Jesus died on the cross. If you trust in Jesus and ask God to forgive you for all your sin, then Jesus was punished on the cross for your sin. You will not have to be punished. You can be forgiven. So you must ask God to forgive you and you must try as much as you can to stop sinning.

PRAYER

Thank you, God that my sins can be forgiven because Jesus died on the cross. Please forgive me for all my sins. Dear Jesus, please help me to live a life that is pleasing to you. Help me to become more like you every day. Amen.

WEEK 26

GOD WANTS US TO BE HUMBLE

This week we are going to learn about how bad it is to be proud. Being proud means that you think that you are better than other people and more important than other people. God hates pride and proud people will be destroyed. God wants you to be humble.

TIME TO REMEMBER

Proverbs 16:5. "The Lord detests all the proud of heart. Be sure of this: They will not go unpunished."

25 June

READ AND UNDERSTAND

Proverbs 6:17a. The Lord hates the proud. So don't be proud, be humble.

Proverbs 21:22. Wisdom is better than physical strength. A wise person will accomplish more than a fool who thinks that his physical strength can protect him. Wise people know that only God can protect them. Be wise and trust in God, not in your own strength.

LOOK AT YOURSELF

Have you ever told people that you could do something but then found out that you were not strong enough or able to do what you thought? Did you go and ask for help? Or did you have a proud heart and not want to admit that you could not do what you thought you could? You must not be proud and think that you are so great. You must rather be humble and wise, and then you will be able to do a lot more things because you know when you need to ask for help.

PRAYER

Thank you, God, that I can always trust in you. Dear Jesus, please help me to trust in you more and not in anything else. Thank you for the abilities that you have given me, help me to not be proud about what I can do, but rather do everything that I can to glorify you. Please help me to live a life that pleases you. Please help me to be humble. Amen.

26 June

READ AND UNDERSTAND

Proverbs 13:10. Pride causes nothing but trouble. It is wiser to ask for advice. So be humble and ask for advice.

Proverbs 16:25. What we think is right, might not always be what God wants. We must study the Bible so that we know what is right.

Proverbs 31:1-2. The proverbs in chapter 31 are from King Lemuel's mother, teaching him, she wants her son to learn. You must remember to listen to your parents teaching.

LOOK AT YOURSELF

Do you listen when your parents teach you? Do you obey them in everything? Do you go to your parents and ask them for help and advice? Remember that wise people will ask for and listen to advice. Wise people will learn from the Bible and learn from their parents. Don't be proud and think that you know everything. God wants you to learn and He has given us the Bible and other people to help us to learn.

PRAYER

Thank you, God, for giving us the Bible. Thank you for giving me parents. Dear Jesus, please help me to not be proud but to ask for advice. Please help me to learn from the Bible and to learn from my parents. Please forgive me for the times when I have not listened and not learned. Please help me to change. Amen.

27 June

READ AND UNDERSTAND

Proverbs 15:25. The Lord will often destroy the homes of the proud people, but He often protects a widow's property. Don't trust in your worldly possessions, the Lord might take them away so that you are humbled.

Proverbs 22:2. Remember that God made everyone, the rich and the poor.

Proverbs 28:6. It is better to be poor and obedient to God than to be a rich person who is wicked. So don't be wicked, love God and obey Him.

LOOK AT YOURSELF

Do you think that money is very important? God says that it is better to be obedient to him than to have a lot of money. Remember that the most important thing is that you love God and obey Him. He wants you to rely on Him and not on money. Money is not bad, but it is not as important as living a life that is pleasing to God. Knowing that you are going to go to heaven is a lot more important than having things on earth.

PRAYER

Thank you, God, that Jesus died on the cross so that my sins can be forgiven and I can be with you in heaven one day. Dear Jesus, please help me to live a life that pleases you. Please help me to remember to trust in you and never to trust in things on this earth. Please forgive me for all my sins and please help me to change and to become more like you. Amen.

28 June

READ AND UNDERSTAND

Proverbs 16:5. God hates proud people; they will be punished. So don't be proud, be humble.

Proverbs 27:19. If you look into still water you will be able to see your face, as if you were looking in a mirror. If you want to see what your character is like you must look at your heart. You will see if you are a godly person, someone whose heart is pure, if your thoughts are pure. You must have a pure heart, then you will not think about wicked or evil things or do them, you will love God and others and you will want to obey God and glorify Him.

LOOK AT YOURSELF

Do you love God? Do you want to please him? Have you asked God to forgive you for all your sin so that you can have a new heart, a pure heart? If you have been saved then you have been given a pure heart. Then you must make sure that you are living a pure life. You must not have wicked thoughts, you must not say wicked things and you must not do wicked things. Rather you must have thoughts, words and actions that show that you love God and want to obey Him.

PRAYER

Thank you, God, that I can have a new heart because Jesus died on the cross to pay for my sins. Dear Jesus, please help me to live a life that is pleasing to you in everything that I think, say and do. Please forgive me for the times when I have not lived in that way, when I have sinned against you. Please help me to change. Please help me to become more like you every day. Amen.

29 June

READ AND UNDERSTAND

Proverbs 16:18. Pride leads to destruction and arrogance leads to a fall. Pride will only get you into trouble.

Proverbs 27:14. It is good to thank your friends for what they have done and to encourage them if they are living a godly life, but be careful of always shouting about how good your friend is. Your friend will get tired of it; he might even wonder what you want from him. You could cause your friend to become proud. So be careful not to praise your friends too much.

LOOK AT YOURSELF

Do you like it when people tell you how good you are? Do you say "Thanks, I know I am good"? Or do you tell them that everything that you can do is because God has given you the ability to do it? You must not be proud. Everything that you do is because God has been kind to you and blessed you with that ability. We must focus on what the Lord has done and is doing rather than on what we can do. If your friend has done something very well, you could tell them that it is wonderful to see them using the talents God has given them.

PRAYER

Thank you, God, for allowing me to be able to do so much. Thank you that everything that I can do is because you allow me to do it. Thank you for my friends and all the things that they can do so well. Dear Jesus, please help me to not be proud about what I can do. Please help me to always give you the praise and glory. Please forgive me for the times when I have not been humble and have been proud. Please help me to change. Amen.

30 June

READ AND UNDERSTAND

Proverbs 6:17b. The Lord hates the lying tongue. Always tell the truth.

Proverbs 17:19b. If you brag all the time destruction might come. Don't try and have the best things to brag about. Be humble and thankful for what you have.

Proverbs 20:25. Think carefully before you promise to offer something to God, that you know how much it will cost you. If you don't it would be like an animal falling into a trap. Think before you promise something; remember that if you promise you must do it.

LOOK AT YOURSELF

Have you ever bragged about what you have done? Have you ever bragged about something that you never actually did? Have you ever promised to give something to someone and never gave it? It is a sin to lie. So be careful of what you say. Make sure that you do what you promise to do. Always tell the truth and keep your promises. When you say that you will try to do something, make sure you try as hard as you can.

PRAYER

Thank you, God, that you never lie. Thank you that I can know that you always tell the truth and that the Bible is true. Dear Jesus, please help me to never tell lies. Please help me to be careful of what I say and what I promise to do. Please forgive me for the times that I have bragged about things that I have done. Please help me to be humble. Please help me to change. Amen.

1 July

READ AND UNDERSTAND

Proverbs 18:12. Pride leads to destruction. People who think they are better than others will fall. Humility comes before honour, humility is what pleases God and so we must be humble.

Proverbs 15:29. Wicked people are far from the Lord; He will not hear their prayer. God hears the prayer of righteous people.

Proverbs 4:19. The way the wicked live is like darkness. They don't know what they are falling over. It is foolish to be wicked, obey God and you will know how to live.

LOOK AT YOURSELF

Have you ever tried to walk in the middle of the night, with no lights? You can fall over things because you don't see them. If you are not a Christian you are living life without the light to show you how to live. God has told us in the Bible how we should live so that we can honour and glorify Him. If you are a Christian you can pray to God and ask Him to help you and guide you, you will be able to live without falling over everything. Remember that if you are a Christian you must not be wicked, you must stop sinning and start living a righteous life. If you think that you are not sinning then you are wrong. We have all sinned and we must go humbly to God and ask Him to forgive us.

PRAYER

Thank you, God, that Jesus died on the cross so that my sins can be forgiven. Please forgive me for all my sins. Dear Jesus, please help me to be humble and not to have pride. Please help me to change and to become more like you. Amen.

WEEK 27

THE IMPORTANCE OF TRUTH

This week we are going to look how important it is to be honest and tell the truth. God hates people who cheat and lie but He is pleased when you obey Him and always tell the truth. We will also see that people will like someone who is honest because they can trust them.

TIME TO REMEMBER

Proverbs 12:22. "The Lord detests lying lips, but he delights in men who are truthful."

2 July

READ AND UNDERSTAND

Proverbs 11:1. The Lord hates people who cheat. He is happy with people who are honest. So you must never cheat, always be honest.

Proverbs 21:15. When justice is done, good people are happy. But destruction will come to those who are evil and so they hate justice and will try to run from it. Obey God and don't be evil, God will punish the wicked.

LOOK AT YOURSELF

When last did you tell a lie? When you lied had you forgotten that God knows everything and that you cannot hide things from Him? God hates lying and cheating. You must obey God and always be honest. Then you will be living a life that is pleasing to God and honouring to Him. Have you ever known that you have done something wrong and that you will get punished for it? Did you lie about it and try and run away from justice. Remember that you must be honest. If you have done something wrong you must not sin again by lying about it. Rather be honest, if you lie you will only make the situation worse.

PRAYER

Thank you, God, that you never lie. Dear Jesus, please help me to become more like you. Help me to remember how much you hate lying and cheating. Please help me to always be honest and tell the truth. Please help me to live a life that is pleasing to you. Amen.

3 July

READ AND UNDERSTAND

Proverbs 21:29. Wicked people will tell a lie and pretend as much as they can, they don't care about truth. A righteous person is consistent; always doing what is right and true and so can carry on without pretending. Don't lie. Always tell the truth.

Proverbs 20:10. The Lord hates people who cheat, people who lie about how much they are selling and give less than what is paid for. Never cheat, always be honest.

Proverbs 12:9. It is better to be an ordinary person working for a living than to pretend you are a great person but go hungry. Enjoy your job and work hard.

LOOK AT YOURSELF

Have you ever lied to your friends about how much your parents have or about what they can do so that your friends will think that you are better than them or special? Have you ever lied about something that you can do, told someone that you were better than you really are? It is wicked to lie and pretend all the time. You must never lie. God wants you to be honest and tell the truth.

PRAYER

Thank you, God, for everything that you have given to me. Dear Jesus, please help me to be thankful for what I have and can do. Please help me to never lie about things. I know that you hate lies, please help me to live a life that is pleasing to you. Please forgive me for the times when I have lied, please help me to change. Amen.

4 July

READ AND UNDERSTAND

Proverbs 12:22. The Lord hates liars, but He is pleased with those who keep their word. So don't lie, obey God and be honest.

Proverbs 5:11. Impure relationships will result in sickness and a horrible life. But marriage will bring happiness because it is the relationship that God said is good.

Proverbs 5:15. Be faithful to your marriage partner and give your love to that person only.

LOOK AT YOURSELF

Did you know that when a man and a woman get married that they promise to love each other for the rest of their lives? If you get married one day you must remember that you have to keep your promise and you must love that person for as long as you both live. Having a relationship with a man or a woman that you are not married to is wrong. If you pretend to be married to someone when you are not you are lying and you are living a life that is displeasing to God. So remember how important marriage is and remember how important it is to always tell the truth.

PRAYER

Thank you, God, for creating marriage. Dear Jesus, please help me to be someone who is honest and who keeps my promises. Please forgive me for the times when I have sinned against you and have not been honest but have lied. Thank you that you died on the cross so that my sins can be forgiven. Please help me to change. Please help me to become more like you. Amen.

5 July

READ AND UNDERSTAND

Proverbs 20:7. It is good for children to have a father who is honest and does what is right.

Proverbs 19:27. If a person stops listening to instruction he is not learning and he will soon forget what he already knows. So remember to always listen when you are taught and never stop learning.

Proverbs 4:18. The godly are like sunrise, shining brighter and brighter. The godly people will keep learning how to live like Christ.

LOOK AT YOURSELF

Do you listen when your parents teach you? Do you appreciate your parents and everything that they do for you and everything that they teach you? Do you see that the father in Proverbs 20:7 is described as a man who is honest and does what is right? Are you an honest person? Do you do what is right? If you are a Christian you should be able to see that over the weeks, months and years of being a Christian that you are obeying God more and more. You should be learning all the time about how to become more like Christ. You should be able to see that, even though you sin, you are changing and sinning less.

PRAYER

Thank you, God, for giving me parents who can teach me. Thank you for everything that they do for me. Dear Jesus, please help me to be an honest person, and someone who always tries to do what is right. Please forgive me for the times when I have sinned against you and not obeyed you. Please help me to change and become more like you. Amen.

6 July

READ AND UNDERSTAND

Proverbs 11:10. A city is happy when good things happen to honest people, they are also happy when wicked people die. Nobody likes wicked people, so don't be wicked, be honest.

Proverbs 29:16. If a leader is wicked then there will be lots of crime, but godly and righteous people will often see those wicked people fall. Remember that God will punish people who are wicked.

LOOK AT YOURSELF

Do your friends see you as someone who will lie to your parents? Or do they know that you will never lie to them? If you obey God in everything that you do, people will know that you are not a wicked person but someone who will always tell the truth and do what is right? If someone asks you to lie you must tell them that you cannot lie, that you need to obey God and always tell the truth.

PRAYER

Thank you, God, for giving me the Bible so that I can learn about what is pleasing to you and what you hate. Dear Jesus, please help me to be a person who loves and obeys you. Please help me to remember how important it is to tell the truth. Thank you that I can always trust what you have said in the Bible because you cannot lie. Please help me to become more like you. Amen.

7 July

READ AND UNDERSTAND

Proverbs 20:23. The Lord hates people who cheat and lie about their money. Never cheat, always be honest.

Proverbs 17:4. Wicked people listen to evil talk, liars listen to words that are destructive. Do not listen to talk that is about evil and wickedness. Listen and talk about what is good and pleasing to God.

Proverbs 16:6b. To stop sinning, you must fear the Lord. So fear the Lord and stay away from evil and sin.

LOOK AT YOURSELF

Has your mum ever given you money to go and buy something for her? Did you give her all the change back, or did you lie about how much it cost and take some money for yourself? You must always be honest and never lie. God cannot lie and He hates lies. Remember that wicked people are those who love to listen to lies and evil talk. You must not be wicked. Do you fear the Lord? Do you hate sin? The way to make sure you are not a wicked person is to study the Bible and learn about God and how holy He is. You then need to remember how much God hates sin. You must want to please Him and live a life in obedience to Him.

PRAYER

Thank you, God, that Jesus died on the cross so that my sins can be forgiven. Thank you that you can help me to stop sinning and that you give the Holy Spirit to those who are Christians to help us to obey you. Dear Jesus, please help me to learn more about you and how holy and perfect you are. Help me to become more like you. Amen.

8 July

READ AND UNDERSTAND

Proverbs 24:26. People will be happy if you give a true answer; if you are honest they will be your friend. So never lie, God hates lies but He is pleased when you are honest.

Proverbs 22:11. If you have a pure heart, good motives and hate wickedness, and if your speech is good and honouring to God, then you will be liked by people - even important and powerful people.

Proverbs 11:22. Beauty in an ungodly woman is like a gold ring in a pig's snout. The most beautiful thing about a woman is her godliness.

LOOK AT YOURSELF

Have you ever thought that you had to do something that was wrong so that people would like you? Perhaps if you were to lie about something they would become your friends? Remember that it is sinful to lie and God hates it. If you live a life that is pleasing to God, if you try to obey Him in everything that you do, people will like you and trust you. Those who lie and cheat may not like you, but they are not good friends to have. Good friends are those who love God and who live godly lives.

PRAYER

Thank you, God, that I know what pleases you and I know that it is never good to lie. Thank you that even if I don't get to be friends with some people because I will not lie, that you are pleased and that is what is more important. Dear Jesus, please help me to be a person who always tells the truth. Help me to have godly thoughts, words and deeds. Please help me to become more like you. Amen.

WEEK 28

GOD BLESSES THE RIGHTEOUS

This week we are going to see how godly people are protected and blessed by God. To be a godly person means to live a life that pleases God, obeying Him in everything that you do. You will never be able to obey God in everything, but you must always try and remember that it is because Jesus died on the cross that you can go to heaven, not because you obey Him. When we look at how God protects and blesses Christians, it does not mean that nothing can ever happen that is not nice or easy. But it does mean that God will work everything out for your good. That nothing will happen to you that is out of His control.

TIME TO REMEMBER

Proverbs 2:7-8 "He holds victory in store for the upright, He is a shield to those whose walk is blameless, for He guards the course of the just and protects the way of His faithful ones."

9 July

READ AND UNDERSTAND

Proverbs 2:7b. God protects those who walk in His ways. So you must obey Him in everything.

Proverbs 21:31. You can do all that you can to have success, but success will only come from God. Remember to trust in God who is in control of all things.

LOOK AT YOURSELF

Do you know that nothing can happen to you that is outside of God's control? Christians can know that all things will work together for their good. God is in control of all things and He knows what is best for His children. So remember to trust in God and live a life that pleases Him. To walk in God's way means to have thoughts, words and actions that are the way God wants.

PRAYER

Thank you, God, that you are in control of all things and that you will protect your children from things that you know are not good for them. Dear Jesus, please help me to live a life that pleases you. Please forgive me for my sin and help me to change. Thank you for dying on the cross so that my sins can be forgiven. Amen.

10 July

READ AND UNDERSTAND

Proverbs 2:8a. God protects those who treat others fairly. So remember to treat others with kindness.

Proverbs 27:6. It is better to get corrected from a friend than to get nice things from an enemy. Remember that if someone really loves you they will correct you and tell you when you are sinning. So listen when you are corrected.

LOOK AT YOURSELF

Has a friend or your mum or dad ever told you that something that you were doing was sinful and disobedience to God? Did you get cross with them for showing you? Or did you realise that they were showing kindness to you by telling you? You must show kindness to people and you must not get angry or upset with people. Jesus showed so much love for us and we must try and show love to others.

PRAYER

Thank you, God, that you have put people in my life who can help me to see when I am not obeying you. Dear Jesus, please help me to remember that it is a kind thing if people tell me if I am sinning. Please help me to stop sinning and to live a life that pleases you. Please help me to show love to others by treating them fairly and kindly. Amen.

11 July

READ AND UNDERSTAND

Proverbs 2:8b. God looks after those who are devoted to Him. So you must obey Him in everything.

Proverbs 31:8-9. A ruler must talk for those who cannot speak for themselves, he must protect people who are helpless and can't protect themselves. A ruler must open his mouth and speak the truth, he must be a godly judge and he must defend the afflicted and needy. So remember that God wants us to help and protect those who are in need.

LOOK AT YOURSELF

Do you help people? Have you ever helped a small child who is trying to walk, by holding his hand? Have you ever helped a younger brother or sister who is trying to build something or play with something? Do you help your mum and dad in the house? You might not be a ruler, but there are lots of places for you to help people who need help. Ask your mum and dad to help you see where you can help someone. God wants you to love Him and He wants you to show love to others as well.

PRAYER

Thank you, God, for showing so much love that you sent Jesus to die on the cross. Thank you that our sins can be forgiven and we can be with you in heaven one day. Dear Jesus, please help me to show love to other people. Please forgive me for sinning and not obeying you. Please help me to become more like you. Amen.

12 July

READ AND UNDERSTAND

Proverbs 2:21. God blesses the obedient. So you must obey God.

Proverbs 25:21-22. God commands us to love our enemies. If a person's fire went out he needed hot, burning coals to light it again. Giving that person coals in a pan to carry home was a kind thing to do, something that friends did for each other. So by heaping burning coals on their head you were showing love to your enemy, just like giving him food when hungry and water when thirsty. If your enemy did not want to make things right with you and become friends, then those coals would show God judging him for his lack of love. God will repay you for showing love to even your enemies.

LOOK AT YOURSELF

Can you think of someone who has not been very nice to you? Have you shown love to that person? Have you done something helpful and kind for that person? That is what God wants you to do. He wants you to show love. If you are obedient, God will bless you. You must not do things just to get something back. You must obey God and do what is right because you love God and want to please Him. Then your obedience will be pleasing to God.

PRAYER

Thank you, God, for showing kindness and love. You sent Christ to save people who were your enemies and who did not obey you. Thank you for saving me even though I disobeyed you. Dear Jesus, please help me to show kindness and love to others. Please help me to live a life that is pleasing to you, obeying you in everything that I do. Please help me to change. Amen.

13 July

READ AND UNDERSTAND

Proverbs 10:3. The Lord will not let good people go hungry, but He will keep the wicked from getting what they want. So always do what is right, always obey God.

Proverbs 26:26. A person who has hate in his heart might be able to hide it for a while, but eventually everyone will see the evil things that he does and will know the wickedness that is in his heart. So don't be wicked.

LOOK AT YOURSELF

Have you ever had hate in your heart towards someone? Even if you did not do anything horrible to them, it is still wrong? Wicked and disobedient people have hate in their heart. If you are a Christian you must ask God to forgive you for any hate you have had, and you must love that person. That means that you must do nice things for that person. This is not an easy thing to do. You must ask God to help you to do what is right. You can show your love for God by showing love to others, even showing love to your enemies.

PRAYER

Thank you, God. You show love to me when I don't deserve it. You forgive me when I have disobeyed you. Please forgive me for the times when I have not been loving and forgiving. Dear Jesus, please help me to show love to other people. Please help me to never have hate in my heart. If I do get hate in my heart, please help me to stop hating and start loving. Please help me to become more like you. Amen.

14 July

READ AND UNDERSTAND

Proverbs 11:8. The righteous are protected from trouble; it comes to the wicked instead. So don't be wicked, live a righteous life.

Proverbs 26:2. If someone says something bad against you, or swears at you, and you don't deserve it, then it will not hurt you. It will be like a bird that flies over your head and does not land; it does not do anything to you.

LOOK AT YOURSELF

Has anyone ever said horrible things about you or to you? Did you get angry and cross with them? Or did you forgive them and trust that God is in control? People may be able to hurt you with their words or actions, but you must remember that God will judge everyone who does not obey Him. So if they are wicked in what they do to you, remember not to be wicked back to them. God will judge them for their actions, so you must not want to get back at them. You must trust in God.

PRAYER

Thank you, God. You see everything and you know everything that happens. Thank you that you will judge people for their wickedness and I don't have to worry if people are horrible to me. Dear Jesus, please help me to not be wicked to other people. You see everything that I do and I want to try and obey you in everything that I think, say and do. Please help me to change. Amen.

15 July

READ AND UNDERSTAND

Proverbs 11:31. When you die you will be rewarded if you are righteous or punished if you are wicked. Often those who are righteous are rewarded here on earth as well. Obey God and live a righteous life.

Proverbs 3:35. The wise will be honoured and the fools will be shamed. You must learn from the Bible and become wise. If you are a fool you will not be respected.

LOOK AT YOURSELF

Do you know who is allowed into heaven? Do you think that if you are good enough you will be allowed in? You would never be good enough on your own to be allowed into the presence of God, He is too holy and every person has sinned. The only way to be allowed into heaven is if you accept Jesus Christ as your Lord and Saviour. You need to ask God to forgive you and trust that Jesus paid the price for your sins when He died on the cross. If you are a Christian you will want to please God and live a life that is obedient to Him. If you do live a righteous life, you will be rewarded in heaven. Remember that doing good things won't get you into heaven.

PRAYER

Thank you, God, that Jesus died on the cross so that I can be with you in heaven one day even though I am sinful. Thank you for your love and forgiveness. Dear Jesus, please help me to live a life that is pleasing to you. Please help me to obey you in everything that I think, say and do. Please help me to become more like you. Amen.

WEEK 29

THE IMPORTANCE OF WISDOM

This week we are going to learn again about wisdom. This week we are going to look at Proverbs 8:1-5. Wisdom is pictured as someone who is calling people to listen and become wise.

TIME TO REMEMBER

Proverbs 8:5. "You who are simple, gain prudence; you who are foolish, gain understanding."

16 July

READ AND UNDERSTAND

Proverbs 8:1. You are called to get wisdom and understanding. So learn from the Bible and become wise.

Proverbs 12:23. Wise people keep quiet about what they know, but stupid people talk so much that everyone knows they are stupid. Don't try and show off if you know something.

LOOK AT YOURSELF

Have you ever wanted to tell someone about what you have learned so that they will think that you are very clever? It is not wrong to tell people about what you are learning, but you must make sure that you are not proud, thinking that you are special and better than other people. Remember that everything that you learn is about God and His world. If you can read you must thank God that you can. If you can remember things about nature and you tell people about it, you must give God the praise for making it. If you learn about history you must see that God is in control. Your focus must be on what God has done and not on how clever you are.

PRAYER

Thank you, God, for giving me the ability to learn. Thank you that I can learn so much about you. Dear Jesus, please help me to not be proud and think that I am special. Please forgive me for the times when I have not obeyed you and I have sinned against you. Please help me to change. Amen.

17 July

READ AND UNDERSTAND

Proverbs 8:2a. Wisdom is not hidden. You must read the Bible and learn from it, and then you will get wisdom.

Proverbs 23:1-3. When you sit down to eat with someone important you must be careful of how you act. If you like to eat a lot you must stop yourself, you must not eat too much. Don't be greedy for all the nice food that he serves; he may be trying to trick you. So if you go to a fancy meal, don't just concentrate on the food, be polite and pay attention to what is happening around you, remember that it is wrong to eat too much.

LOOK AT YOURSELF

Do you like food? Do you pile your plate with lots of food or lots of pudding? God says that it is wrong to eat too much. You must make sure that you are not just eating lots of food because it tastes nice. You can enjoy your food, but you don't have to rush to the table first and take some of every pudding. You must think about other people and let them go first. You must also not take too much so that there will be enough for everyone.

PRAYER

Thank you, God, for all the food that you have made. Thank you for making so many tastes and flavours. Dear Jesus, please help me not to eat too much. Please help me to be thankful for the food that you have given and to be aware of other people. Please help me to learn to share and show kindness to others. Amen.

18 July

READ AND UNDERSTAND

Proverbs 8:2b-3. Wisdom will direct us. If we learn from the Bible, the Bible will tell us how to live.

Proverbs 27:8. If a bird leaves her nest and does not stay close by, it will be dangerous for the eggs or chicks that are in the nest. It is also true that if a baby bird leaves its nest too soon, it will also be in danger. So remember that there is safety at home. Children must appreciate the protection that their parents give, and parents must be close to their children so that they can protect them.

LOOK AT YOURSELF

Do you thank God for giving you parents? Do you appreciate your parents and everything that they do for you? Your parents can protect you, so you must listen to them when they teach you and you must obey them. God commands children to honour and obey their parents. That means you must respect your parents and obey them. God has put them over you to protect you. When you obey your parents you are obeying God.

PRAYER

Thank you, God, for my parents. Thank you that they protect me and look after me. Dear Jesus, please help me to always listen to my parents and to obey them. Please forgive me for the times when I have not obeyed. Please help me to change. Amen.

19 July

READ AND UNDERSTAND

Proverbs 8:4. Wisdom is offered to everyone. So YOU must read the Bible and learn from it. You can become wise.

Proverbs 30:21-23. There are four situations where things are not the way they should be. When a servant becomes a king, when a fool is rich, when a hated women gets married and when a maid takes the place of the lady she works for. People should not take positions that they are not able to handle, a fool does not know how to handle money and a servant does not know how to rule.

LOOK AT YOURSELF

If you were asked to run a big grocery shop, there would be many things to organise. You need to have all the goods to sell. You must make sure that all the things that need to be kept cold are all kept cold and that nothing has gone bad. You should make sure that the tills have enough change in them and that no money gets stolen. It is a very big job and perhaps you will be able to do it one day. But you must learn how to do it first. You should learn from someone else about how to do it. Do not try to do things that you cannot do on your own. Maybe one day you will be able to do it, but if you are wise you will ask for help. Only do what is just a little bit more difficult than what you have done before.

PRAYER

Thank you, God, that I can learn and grow every year. Thank you for giving the ability to learn. Dear Jesus, please help me to enjoy learning. Please help me to become wise. Amen.

20 July

READ AND UNDERSTAND

Proverbs 8:5a. Are you immature? Wisdom will teach you how to be mature. Learn from the Bible and become wise.

Proverbs 14:10. Your joy is your own; your sadness is your own. No one can understand completely how someone else feels.

Proverbs 17:26. It is not good to punish innocent people. It is also not good to punish leaders who are being honest and just. God hates injustice, so always be fair and honest.

LOOK AT YOURSELF

Have you ever allowed someone else to get into trouble for something that you did? Have you ever been punished for what someone else did? God is happy when the people who are disobedient get punished and the innocent people are not punished. That is being just and fair. Remember that God always knows what has happened. He knows the truth. Sometimes justice is not done; but you must remember that the Lord knows and He will punish those who are wicked.

PRAYER

Thank you, God. You know everything and justice is important to you. Thank you that I can be forgiven because Jesus died for me. Dear Jesus, please help me to always be honest, fair and just. Please help me to learn from the Bible and become wise. Amen.

21 July

READ AND UNDERSTAND

Proverbs 8:5b. Are you foolish? Wisdom will teach you how to have understanding. Learn from the Bible and become wise.

Proverbs 19:4. Rich people may have lots of friends but the friends may only want their money. Poor people may lose their friends but those were not true friends. So remember to choose your friends wisely. Also remember to be a true friend, someone who is a friend no matter what.

LOOK AT YOURSELF

Are you a good friend? Do you help your friends when they need help? Do you listen to your friends? Remember that we must consider others more important than ourselves. If your friend does not have a lot of money, you must not always go places where you need money. You must try and do things that do not cost money, or you must try and save up so that you can pay for your friend. Remember that having lots of money is not the reason to be friends with someone; you should find friends who love God and want to obey Him.

PRAYER

Thank you, God, for all the friends that I have. Thank you that people care about me. Dear Jesus, please help me to be a good friend. Please help me to care about other people and not to be worried about what I can do or get. Please help me to show love to others. Amen.

22 July

READ AND UNDERSTAND

Proverbs 4:22. Wisdom gives life and health. So learn from the Bible and become wise.

Proverbs 8:6. Listen to what the Bible teaches. It teaches the truth.

Proverbs 14:18. Simple people only get more foolish, but wise people get more knowledge. So be wise and learn as much as you can from the Bible.

LOOK AT YOURSELF

Do you enjoy reading your Bible? Do you enjoy learning more about God? If you are a Christian you will be able to understand the Bible. The more you study the Bible the more you will learn. You must ask God to give you wisdom because He is the source of wisdom. Wisdom is the best thing that you can get. Wisdom will help you throughout your life. If you are a Christian you should want to live a life that pleases God. The more you read the Bible the more you will learn about how God wants you to live.

PRAYER

Thank you, God, that you have given us the Bible so that we can learn more about you. Thank you that you know everything and you can help me to become wise. Dear Jesus, please help me to enjoy studying the Bible. Please help me to obey you when I learn about how you want me to live. Please help me to become more like you. Amen.

WEEK 30

YOUR WORDS CAN PLEASE GOD

This week we are going to look at how good it is to have wise and godly speech. This week you are going to have to look at your speech and see if you have speech that is pleasing to God or if your speech is not what it should be.

TIME TO REMEMBER

Proverbs 15:1. "A gentle answer turns away wrath, but a harsh word stirs up anger."

23 July

READ AND UNDERSTAND

Proverbs 10:11. The speech of the righteous is a fountain of life; it is profitable for the people who hear. The speech of the wicked hides their violence. So make sure your speech is good.

Proverbs 14:9. Foolish people don't care if they sin, but righteous people want to do what is right and want to be forgiven of their sin. So don't be foolish, obey God and live a righteous life.

LOOK AT YOURSELF

Do you care if you sin against God? Do you care if your speech is not pleasing to God? Only a fool will not want to be forgiven. You must go to God and ask Him to forgive you for all your sin. You sin every day against God. The only way you can be forgiven is if Jesus is your Lord and Saviour. Then your sins were paid for when Jesus died on the cross. If you are a Christian you must live a life that pleases God, obeying Him in everything. If you are sorry for sinning, you will try your best not to sin again.

PRAYER

Thank you, God, that my sins can be forgiven. Thank you that Jesus died on the cross so that I can be with you in heaven one day. Dear Jesus, please forgive me for sinning against you. Please help me to stop sinning and to live a life that pleases you. Help me to have speech that is pleasing to you. Amen.

24 July

READ AND UNDERSTAND

Proverbs 10:21. A good person's words will benefit lots of people, but stupid people can cause trouble on themselves, even getting themselves killed because of what they say. So think before you speak.

Proverbs 14:21. It is a sin to hate anyone. If you want to be happy, be kind to the poor. Remember the command to love your neighbour.

Proverbs 20:9. Who can say that they have cleaned their hearts and that they do not sin? Nobody can. All have sinned.

LOOK AT YOURSELF

Have you ever said something that hurt another person? Have you ever thought about something horrible to say but did not say it? God wants you to show love to other people, it is a sin to hate anyone. If you love God you will want to obey Him and you will want to show love and kindness to others. Remember to think before you speak. Your words can hurt people and they can be displeasing to God. So try your best to have speech that is kind, gentle and loving.

PRAYER

Thank you, God, even though I have sinned, I can be forgiven. Dear Jesus, please help me to think before I speak. Please help me to have speech that is kind. Please help me not to get angry or hate anyone but to rather show love. Please help me to become more like you. Amen.

25 July

READ AND UNDERSTAND

Proverbs 15:4. Kind words bring life and healing, but cruel words and lies bring pain and sadness. Love other people and always speak kind words.

Proverbs 15:1. A gentle answer will often stop people from being angry, but a painful word can make people angry. Even if people are fighting with you, you must have speech that is kind.

Proverbs 16:20. Pay attention to what you are taught.

LOOK AT YOURSELF

Has anyone ever started shouting and arguing with you about something? What did you do? Did you get angry and shout back, making the argument worse? Or did you answer with kind words, keeping yourself from shouting, and try and stop the argument? God wants us to have speech that is loving and kind. He wants you to show love to other people and think about them before you think about yourself. God showed so much love for us in saving us; we must show love to Him by obeying Him and showing love to others.

PRAYER

Thank you, God. You showed love to me by saving me even though I sin against you. Dear Jesus, please help me to stop sinning and to obey you. Please help me to have speech that is kind. Please help me not to argue and fight but to show love. Please help me to change and become more like you. Amen.

26 July

READ AND UNDERSTAND

Proverbs 15:7. Knowledge is spread by the speech of wise people, not by fools who have no knowledge in their hearts. Think about what you say, you don't want to be a fool talking only about foolish things.

Proverbs 18:13. Listen before you answer, listen to all the facts before you give your advice. If you don't you are being stupid and insulting.

LOOK AT YOURSELF

A wise person will listen to everything before answering because then he will be able to give a wise answer. If someone wants to ask you something, don't interrupt them and answer them before they are finished. That will be foolish; you will be talking about something that you don't know everything about. So remember to listen when people talk, don't just think about what you are going to say.

PRAYER

Thank you, God, for giving me the Bible so that I can learn about what is wise and pleasing to you. Dear Jesus, please help me to have speech that is pleasing to you. Please help me to listen properly and not interrupt people. Please help me to think before I speak and to have speech that is wise. Amen.

27 July

READ AND UNDERSTAND

Proverbs 15:23. It will bring joy and delight if you say the right thing at the right time. Think about what you are going to say before you say it.

Proverbs 24:13-14. Honey is known to be good for you, it also tastes nice and sweet, and so it is very good and nice to eat honey. It is the same thing with wisdom, it is good for you, and it is sweet to your soul. If you are wise you will have a good future, there is hope for the wise. So be wise, it is so good for you.

LOOK AT YOURSELF

Did you realise that if you are wise and if you say the right things at the right time that it will be good for you? Not only is it pleasing to God if you are wise and have godly speech, it is also good for others and it is good for you. God knows what is best for you and so you must always obey Him. Sometimes you might think that it would be better to lie, but it won't. It is always better to obey God.

PRAYER

Thank you, God. You know what is best for me and you have told me how to live in the Bible. Dear Jesus, please help me to have wise speech. Please help me to think before I speak so that I know what to say and when to say it. Please help me to live a life that pleases you in what I think, say and do. Amen.

28 July

READ AND UNDERSTAND

Proverbs 16:24. Kind words are like honey, sweet to the taste and good for your health.

Proverbs 24:28-29. You must not lie in court so that your neighbour gets into trouble, you must not want to be horrible to him if he was horrible to you. God says that you must do good to those who hate you, you must show them love. You must also always tell the truth.

LOOK AT YOURSELF

Have you ever lied so that someone you were cross with would get into trouble? Have you ever wanted to do something horrible to someone because they were horrible to you? God says that you must love others and be kind to them even if they were horrible to you. Remember to always have kind words and to show kindness to others.

PRAYER

Thank you, God. You show love to me even though I sin against you. Dear Jesus, please forgive me for sinning against you. Please help me to be kind to others and to have speech that is kind. Please help me to change and become more like you. Amen.

29 July

READ AND UNDERSTAND

Proverbs 18:4. A wise person's words can be like life-giving water, as deep as the ocean and as fresh as a flowing stream. So be wise so that your speech can be wise, cleansing and refreshing.

Proverbs 17:10. A wise person will learn more from one rebuke than a fool will learn from being hit a hundred times. So be wise and listen when you are corrected, learn as much as you can.

LOOK AT YOURSELF

If your parents show you that you are sinning, do you listen and learn from them? If you do you are being wise. A wise person will learn from being corrected and they will try to stop sinning and start obeying God. You must try and obey God by having speech that is godly. Think before you speak and listen when you are corrected.

PRAYER

Thank you, God, for people who are wise and can help me to see when I am sinning against you. Dear Jesus, please help me to be wise and be able to have speech that helps others and pleases you. Please help me to remember what I have learnt this week about speech and help me to change. Amen.

WEEK 31

PURITY AND MARRIAGE

This week we are going to study Proverbs 7:4-18. It is the story of a man who had a relationship with a woman who was not his wife. Relationships outside of marriage are sinful and we will see how this man is tempted to sin. We can then learn so that we do not sin.

TIME TO REMEMBER

Proverbs 7:4-5. "Say to wisdom, 'you are my sister,' and call understanding your kinsman; they will keep you from the adulteress, from the wayward wife with her seductive words."

30 July

READ AND UNDERSTAND

Proverbs 7:4-5. This is the introduction to the story. Right at the beginning you are told that wisdom and understanding can keep you from the trouble of a relationship outside of marriage. You must treat wisdom as your sister and understanding as your closest friend. That means that they must be important to you. You must want to learn from the Bible so that you can become wise.

LOOK AT YOURSELF

Do you like to learn from the Bible? Do you want to be wise and have understanding? The wisdom and understanding that you can get from the Bible will help you to know how to live. The Bible will tell you how you should obey God and live a life that pleases Him. So read your Bible and learn about how you should live.

PRAYER

Thank you, God. You have given me the Bible so that I can get wisdom and understanding. Dear Jesus, please help me to obey what I learn from the Bible. Please help me to obey you and to live a life that pleases you. Please help me to change. Amen.

31 July

READ AND UNDERSTAND

Proverbs 7:6-8. The story is told by someone who is looking out their window and sees the young man. He is showing that he is foolish and not wise because he walks on the streets close to her house and then he takes the street that goes to her house. This man knows were she lives, he knows that it is sin, but he is foolish and he goes close to her house.

LOOK AT YOURSELF

Have you ever wanted to do something that you knew was wrong? Imagine that your mum had baked some biscuits and had told you that you could not eat any now because they were for afternoon tea when guests were coming over. Would you go into the kitchen when nobody was there to look at the biscuits? Would you look around and see if anyone was looking? Wanting to take one but knowing you should not? That is what the Bible says is foolish. Don't see how close you can get to sin, stay far away from it. You should not even go into the kitchen if you know the biscuits are there. Think about your life. Think about something that you know you would like to do but must not. Make sure that you try and stay as far away from that sin as possible.

PRAYER

Thank you, God, that my sins can be forgiven because Jesus died on the cross for me. Dear Jesus, please help me to stop sinning. Please help me to stay away from situations that I know will make me want to disobey you. Please help me to live a life that pleases you. Amen.

1 August

READ AND UNDERSTAND

Proverbs 7:9. We see that the man walked by her house when it was night. He was trying to hide his sin. But that is foolish, God can see everything, you cannot hide your sin from Him.

Proverbs 7:10. Here we see the woman that he is going to. She is an ungodly woman, she does not dress modestly and she has evil plans in her heart.

LOOK AT YOURSELF

Have you ever thought that you could sin and that no one would know? Would you take a biscuit that you knew you could not have if nobody was looking, thinking that you could hide your disobedience? God can see everything that you do. You cannot hide your sin from Him. You must also not have evil plans in your heart. God knows what your thoughts are, He knows if you are thinking about evil things. So obey God in your thoughts, word and actions.

PRAYER

Thank you, God, that I cannot hide my sin from you. You know everything and that can help me to stop sinning. Dear Jesus, please help me to obey you in everything that I do. Please help me to remember that I cannot hide my sin from you. I must always obey you. Please help me to change and become more like you. Amen.

2 August

READ AND UNDERSTAND

Proverbs 7:11-12. These verses describe the ungodly woman in our story. She is rebellious and her home is not important to her. She is just looking for an opportunity to do something evil. A godly woman's home is important to her and she will submit to her husband. A godly woman will not be wicked but will look for opportunities of doing something good.

LOOK AT YOURSELF

Do you look for ways that you can disobey your parents? Are you rebellious or do you submit to them? Do you look for ways to get away with doing things that you know are wrong? God wants you to look for good things to do, He wants you to show love to other people and respect other people. You must not look for evil things to do. You must look for godly things to do. You must submit to God and to your parents and you must be obedient.

PRAYER

Thank you, God, for my parents. Dear Jesus, please help me to not be rebellious and disobedient. Please help me to obey you and obey my parents. Please forgive me for the times when I have been horrible to other people. Please help me to look for things to do that will show love to others. Amen.

3 August

READ AND UNDERSTAND

Proverbs 7:13-14. Today we see how the lady tries to tempt the man to sin with her. She wants him to get involved in her wickedness and disobedience. She pretends that she is right with God, she says that she has gone and prayed and that God is happy with her. But she is lying. She does not care about God; she does not want to obey Him. So remember that you must not get involved when people tempt you to sin with them. You must not believe people who say that God is pleased with them if you can see that they are disobeying God and they don't care about what God says is sinful.

LOOK AT YOURSELF

Has anyone ever asked you to do something that you knew was sinful? Did they make it sound nice, like something that you really want to do? This is being tempted to sin. When you are tempted, when sin is made to seem nice, you need to remember that sin is displeasing to God. If you are a Christian you will want to obey God and live a life that pleases Him. Sin is never worth it.

PRAYER

Thank you, God, that you have warned me that people will make sin sound nice. Dear Jesus, please help me to remember that I must always obey you. Please forgive me for the times when I have not obeyed you and have sinned. Please help me to stop sinning and to live a life that is pleasing to you. Amen.

4 August

READ AND UNDERSTAND

Proverbs 7:15-16. Again today we see how the lady lies to the man. She says that she has come out to meet him when she had actually gone out to find anyone. She tempts him to sin again by making sin seem nice, she describes the coloured covering and makes it sound so nice. Remember that it is never nice to sin because you will know that you have disobeyed God. You must not listen to people who want you to sin.

LOOK AT YOURSELF

Have you ever lied to someone so that they would do something that was wrong? It is horrible to lie and it is horrible to tempt someone else to sin. You must make sure that you don't do things that are sinful because other people tell you that it does not matter. Remember that sin is never nice; it is horrible to have disobeyed God. Jesus died on the cross so that your sins can be forgiven. If you are forgiven you should want to show love to God for what He has done for you. You can show love to God by obeying Him.

PRAYER

Thank you, God. You never lie. Thank you that I can know that everything that you said in the Bible is true. Dear Jesus, please help me to always tell the truth. Please help me to not believe people when they lie about sin, and say that it is nice. Please forgive me for sinning against you and displeasing you. Please help me to change and become more like you. Amen.

5 August

READ AND UNDERSTAND

Proverbs 7:17-18. Today we see that the lady again tempts the man to sin. She makes sin seem nice by describing nice smells and pleasant feelings. She tells the man that if he sins with her, he will enjoy sinning and he will feel good. She is lying to him. Disobedience will not bring good feelings; after you have sinned you will have guilt and shame. Obeying God is more important than enjoying things. Obeying God is always the right thing to do, even if you don't feel like obeying.

LOOK AT YOURSELF

Have you ever disobeyed because you wanted to enjoy doing what was wrong? Often we enjoy the sin but then the Holy Spirit shows us that we have sinned against God and that God is not pleased when we sin. Then we feel guilty and we feel bad that we have sinned against God. Remember that even if sin seems to be enjoyable, it is not enjoyable to know that you have disobeyed God. If you are a Christian you will want to please God, you will want to obey Him in everything.

PRAYER

Thank you, God, that Jesus died on the cross so that my sins can be forgiven. Dear Jesus, please forgive me for my sins. Please help me to remember that it is not pleasing to you if I sin. Please help me to stop sinning and to become more like you. Amen.

WEEK 32

GOD PUNISHES SIN

This week we are going to see how God hates wicked people and that sin will be punished. God will judge evildoers. Remember that we are all disobedient to God and all need to be judged for our sin. But Jesus died on the cross so that you can be forgiven. If you are a Christian and have asked God to forgive you, you will not be judged for your sin. But remember that if you are a Christian you will want to obey God and you will try to stop sinning.

TIME TO REMEMBER

Proverbs 4:27. "Do not swerve to the right or the left; keep your foot from evil."

6 August

READ AND UNDERSTAND

Proverbs 3:32a. God hates the wicked man. So don't be wicked, obey Him.

Proverbs 21:18. Wicked people bring on themselves the bad things they try to do to good people. God will judge their intentions and actions and punish them for it. Don't be wicked, God commands us to love.

LOOK AT YOURSELF

Has anyone ever done horrible things to you? Did you get angry or upset about it? Or did you go to God in prayer and ask Him to give you love for those people? God wants you to show love to others and not to be wicked. God knows peoples thought as well as their actions and He will judge and punish those who are wicked.

PRAYER

Thank you, God, there is forgiveness through Christ. Thank you that you can forgive me for my sin so that I do not have to be judged. Dear Jesus, please help me to obey you. Please help me to show love to other people and not to be wicked. Please help me to become more like you. Amen.

7 August

READ AND UNDERSTAND

Proverbs 3:33a. God curses the house of the wicked. So don't be wicked, obey God.

Proverbs 30:29-31. There are four things that can walk with power and authority: a lion, who is strongest of all animals and afraid of none; a cockerel who is strong and important; a male goat who is the leader of the flock; and a king who has his army with him. If animals and people can have power and importance, how much more important and powerful is God who made them all.

LOOK AT YOURSELF

When you look around you and see all the things in nature, do you praise God for making it all? When you see something amazing about an animal or a plant, do you remember that God is so wonderful and powerful that He designed it that way? If God is so powerful and important, don't you think that He has the most authority? That means that you should obey God and desire to please Him. You must not be wicked but rather you must show love as God has commanded.

PRAYER

Thank you, God, everything that you have made is so wonderful and amazing. Thank you that I can learn more about you when I read my Bible and I can learn about how you want me to live. Dear Jesus, please help me to obey you. Please help me to show love to people and to become more and more like you. Amen.

8 August

READ AND UNDERSTAND

Proverbs 6:17c. The Lord hates murderers. You must never murder.

Proverbs 24:1-2. Don't be jealous of evil people, and don't try to make friends with them. Evil people are always thinking about hurting others; they talk about making trouble. Be careful of who your friends are, don't be friends with anyone who is evil.

Proverbs 24:19-20. Don't let evil people worry and upset you. Don't want what evil people have. They have no future, when they die all there things will be gone and they will not be going to heaven. It is better to be godly and have the future hope of heaven. Don't be wicked.

LOOK AT YOURSELF

Have you ever hurt someone? Have you ever wanted to hurt someone? It is evil and wicked to hurt or want to hurt other people. God wants you to show love to other people and to do good things for them. God has shown so much love to us by sending His son to die for us. We need to become more and more like God, learning every day how we can show more love to others.

PRAYER

Thank you, God, for showing so much love. Dear Jesus, please help me to become more like you. Please help me to show love to others and help me to never want to hurt others. Please forgive me for the times when I have not shown the love that I should have. Please help me to change. Amen.

9 August

READ AND UNDERSTAND

Proverbs 28:28. If a wicked person is in charge, then people will hide. But when the wicked person dies then godly people will rule again. Don't be wicked, obey God and you will be a blessing to others.

Proverbs 6:18b. The Lord hates those who are always doing evil things. Don't be wicked, don't do evil things.

Proverbs 4:27. Avoid evil and walk straight ahead. Don't go one step off the right way. Always obey God.

LOOK AT YOURSELF

Have you ever walked on a balancing beam? It is so important that you concentrate on each step that you take. If you don't look and think about what you are doing, you can easily miss the beam and fall off. It is the same with living a life that pleases God. You must concentrate and make sure that you live a life that is obedient to God. You must try the best that you can to live a life that pleases God in everything that you do. It is very easy to fall off the right way and to do evil and disobedient things. So remember how important it is to obey God in everything.

PRAYER

Thank you, God, for showing me in the Bible how I should live. Dear Jesus, please help me to always obey you and to not forget what I have learned. Please help me to live a life that pleases you. Please forgive me for the times when I have disobeyed you and not walked in the way that you want. Please help me to change and become more like you. Amen.

10 August

READ AND UNDERSTAND

Proverbs 5:3-6. Impure relationships seam nice but they will end in pain and death. The best relationship is that of marriage.

Proverbs 14:17b. People who plan evil are hated. So don't plan evil, obey God and live a righteous life.

Proverbs 27:1. Don't brag about what you will do tomorrow, you don't have control over tomorrow; you have no way of knowing for sure what will happen. So don't brag. Remember that the future is in God's control, not yours.

LOOK AT YOURSELF

Have you ever made plans to do something? It is fine to make plans as long as you always make plans to do things that will please God. Never plan to do something that is evil. If you plan something that is good and pleasing to God, you must remember that God is in control and you will only be able to do what you have planned if God allows it. Remember that God is in control of everything.

PRAYER

Thank you, God. You are in control of everything. Thank you that nothing can happen that is out of your control. Dear Jesus, please help me to never plan to do evil. Please help me to live a life that pleases you. Amen.

11 August

READ AND UNDERSTAND

Proverbs 21:27. Outward acts of worship, like going to church or reading our Bible, are things that God wants, but He hates those things if you are wicked. If people do those things with evil motives God will punish them. So you must obey God because you love Him and want to glorify Him.

Proverbs 6:21. Remember to obey your father and your mother. This is a command; you must honour and obey your parents.

LOOK AT YOURSELF

Do you love God? Do you want to obey Him and live a life that pleases Him? Remember that God knows your heart and He knows if you are obeying Him because you love Him.
Do you obey your parents? Do you respect your parents? Remember that God commands you to respect and obey them. You must obey God by obeying your parents.

PRAYER

Thank you, God, for my parents. Dear Jesus, please help me to obey you by obeying my parents. Please help me to remember what I have learned and to remember that you want me to obey you and live a life that pleases you. Please help me to change and to become more like you. Amen.

12 August

READ AND UNDERSTAND

Proverbs 24:8-9. If you are someone who plans to do evil things, people will think of you as a troublemaker. It is foolish to plan evil things because it is sin, people will hate you if you are evil. So don't cause trouble, don't do evil things.

Proverbs 28:2. If there is wickedness in a country the leaders will change often. But a leader who is wise and has understanding and knowledge, he will be able to lead for a long time. Then the country will be able to have peace and there will not be so much rebellion. Wisdom has a lot of benefits.

LOOK AT YOURSELF

Do you cause trouble between people? Do you like starting fights and arguments? It is wrong to start fights and to cause trouble. People will not like you if you are a troublemaker. You should rather try to obey God and be a person who shows love to others, someone who has wisdom and who tries to make peace.

PRAYER

Thank you, God, that Jesus died on the cross so that I can be forgiven. Dear Jesus, please help me to stop sinning. Please forgive me for the times when I have caused trouble and not made peace. Please help me to show love and not to do evil. Please help me to become more like you. Amen.

WEEK 33

WISDOM AND FAMILY LIFE

This week we are going to look at verses that tell parents how they should discipline and instruct their children. If your parents are Christians they will want you to learn to live a life that pleases God. They can help you to learn about what God wants by correcting you and punishing you when you disobey. By disciplining their children, Christian parents are showing love to their children, wanting them to obey God and please Him.

TIME TO REMEMBER

Proverbs 29:15. "The rod of correction imparts wisdom, but a child left to himself disgraces his mother."

13 August

READ AND UNDERSTAND

Proverbs 3:12b. Parents discipline a child that they love. They want you to obey God and become more like Christ.

Proverbs 20:11. Even children show who they are on the inside by what they do on the outside. You can tell if they are honest and good, and if they do what is honouring to the Lord. So obey God and do what is right.

LOOK AT YOURSELF

Did you know that God disciplines His children because He loves them? Christian parents will also discipline their children because they love them. The best thing that you could learn is to obey God and live a life that is pleasing to Him. Your parents want to help you to learn how to live. They can see when you are living in a way that is not pleasing to God, and they will want to help you to change.

PRAYER

Thank you, God, for my parents. Thank you that my parents can help me to become more like you, by showing me and correcting me when I sin against you. Dear Jesus, please help me to obey my parents. Please help me to remember that they discipline me to help me become more like you. Please help me to change and to become more like you. Amen.

14 August

READ AND UNDERSTAND

Proverbs 13:24. If parents don't punish their children, they don't love them. If your parents love you, they will discipline you.

Proverbs 17:25. A foolish child will make his father angry and his mother sad. Don't be a fool, be wise and you will bring joy to your parents.

Proverbs 26:7. A fool does not understand Proverbs and he does not apply the teachings. The Proverbs are as useless to him as legs are to a paralyzed man. So don't be a fool. Learn from the Proverbs and apply them to your life.

LOOK AT YOURSELF

Have you ever gotten cross with your parents when they disciplined you? You must remember that God told parents that if they love their children they will discipline them. God has given parents the job of helping children to learn how to live a life that pleases Him. So don't be a foolish child. You must learn from the Bible and obey it. Your parents can help you to do this.

PRAYER

Thank you, God, for my parents. Thank you that they can help me to see where I am sinning and they can help me to change. Dear Jesus, please forgive me for the times that I have sinned against you. Please help me to learn from my parents and to stop sinning. Please help me to become more like you. Amen.

15 August

READ AND UNDERSTAND

Proverbs 19:18. Parents are commanded to discipline their children when they are young enough to learn. If they don't, they are helping the children to destroy themselves. Remember that parents who love their children will discipline them. Don't rebel against your parents discipline, learn from it and glorify God.

Proverbs 24:10. If you can't cope when there is a difficult time then you are weak. You can be strong though, you must trust in God and He will help you in difficult times. You must also ask for advice.

LOOK AT YOURSELF

Have you ever wished that nobody would tell you how to live and that nobody would tell you when you are doing something wrong? God says that if you were left on your own, and not corrected and helped, you would probably get involved in so much sin that it would destroy your life. So you must be thankful for the people, especially your parents, who can help you to know how to live a life that pleases God. They may be able to help you to save your life.

PRAYER

Thank you, God, for my parents and for other people who can help me to learn about how I should live. Dear Jesus, please help me to listen and to learn when I get corrected and disciplined. Please help me to remember that they are helping me to become more like you. Please forgive me for the times when I have not wanted to know what I was doing that was sinful. Please help me to change. Please help me to hate the sin in my life. Amen.

16 August

READ AND UNDERSTAND

Proverbs 13:1. Wise children accept their parent's discipline. Proud people never admit when they are wrong. So don't be proud, when you are wrong you must admit it.

Proverbs 22:6. Parents must teach and train their children how they should live when they are young, then they will remember it all their lives. So listen when your parents teach you.

Proverbs 29:22. People who get angry quickly will cause fighting; they will sin in a lot of ways. So don't get angry, it will only lead you into more sin.

LOOK AT YOURSELF

Have you ever gotten angry when someone told you that you were doing something wrong? Remember that it is sinful to get angry and if you get angry it will be easy to sin in so many other ways. So it is much better to be humble and to listen when you are corrected. You must listen when your parents teach and train you, because it can help you throughout your whole life to know how to live a life that pleases God.

PRAYER

Thank you, God, that you have put people in my life who will help me to know how to live a life that pleases you. Dear Jesus, please help me to be humble and to listen when I am corrected. Please forgive me for the times when I have gotten angry and not wanted to change. Please help me to see where I need to change and help me to change. Amen.

17 August

READ AND UNDERSTAND

Proverbs 23:13-14. God tells parents that they must discipline their children; the children won't die if they get spanked. Sometimes it is the punishment that parents give their children that helps the children know how God wants them to live. So they may end up living a longer life or they don't die young because of a foolish way of living.

Proverbs 21:2. You may think that everything you do is right, but God looks to see why you are doing it.

LOOK AT YOURSELF

Do you obey your parents? Do you do things that you know are the right things to do? Why do you obey and do the right things. You should want to obey your parents and do what is right so that God can be pleased and glorified. Everything that you do should be done to please God. God is pleased if you obey your parents and do what is right because you want to please and obey Him.

PRAYER

Thank you, God, for giving me the Bible to learn about how you want me to live. Dear Jesus, please help me to obey and please you. Please help me to obey my parents. Please help me to remember that I must do what is right so that you will be pleased and glorified. Amen.

18 August

READ AND UNDERSTAND

Proverbs 29:15. Parents who correct and discipline their children help them to become wise. But if they let their children do what they want and don't give them rules, then those children will not be wise and will make their parents embarrassed by the way they live.

Proverbs 22:13. Lazy people are always giving excuses why they don't work, they say "If I go outside, there might be a lion and I would be killed", even if he had never seen a lion in his life. So don't make excuses, you must work when there is work to be done.

LOOK AT YOURSELF

Do you sometimes wish that you did not have any rules to obey? Or do you realise how much rules can help you and protect you? If you had no rules, you could get hurt. If your parents did not tell you that you could not touch the pots on the stove, you could get burnt. Some rules protect you from hurting your body and some rules help to protect you as a person. Rules can help you to act in a wise way rather than a foolish way. Rules can help you to live a life that is pleasing to God. Remember that if you want to please God, you have to be saved; you must trust in Jesus, you have to be a Christian.

PRAYER

Thank you, God, that Jesus died on the cross so that my sins can be forgiven. Thank you that Christians can be with you in heaven one day because of what Jesus did. Dear Jesus, please help me to live a life that pleases you. Please help me to show you how thankful I am that you saved me by obeying you and pleasing you. Please help me to become more like you. Amen.

19 August

READ AND UNDERSTAND

Proverbs 29:17. Parents who correct and discipline their children will be happy and at peace, their children will be wise and they will bring the parents joy.

Proverbs 21:23. Be careful and wise in what you say and you will keep yourself out of trouble. So think before you speak. Your speech must always bring glory to God.

Proverbs 10:1. If you are wise your parents will be happy. But if you are foolish your parents will be sad. So learn from the Bible and become wise.

LOOK AT YOURSELF

Wouldn't it be wonderful to have a family where everyone is happy and at peace? If the people in that family are Christians it is possible. If you are a Christian you should want to become wise. If you learn from the Bible you will be able to become wise. Wisdom will help you to have speech that is pleasing to God and it will help you to bring joy and happiness to your parents.

PRAYER

Thank you, God, for giving me the Bible so that I can become wise. Dear Jesus, please help me to become wise and to have speech that is pleasing to you. Please help me to bring joy and happiness to my parents by obeying you and living a godly life. Please forgive me for the times when I have not obeyed you. Please help me to change. Amen.

WEEK 34

THE IMPORTANCE OF WISDOM

This week we are going to work though Proverbs 8:8-14. These verses are going to teach us about wisdom. Wisdom is the most important theme in the book of Proverbs. So it must be very important that we learn about wisdom and become wise.

TIME TO REMEMBER

Proverbs 8:11. "For wisdom is more precious than rubies, and nothing you desire can compare with her."

20 August

READ AND UNDERSTAND

Proverbs 8:8. The wise will speak what is righteous and will not have any wickedness within them. So you must be wise and always tell the truth.

Proverbs 19:28. A wicked witness mocks justice when he lies in court to hurt someone else. Wicked people love the taste of evil. So don't be wicked, remember God commands us to love our neighbour.

LOOK AT YOURSELF

Have you ever told a lie that got someone else into trouble? If you are a Christian you should want to always tell the truth. God hates lies and He hates the wicked witness who lies and gets someone into trouble. Remember how important it is to God that you always tell the truth. Ask God to help you to be a righteous person; a person who lives a life that pleases God in everything that you think, say and do.

PRAYER

Thank you, God, that you always tell the truth. Dear Jesus, please forgive me for the times when I have lied and sinned against you. Please help me to always tell the truth. Please help me to change and to become more like you. Amen.

21 August

READ AND UNDERSTAND

Proverbs 8:9. To someone with wisdom and understanding the Bible is clear and plain. The more you read the Bible the more you will understand.

Proverbs 9:7a. If you try and correct someone who mocks the Bible, he will mock you.

Proverbs 24:7. Wisdom is too deep for foolish people to understand, when important people and leaders get together, he will have nothing to say. So don't be a fool; fear God and become wise.

LOOK AT YOURSELF

Do you understand everything that is written in the Bible? You will never be able to understand it all. But you can ask God to help you to understand, you must ask God to give you wisdom. If you are a Christian, God will help you to understand. The more you read and think about the Bible, the more you pray to God and ask Him to help you to understand, the more God will help you to get wisdom and understanding.

PRAYER

Thank you, God, for the Bible. Thank you that you can help me to understand what you have said in the Bible. Dear Jesus, please help me to read and understand the Bible. Thank you that the Bible tells me how I must live, please help me to change and become more like you. Amen.

22 August

READ AND UNDERSTAND

Proverbs 8:10. Choose wisdom and knowledge instead of silver and gold. Wisdom is the most important thing you can get.

Proverbs 28:11. Some rich people think that they are so wise even if they are not. But a poor, wise person will be able to see that the rich man is not wise. So don't let money make you blind. The most important thing to have is true wisdom.

LOOK AT YOURSELF

Do you think that having lots of money and lots of things is the most important thing in life? The Bible tells us that having wisdom is the most important thing that you could have. You must never think that you know everything though. Only God knows everything. Everyone needs to keep learning and keep asking God for wisdom.

PRAYER

Thank you, God, that you know everything. Thank you that I can get wisdom from you by studying the Bible. Dear Jesus, please help me to learn from the Bible and become wise. Please help me to remember that wisdom is more important than having lots of things. Please help me to obey you and to live a life that pleases you. Amen.

23 August

READ AND UNDERSTAND

Proverbs 8:11. Wisdom is more precious than jewels, nothing you want can compare with it. So learn from the Bible and become wise.

Proverbs 19:6. Many people will try to get things from important people. Everyone will be friends with someone who gives gifts. Remember that true friendship is being a friend no matter how many things that person has.

LOOK AT YOURSELF

How do you choose your friends? Do you want friends who have lots of things and who will share their things with you? Or do you want a friend who loves God and wants to be wise and godly. If wisdom is the most important thing for you to have, more important than presents and gifts, then you will want a friend who has wisdom. The most important thing in life is to know God. So remember to choose your friends carefully.

PRAYER

Thank you, God, for giving me the Bible so that I can learn more about you and about how you want me to live. Dear Jesus, please help me to find friends who love you and what to obey you. Please help me to love and obey you. Please forgive me for the times when I have not obeyed you. Please help me to change. Amen.

24 August

READ AND UNDERSTAND

Proverbs 8:12. If you are wise you will have common sense and knowledge. You will be able to tell the difference between good and evil as well as truth and falsehood. So learn from the Bible and become wise.

Proverbs 8:13a. To fear the Lord is to hate evil. God hates evil and so must you.

Proverbs 6:32. You are stupid if you have a relationship outside of marriage. You are destroying yourself.

LOOK AT YOURSELF

If you read the Bible you will see that God is holy and that He cannot sin. God is so perfect and we are so sinful. If you understand how wonderful God is you will fear Him, you will respect Him and you will want to obey Him. If you are a Christian you will be able to know how God wants you to live and you will want to obey Him in everything that you do.

PRAYER

Thank you, God, that I can learn about how wonderful and perfect you are. Thank you that even though I am sinful I am able to pray to you because Jesus died on the cross for me. Dear Jesus, please help me to learn from the Bible about what is right and wrong. Please help me to always obey you and to live a life that pleases you. Amen.

25 August

READ AND UNDERSTAND

Proverbs 8:14b. Wisdom gives people understanding and power. So learn from the Bible and become wise.

Proverbs 8:15. Wisdom helps kings to rule well and it helps rulers to make good laws. The Bible teaches kings and rulers how to be wise.

Proverbs 14:28. A fancy position or name means nothing if you have no responsibilities. The important thing is that you work hard when you have work to do.

LOOK AT YOURSELF

If you get a job to do, do you make sure you do the best job that you can? Do you work hard and get it done as soon as you can? If you are wise you will always do the best job that you can. Remember that everything that you do must be done for God. You must want to please Him in what you do as well as how you do it. So work hard and do your best for God.

PRAYER

Thank you, God. You have given me the Bible so that I can become wise. Dear Jesus, please forgive me for the times when I have not done the best job that I could have done. Please help me to work hard and to do my best. Please help me to obey you and live a life that pleases you. Amen.

26 August

READ AND UNDERSTAND

Proverbs 9:6. If you want to be wise you must stop being foolish. Then you will get understanding.

Proverbs 18:15. People with understanding want to use their mind and get more knowledge. A wise person listens out for knowledge. So be wise and understanding, the more you know the more you can glorify God.

LOOK AT YOURSELF

Do you want to become wise? If you study the Bible and ask God to give you wisdom then you will be able to get it. Wisdom will help you throughout your life. You must want to learn about God so that you can live a life that pleases and glorifies Him.

PRAYER

Thank you, God, for giving me the Bible so that I can learn more about you. Dear Jesus, please help me to learn from the Bible and become wise. Please help me to know how I must live. Please forgive me for the times when I have not obeyed you. Please help me to change. Amen.

WEEK 35

STUDYING GOD'S WORD

This week we are going to see how important it is to learn from the Bible and to remember what we learn. We are going to look at Proverbs 22:17-21. This passage talks about how important it is to learn from the Bible. We will see that the Bible can teach us so many things and it can help us to learn to trust in God.

TIME TO REMEMBER

Proverbs 22:17-18. "Pay attention and listen to the sayings of the wise; apply your heart to what I teach, for it is pleasing when you keep them in your heart and have all of them ready on your lips."

27 August

READ AND UNDERSTAND

Proverbs 7:2a. Keep the commandments and you will live. If you are a Christian you will desire to obey God. Only Christians will be able to live with God in heaven.

Proverbs 29:10. Murderers hate honest and godly people and would want to kill them. But godly and righteous people will want to protect honest people. Don't be wicked; love the truth and those who are honest and godly.

LOOK AT YOURSELF

Are you a Christian? Do you know that you are sinful and that you need forgiveness? The only way to have forgiveness is if Jesus is your Lord and Saviour. If He is your Lord it means that you will want to obey Him and live a life that pleases Him. Remember that God wants you to obey His commandments and He wants you to love Him and to love others. So don't be wicked, show love to other people.

PRAYER

Thank you, God, that I can be forgiven because Jesus died on the cross. Dear Jesus, please help me to love you more. Please help me to show love to others and never hatred and anger. Please forgive me for all my sins and help me to change. Amen.

28 August

READ AND UNDERSTAND

Proverbs 7:2b. The Bible must be as important to you as your eyes are. You must learn from it and obey it.

Proverbs 14:1. Homes are made by wise women, but they are destroyed by foolish women. A godly woman is a wise woman.

Proverbs 14:6. Proud people can never become wise, but if you have understanding you will be able to get more knowledge. So humbly learn from the Bible and you will get understanding and knowledge.

LOOK AT YOURSELF

Do you think that you know everything that you need to know from the Bible? You will never be able to say that you know everything. The more you study the Bible the more you will learn. The wisdom that you can get from the Bible will help you in so many ways. So be humble and remember that you always need to learn more.

PRAYER

Thank you, God, for giving me the Bible so that I can become wise and know how to live. Dear Jesus, please help me to become wise. Please help me to live a life that pleases you. Please forgive me for the times when I have sinned against you. Please help me to change. Amen.

29 August

READ AND UNDERSTAND

Proverbs 22:17. You must listen to the instruction that is given in the Bible and you must think about how it applies to your life. You must read the Bible and obey it.

Proverbs 28:23. It is much better to tell someone when they are wrong than to always tell them how nice they are. People can grow from being told were change is needed; they can't grow if they are always flattered. So to be a good friend you will tell your friend when they are wrong so that they can change, then your friend will appreciate you. You must also appreciate your friends who tell you when you must change.

LOOK AT YOURSELF

Do you want to learn more about how God wants you to live? Do you want to change; to stop sinning and to live a life that pleases God? You must keep learning from the Bible and you must think about how God wants you to change. You must also appreciate other people who help you to see where you are sinning. If you want to show God how much you love Him, you will want to become more like Him.

PRAYER

Thank you, God, that the Bible can help me to change. Dear Jesus, please forgive me for sinning against you. Please help me to stop sinning. Please help me to learn from the Bible about how I must live so that I can please you. Please help me to become more like you. Amen.

30 August

READ AND UNDERSTAND

Proverbs 22:18. It is a good thing to memorise Scripture because then you will be able to quote them and talk about them when they are needed.

Proverbs 17:15. Punishing innocent people or letting the wicked go free, both are hated by God. It is sin to not be fair and just.

Proverbs 29:12. If a leader listens to lies then all the people who work for him will become liars. If you lie you will be surrounded by people who lie. So you must hate lies.

LOOK AT YOURSELF

Do you lie? Do you know that lying is wrong? You should memorise a Bible verse that tells you how bad it is to lie. Then when you want to lie you will remember that it is wrong and that God hates lies. Do you want to please God? Do you want to live a life that glorifies Him? Then you must always tell the truth and you must be fair and just.

PRAYER

Thank you, God. You gave me the Bible so that I can know how to live. Dear Jesus, please help me to remember what I have learnt in the Bible. Please help me to obey you in everything. Please forgive me for the times when I have lied. Please help me to change and to always tell the truth. Amen.

31 August

READ AND UNDERSTAND

Proverbs 22:19. If you read the Bible it will teach you, yes you, to trust in God.

Proverbs 19:7. If the family of a poor person sometimes hate him because he is poor, how much more will his friends. They will avoid him. The poor person calls for them but they are gone. Remember to be a true friend, even if your friend becomes poor.

LOOK AT YOURSELF

How do you choose your friends? Do you look for friends who have a lot of money? Or do you look for friends who love God and want to serve Him? It should not matter how much money your friend has. You must always be a good friend, no matter how much money they have. Remember that you must have friends who want to please God in everything that they do. Then they will be able to help you to live a life that pleases God.

PRAYER

Thank you, God, for friends. Dear Jesus, please help me to be a good friend. Please help me to be kind to my friends and to always try and help them when they need help. Please help me to find friends who love and serve you. Please help me to love you more and to live a life that pleases you. Amen.

1 September

READ AND UNDERSTAND

Proverbs 22:20. The proverbs are saying that they will give you good advice and will teach you how to have knowledge and be wise. So learn from the Proverbs.

Proverbs 18:23. When poor people speak, they plead for mercy, they beg politely. But sometimes when rich people answer they are rude and insulting. Remember that rich and poor should speak with gentle words and with kindness. Rich people are not better than the poor.

Proverbs 14:20. Worldly people hate poor people and they love rich people. The righteous do not do this. God commands us to love our neighbour, and that means everyone.

LOOK AT YOURSELF

Have you got a lot of money? Do you think that you are special because of the money that you have? Or do you think that you are less important because you don't have a lot of money? God says that He made everyone and nobody is better than anyone else. Everyone needs to go to God and ask Him for forgiveness. Everyone needs Jesus as their Lord and Saviour. So remember that money is not important. What is important is that you are a Christian. If you are a Christian you must remember to show love to everyone, to the rich and to the poor.

PRAYER

Thank you, God, for making me. Dear Jesus, please help me to show love to everyone. Please forgive me for the times when I have sinned against you. Please help me to change and to become more like you. Amen.

2 September

READ AND UNDERSTAND

Proverbs 22:21. If you study the Proverbs you will know what the truth is and you will be able to tell other people about the truth. So study the Proverbs and learn from them.

Proverbs 29:8. People who don't care about others will say horrible things about them and will get a lot of people upset and angry. But a wise person does not get angry but can be calm and kind when someone is horrible to them.

LOOK AT YOURSELF

Do you get cross when someone is horrible to you? Do you get angry with them and say horrible things to them? Or do you stay calm and speak with kind words to those people? Jesus showed love to the people who killed Him. We must learn to show love to others and then we will be able to tell them that Jesus showed love by dying on the cross.

PRAYER

Thank you, God, that Jesus died on the cross so that I can be forgiven. Dear Jesus, please forgive me for the times when I have gotten angry and the times when I have not showed love. Please help me to become more like you and show love to everyone. Amen.

WEEK 36

FEARING GOD

This week we are going to see how many benefits there are to fearing God. To fear God means that you know how perfect and how powerful He is. It means that you respect Him and honour Him because of how wonderful He is. God should be feared because He says that He will punish those who sin. You can be thankful that Jesus died on the cross so that you can be forgiven and so He can love you instead of hating you for your sin. If you fear God you will go to Him and repent of your sin. You will ask Jesus to be your Lord and Saviour and then God will forgive you. If you fear God you will want to obey Him and live a life that pleases Him.

TIME TO REMEMBER

Proverbs 14:27. "The fear of the Lord is a fountain of life, turning a man from the snares of death."

3 September

READ AND UNDERSTAND

Proverbs 10:27. If you fear the Lord you will have a good life. The life of the wicked will often be shortened because of their wickedness.

Proverbs 21:12. God, the righteous One, knows what goes on in the homes of wicked people. He will judge and punish them for their wickedness. Remember that you can't hide from God, so don't be wicked.

Proverbs 4:4b. Keep the commandments and live. God has given the Bible to us and we must obey it.

LOOK AT YOURSELF

Do you know that you sin and disobey God? Have you asked God to forgive you and to help you to change? God will punish you for your sin if you don't go to Him and repent. The only way to be with God in heaven one day is if you are a Christian. And if you are a Christian you will want to obey Him.

PRAYER

Thank you, God, that Jesus died so that I can be forgiven. Dear Jesus, please forgive me for my sins. Please help me to change and to live a life that pleases you. Amen.

4 September

READ AND UNDERSTAND

Proverbs 14:2. If you fear the Lord you will live righteously. If you are wicked you show that you hate God. Fear God and live righteously.

Proverbs 25:26. If a godly person sins, it is like putting mud into clean water. You must not disobey God to please man; the only thing that will happen is that you will get a bad reputation. You must obey God and be pure and clean, like clean and pure water from a spring or well. If that well or spring gets dirty, it becomes useless.

LOOK AT YOURSELF

Do you hate sin? Do you want to live a life that is like the pure clear water from a spring? Or are you happy to have a life that looks like a muddy puddle because of your sin? If you fear God, you will want to obey Him and have a pure and clean life. Ask God to forgive you for your sins and ask Him to help you to obey Him.

PRAYER

Thank you, God. You have shown me in the Bible how I must live. Dear Jesus, please forgive me for my sin. Please help me to change and to live a life that is obedient to you. Help me to obey you in everything that I think, say and do. Please help me to become more like you. Amen.

5 September

READ AND UNDERSTAND

Proverbs 14:26. Fear the Lord and you will have security and protection, for you and your children. Nothing can happen to God's people without God allowing it. If something happens that seems bad to someone who is a Christian and who fears God, you can know that it is for their good because God loves them and knows what is best for them.

Proverbs 22:22-23. It is wicked to rob the poor just because he is poor, or to be horrible to people who need help and mercy. God will look after the poor and the needy and if you are horrible to them, God will punish you. So remember to show kindness and mercy to the poor and those in need, this is what God commands us to do.

LOOK AT YOURSELF

Do you always show kindness to people? Do you show kindness to people who you think are not important? God wants you to show love and kindness to everyone. No matter who they are and no matter how much money they have. God knows how you treat people, so make sure you are showing love and kindness. That is what will please God.

PRAYER

Thank you, God. You showed love and kindness to me in letting Jesus die so that I can be forgiven. Dear Jesus, please help me to show love and kindness to all the people that I meet. Please help me to live a life that pleases you. Please help me to become more like you. Amen.

6 September

READ AND UNDERSTAND

Proverbs 14:27. Do you want to avoid going to hell? The fear of the Lord is a fountain of life. Only Christians will be able to be with God in heaven one day.

Proverbs 26:3. If a farmer wanted his horse to do something he would use the sound of a whip to make the horse know what to do, he would also use a bridle to control a donkey. The only way to control a fool is by physical punishment. Don't be a fool, you must listen when you are instructed and corrected, then you will not have to be punished.

LOOK AT YOURSELF

Do you listen when your parents tell you to do something? Or do you disobey them and then get a hiding or punished in another way? If you are wise you will listen when your parents speak. You must obey them and listen to them when they teach you. Then you will be able to learn without getting punished.

PRAYER

Thank you, God, that Christians can be with you in heaven one day. Thank you that Jesus died so that my sins can be forgiven. Dear Jesus, please help me to listen when my parents tell me what to do and when they teach me. Help me to obey you by obeying them. Please help me to become more like you. Amen.

7 September

READ AND UNDERSTAND

Proverbs 19:23. A person who fears the Lord has life, and is secure and at peace, protected by God. So fear God and obey His commandments. When something bad happens to a Christian it is in God's control and He allowed it to happen for a good purpose. Christians can always be at peace because God cares for them and He is in control.

Proverbs 3:34b. God looks after those who are humble and those who are suffering. He is loving and kind. God cares for the humble and those who rely on Him.

Proverbs 21:1. The Lord controls the minds of leaders as easily as a farmer directs water by digging paths for it to flow through. Remember that God is in control of everything, nothing is out of His control.

LOOK AT YOURSELF

Have you ever felt scared? Have you ever been worried about something? If you are a Christian you don't need to be afraid of anything. God is in control and He only allows things to happen to His people that will be good for them. Sometimes something might happen that is not nice, but it is your loving God who is in control. If the bad thing makes you trust God more then it is good that it happened. Don't be afraid or worry about things. Ask God to help you to trust in Him and give you peace.

PRAYER

Thank you, God. You are in control of everything. Nothing will happen to me that will not be for my good. Dear Jesus, help me to trust you more. Help me to trust you if bad things happen. Thank you for your love and kindness. Amen.

8 September

READ AND UNDERSTAND

Proverbs 22:4. We must fear the Lord and humbly submit to His authority and power. Then we will have riches, honour and life. We must remember to worship God, trust in Him, obey Him and serve Him. It does not mean that all Christians will have a lot of money or that they will live a long life. But it does mean that God will provide for them and that they will be with Him in heaven one day.

Proverbs 19:20. If you listen to advice, instruction and counsel and you learn from being disciplined, then you will be able to become wise.

Proverbs 13:12b. Put your hope in the promises of God, He is faithful. When the promises are fulfilled you will be very happy.

LOOK AT YOURSELF

Do you want to go to heaven when you die? Do you want to live with God in heaven forever? The only way to go to heaven is to be a Christian. Only if your sins have been forgiven because of Jesus dying on the cross, can you be with God in heaven. If you are a Christian you can look forward to being with God one day.

PRAYER

Thank you, God, Jesus died on the cross so that my sins can be forgiven. Dear Jesus, please forgive me for all my sins. Please help me to stop sinning and to live a life that pleases you. Thank you that because of your love I can be with you in heaven one day. Please help me to love you and to obey you. Amen.

9 September

READ AND UNDERSTAND

Proverbs 28:14. You must fear the Lord and you must fear the consequences of sin, then you will be happy and blessed. But if you harden your heart, if you don't care if you sin, then you are headed for trouble. So don't sin, fear God and obey Him.

Proverbs 19:15. A lazy person sleeps a lot and day dreams, doing nothing. Lazy people don't get a lot of work done and they will often go hungry because they haven't worked for food. So remember to always work hard and don't be lazy.

LOOK AT YOURSELF

Do you know how bad it is to disobey God and to sin? Do you know how much God hates sin? If you do know then you will want to stop sinning and you will want to live a life that pleases God. One way you can please God is if you work hard and do the best job that you can. Everything that you do you must do for God. And you should always want to do the best job for Him.

PRAYER

Thank you, God. You have given me the Bible so that I can know how to live a life that pleases you. Dear Jesus, please help me to obey you. Please forgive me for the times when I have disobeyed you and have sinned against you. Please help me to change and to become more like you. Amen.

WEEK 37

GOD BLESSES THE RIGHTEOUS

This week we are going to see how God looks after godly people. Everything that happens to God's people will be for their good and they will be happy if they trust in God. But people who hate God and who disobey Him will have trouble and they will be sad. Sometimes evil people may seem happy in this life, but they will be punished for their sin, and then they will definitely be sad.

TIME TO REMEMBER

Proverbs 17: 22. "A cheerful heart is good medicine, but a crushed spirit dries up the bones."

See the explanation on the 14th September.

10 September

READ AND UNDERSTAND

Proverbs 12:21. Nothing bad happens to righteous people, but the wicked have nothing but trouble. Even if you think something is bad, if you are a Christian, you can know that it is for your good. Remember that if you are a Christian you will want to obey God and live a righteous life.

Proverbs 21:28. If you tell lies in court, you will be punished. You must always tell the truth and then justice will be done. Lying is a sin God hates it.

LOOK AT YOURSELF

When did you last lie? Did you forget how much God hates lies? If you are a Christian you will want to obey God and you will want to live a life that pleases Him. That means that you will always tell the truth. Remember that telling lies will often cause more trouble. So don't lie, tell the truth.

PRAYER

Thank you, God, Jesus died on the cross so that I can be forgiven. Dear Jesus, please forgive me for the times when I have lied and sinned against you. Please help me to change and to always tell the truth. Please help me to become more like you. Amen.

11 September

READ AND UNDERSTAND

Proverbs 13:21. Trouble follows sinners everywhere, but righteous people will be rewarded with good things. So obey God and live a righteous life.

Proverbs 25:8-10. Don't be in a hurry to take someone to court because you saw them doing something. You might be embarrassed if you were wrong. It is better to talk to that person first and don't tell anyone else. If you talk about it to other people, people might think of you as a gossip, someone who can't keep a secret and then you will not be respected.

LOOK AT YOURSELF

Have you ever told someone about what you saw someone else do that looked wrong? You must not do that, it is gossiping. You should go to the person that you saw and find out what they were doing. Maybe you saw wrong, and what they were doing was not wrong. If they were doing something wrong you can help them to see that God wants them to obey Him. Then they will be able to repent and to ask God to forgive them.

PRAYER

Thank you, God, that all Christians will be able to be with you in heaven one day. Dear Jesus, please forgive me for the times when I have gossiped and said things that I should not have said. Please help me to have speech that is pleasing to you. Please help me to change and to become more like you. Amen.

12 September

READ AND UNDERSTAND

Proverbs 15:6. Righteous people will get paid with riches and blessings, but wicked people will get paid with trouble. Not all Christians have a lot of money, but all Christians have a relationship with God and that is the best thing to have.

Proverbs 28:3. If a poor person gets to be a leader and then is horrible to poor people, it is terrible. It is like rain that is so hard that it washes all the crops away, instead of watering the crops and helping them to grow. So that horrible leader is wrong, he should be showing kindness and love to the poor. Remember to show love to those who are in need.

LOOK AT YOURSELF

Are you kind to people? Are you kind to people who you don't know, people who are poor and need help? God wants you to love Him and if you do you will also show love to others as well. If you are a Christian, God has shown so much love to you in saving you. You should show love to others because you are God's child and you should be like Him. Ask God to help you to live a righteous life, a life that is pleasing to Him and obedient to Him.

PRAYER

Thank you, God. You showed so much love to me by letting Jesus die for my sins. Dear Jesus, thank you for dying for me. Thank you for showing me so much love. Please help me to become like you and to show love to others. Please help me change and to live a life that pleases you. Amen.

13 September

READ AND UNDERSTAND

Proverbs 16:7. If you please the Lord in the way that you live, you will be at peace with even your enemies. So make sure you are obeying God and pleasing Him. Then you will not have any hatred in your heart.

Proverbs 18:18. If two powerful people are fighting in court, casting lots can settle the issue. It may be easier to decide who goes first by flipping a coin. Then there is no fighting.

LOOK AT YOURSELF

Do you get angry and upset with people who are horrible to you? Or do you forgive them for what they have done and pray for them? Jesus forgave and prayed for the people who killed Him. If you are a Christian you can also have love in your heart for people who hate you and are horrible to you. You must remember that God is in control of everything and that He will punish people who are wicked and do horrible things. Be thankful that Jesus is your Saviour and because He died on the cross, you won't have to be punished for your sin. Pray for the people who are horrible to you. If they are not Christians pray that they may come to know God. If they are Christians you must pray that they would learn more about how God wants them to live and that He would help them to change.

PRAYER

Thank you, God. You can give me peace in my heart when people are horrible to me. Dear Jesus, please forgive me for the times when I have gotten angry and upset and sinned against you. Please help me to change and to become more like you. Please help me to love others the way you loved me. Amen.

14 September

READ AND UNDERSTAND

Proverbs 17:22. Being happy can keep you healthy, but being gloomy and sad can use up all your strength. So rejoice in the Lord always.

Proverbs 15:13. When people are happy, they smile, but when they are unhappy in their heart, they look sad. Our thoughts can control how we feel and how we look.

LOOK AT YOURSELF

Do you sulk about things when you don't get what you want? Are you sad for the rest of the day when you don't get to do what you hoped to do? You should rather be thankful for what you do have and what you have had to do. If you spend all your time being unhappy and thinking about something that you missed, you will waste a day that the Lord has given to you. You must rejoice in the Lord and enjoy every day that He has given.

PRAYER

Thank you, God. You have given me so much. Thank you for my family and all the things that we can do together. Dear Jesus, please forgive me for the times when I have gotten upset because I did not get something that I wanted. Please help me to see all the things that I do have. Please help me to be more thankful. Amen.

15 September

READ AND UNDERSTAND

Proverbs 18:14. A physically sick person can cope if his spirit is rejoicing and trusting in God. But if his spirit is down, he will have no hope. Remember to have a right relationship with God, and then you can have hope and joy.

Proverbs 25:20. Singing cheerful songs to a person who is sad and going through a difficult time is not being nice to them. It is like stealing someone's jacket when it is cold. It is like pouring vinegar on soda, it makes a big reaction. So you must show love when someone is feeling sad, you must be kind and sensitive.

LOOK AT YOURSELF

Have you ever visited someone who was very sick or very sad? If you do you must remember not to be too loud and noisy. You must show kindness and love to them. You can encourage them that God is in control of everything and that they can trust in Him through the difficult time. Then the person will be able to cope better, because they can trust in God and His love. They will be able to have joy because of everything that God has done for them, even if they are feeling sick or sad about something.

PRAYER

Thank you, God. You are in control of everything and I can always trust in you. Thank you that for a Christian everything works together for good. Dear Jesus, please help me to show love and kindness to people who are sick or sad. Please help me to tell them about your love and care, and about how you are in control of everything and that they can trust in you. Please help me to trust in you if I go through a difficult time. Amen.

16 September

READ AND UNDERSTAND

Proverbs 29:18. If people don't care about God's Word and what God says is good and what is sin, then there will be so much sin and wickedness. But if people listen to God's law and obey it then there will be happiness.

Proverbs 29:4. When a leader rules with justice, and is fair and does what is right, then the nation will be strong. But if he is only concerned about money and getting bribes, then he will ruin the country. Remember that God hates bribes and that it is unjust and will bring disaster.

LOOK AT YOURSELF

Do you care about obeying God? Do you want to do what is right? If you are a Christian you should want to obey God and live a life that pleases Him. If a family want to listen to God's word and want to obey what He says, that family will be happy. God will be pleased with them and they will be showing love towards each other, which will make it a lovely family to be in.

PRAYER

Thank you, God. You have given the Bible so that I can know what pleases you. Dear Jesus, please help me to obey your word. Please forgive me for the times when I have sinned against you. Please help me to change and to become more like you. Amen.

WEEK 38

GOD IS OUR LEADER

This week we are going to see how leaders are pleased and how they are made angry. Just like a worldly leader would be happy if you lived a good life, so God who is the most important leader in our life will be pleased if we obey Him and live a life that pleases Him.

TIME TO REMEMBER

Proverbs 14:35. "A king delights in a wise servant, but a shameful servant incurs his wrath."

17 September

READ AND UNDERSTAND

Proverbs 14:35. Kings are pleased with servants who act wisely, but they punish those who act foolishly. So don't be foolish, think before you do something.

Proverbs 29:19. If someone is a bad worker and does not want to work or does his work badly, it is not enough to just tell him what he is doing wrong. If he is foolish he will need to be corrected in other ways as well.

LOOK AT YOURSELF

Your king is Jesus, so you must live in a way to please Him. If you have work to do, you must do the best job that you can. Everything that you do, you must do for God. You should want to please God and do the best job that you can for Him. You must not be foolish, but rather be wise and learn from the Bible. When you learn about how God wants you to live, you must obey Him and live in the way that you have learned that you should.

PRAYER

Thank you, God, for being my king. Dear Jesus, please help me to be wise and to live a life that pleases you. Please forgive me for the times when I have not obeyed you, the times when I have done what I knew I should not do. Please help me to change and to become more like you. Amen.

18 September

READ AND UNDERSTAND

Proverbs 13:13. The people who hate the Bible will be punished. Those who fear the Lord and His word will be rewarded. So fear God and read His word.

Proverbs 16:13. Leaders want to hear the truth; they love those who speak the truth.

Proverbs 19:9. If you tell lies in court, you will be punished. If you are a liar you will not be able to escape punishment. So remember to always tell the truth. God hates lies and will punish liars.

LOOK AT YOURSELF

Do you always tell the truth? Remember that is what God wants. God hates lies and so do people. If you want to live a life that pleases God you will obey Him and always tell the truth. People who do not care about what God wants and people who do not care about the Bible will be punished. So don't be foolish. Learn from the Bible and obey God.

PRAYER

Thank you, God. You have given me the Bible so that I can learn about how you want me to live. Dear Jesus, please help me to obey the Bible. Please forgive me for the times when I have lied and sinned against you. Please help me to always tell the truth. Please help me to change. Amen.

19 September

READ AND UNDERSTAND

Proverbs 19:12. A leader's anger is like the roaring of a lion, frightening and scary. But his favour is like dew on the grass, comfortable and refreshing. So remember to respect leaders and submit to them.

Proverbs 6:34-35. The anger caused by impure relationships will not be put out. Marriage is a pure relationship. It was created by God and it is good. People must not act like they are married if they are not. Marriage is for one man and one woman for as long as they live.

LOOK AT YOURSELF

Do you know who the leaders are in your life? The most important leader is God. You must listen to what He teaches in the Bible and you must obey Him. You must respect God and live a life that pleases Him. The next people who are your leaders are your parents. You must listen to your parents when they tell you to do things and when they teach you. You must respect them and you must obey them. If you obey God and your parents you will find favour with them.

PRAYER

Thank you, God. You have told me how to live in the Bible. Thank you also for my parents who can help me to know how to live. Dear Jesus, please forgive me for my sins. Please help me to obey you and to obey my parents. Please help me to live a life that pleases you. Amen.

20 September

READ AND UNDERSTAND

Proverbs 16:15. If a leader is happy with you it is like rain clouds that bring life.

Proverbs 12:8. If you are wise you will be praised, but if you are stupid people will have no respect for you. So learn from the Bible and become wise.

Proverbs 27:2. Don't praise yourself for things you have done. Rather let another person praise you if you deserve it. It would be better to be praised by a stranger than to be praised by your own lips. So don't be proud, wanting to be praised and even praising yourself.

LOOK AT YOURSELF

Do you want people to tell you how good you are? Do you tell other people how good you are? If you do you are being proud. God wants you to be humble. He wants you to learn from the Bible and become wise. But you must remember that you will never know everything. You will always need to learn more. You can't be proud about what you know, there are so many other people who know a lot more than you, and God knows more than anyone. So be humble and always want to learn more.

PRAYER

Thank you, God. You know everything and you have given me the Bible so that I can learn about you. Dear Jesus, please forgive me for being proud and thinking that I am better than others. Please help me to be humble. Please help me to remember how little I know and how much I need to learn. Please help me to learn more about you so that I can live a life that pleases you. Amen.

21 September

READ AND UNDERSTAND

Proverbs 16:14. A wise person will try to keep the leaders happy. It is not nice to have angry leaders.

Proverbs 20:20. If you hate your parents, disobey them and rebel against them, you are sinning and your sin will result in death. So remember that God commands you to honour and obey your parents and if you don't you are sinning.

Proverbs 23:19. You must be wise and listen to instruction; you must desire to live in a way that pleases God. So listen to instruction and become wise.

LOOK AT YOURSELF

How do you treat your parents? Do you listen to them? Do you obey them? If you want to please God you must obey your parents. God has put them over you to help you and to teach you. So you must listen when your parents teach you and you must obey them when they tell you to do something. The only time you can disobey your parents is if they tell you to disobey God. You must always obey God.

PRAYER

Thank you, God, for my parents. Thank you that they can teach me and help me to know how to live a life that pleases you. Dear Jesus, please help me to love and obey you. Please help me to love and obey my parents. Amen.

22 September

READ AND UNDERSTAND

Proverbs 20:2. An angry leader is like a roaring lion, to make him angry is to risk your life. So submit to authority and don't rebel.

Proverbs 9:14. Foolishness will interest all people, but you must be wise and not foolish.

Proverbs 1:30. The foolish never want advice and never pay attention to correction. You must be wise and listen to advice; you must listen when you are corrected.

LOOK AT YOURSELF

If someone comes and shows you that you are sinning, do you get angry and not listen to them? Or do you listen and learn from what they are saying? Do you humbly go to God and repent of your sin? If you are wise you will learn when people correct you. You will want advice and you will not think that you know everything. So don't be foolish, rather be a wise person who listens to advice and correction.

PRAYER

Thank you, God, for people who can help me to see where I am sinning and how I need to change. Dear Jesus, please forgive me for the times when I have been foolish and not wanted to listen. Please help me to be wise and to listen to advice and correction. Please help me to change. Amen.

23 September

READ AND UNDERSTAND

Proverbs 29:14. If a leader is fair to the poor, and judges with honesty and truth, he is a good leader and God will bless him. People also like leaders who are fair, and so he will rule for a long time.

Proverbs 14:34. Righteousness makes a nation great; sin is an embarrassment to any nation. So don't sin, obey God and live a righteous life.

LOOK AT YOURSELF

you might not be a leader of a country, but God wants you to also be kind to people. He wants you to be an honest person who always tells the truth. He wants you to be fair and to do what is right. So remember that you must try to live a life that pleases God. You must repent of your sin and ask God to help you to change.

PRAYER

Thank you, God, for showing me in the Bible how I should live. Dear Jesus, please forgive me for the times when I disobey you and sin against you. Please help me to be honest. Please help me to show love to people and to be a kind person. Please help me to become more like you. Amen.

WEEK 39

DON'T BE FOOLISH

This week we are going to see how bad it is to be foolish. We will see that foolish people will get punished and they will get ruin and death. To be a foolish person means that you do not care about God or His word and you think that you can live the way you like. If you are wise, and not foolish, you will love God and want to please Him. You will study the Bible and learn about how God wants you to live. Remember that only Christians will have eternal life with God in heaven. So foolish people will not have that life, they will have death.

TIME TO REMEMBER

Proverbs 5:23. "He will die for lack of discipline, led astray by his own great folly."

24 September

READ AND UNDERSTAND

Proverbs 1:31. The fool will get what he deserves, death. So don't be foolish, be wise.

Proverbs 25:4-5. It is good to take dirt out of silver before you make something beautiful with it. In the same way you must not have someone that is wicked giving the leader advice. If you get rid of those wicked people, then the leader will rule well and be respected.

LOOK AT YOURSELF

Just as important as it is for a king to have godly people giving him advice, so it is important that you have Christian friends. If your friends are not Christians, and don't care about obeying God, you might get trapped into doing wicked things with them. So remember to be surrounded by people who love God and want to serve Him. Then they will be able to help you to live a life that pleases God.

PRAYER

Thank you, God, Jesus died on the cross so that my sins can be forgiven. Dear Jesus, please forgive me for my sins. Please help me to live a life that pleases you in everything that I think, say and do. Please help me to be wise and not foolish. Thank you that I can be in heaven with you one day because of the love that you showed to me when you died on the cross. Please help me to become more like you. Amen.

25 September

READ AND UNDERSTAND

Proverbs 1:32. The foolishness of the fool will lead to destruction. So you must not be foolish, you must be wise.

Proverbs 11:11. A city becomes great when righteous people give it their blessing, but a city will be ruined by the words of the wicked. Think before you speak.

Proverbs 28:12. When good people are in charge they do well and everyone is glad. But if a wicked person is in charge, people have to hide.

LOOK AT YOURSELF

Can you see that when there is foolishness and wickedness there is destruction, ruin and sadness? It is so much better to be a person who is wise, someone who thinks before you speak and someone who obeys God and is not wicked. Look at your life and see where you are not obeying God. Ask God to forgive you and ask Him to help you to change.

PRAYER

Thank you, God. You have given me the Bible so that I can learn and become wise. Thank you that you know everything and I can learn from you through the Bible. Dear Jesus, please forgive me for disobeying you and sinning against you. Please help me to change and to live a life that pleases you. Please help me to be wise and not foolish. Please help me to obey you. Amen.

26 September

READ AND UNDERSTAND

Proverbs 5:14. Foolishness will lead to ruin. So don't be foolish, learn from the Bible and become wise.

Proverbs 24:27. Most of the Israelites were farmers. It was very important that they do the work on the farm so that they would have food. In that time they would live in tents or houses. This verse is telling us that you must have your priorities right. If you want a fancy house rather than a tent and so you build a house rather than working on the farm, you might not have enough food. It would be foolish to do that.

LOOK AT YOURSELF

If you have more than one thing to do, do you do the most important thing first? If you have work to do, will you do the work first or will you go and play first? If you are wise you will do your work first and you will do the most important work first. If you have more than one thing to do, you can ask your parents what is more important and what you should do first. And remember if you do your work before you go and play, you will know that the work will get done, and that will be pleasing to God.

PRAYER

Thank you, God, for keeping the world together. You make everything work and you never stop giving me air to breath. Thank you for everything that you do for me. Dear Jesus, please help me to do my work for you. Please help me to do the best job that I can. Please help me to live a life that pleases you. Amen.

27 September

READ AND UNDERSTAND

Proverbs 5:23. The fools will die because they don't want instruction. Foolishness will lead you off the right path. So don't be foolish, learn from the Bible and become wise.

Proverbs 6:19b. The Lord hates people that make trouble between friends. You must not make trouble, you must make peace.

Proverbs 29:5. If you say nice things about your friends so that you can get things it is wrong and sinful, you will get caught in the trap that you are trying to get your friend caught in. So don't flatter.

LOOK AT YOURSELF

Do you like causing trouble between other people? Do you like getting your brother and sister cross so that they will get into trouble? If you are a Christian you should be a person who makes peace between others and not trouble. If your brother and sister are fighting you should help them to stop fighting and help them to show love towards each other. Also remember not to say nice things to people so that you can get something. You are being selfish and dishonest if you do that. It is not wrong to say nice things, but the reason for saying it should be to encourage them to live a life that pleases God.

PRAYER

Thank you, God. You have given me the Bible so that I can learn and not be foolish. Dear Jesus, please forgive me for the times when I have caused trouble instead of bringing peace. Please help me to be a kind person who shows love to others. Thank you for the love that you showed to me in dying on the cross. Please help me to change and to have more love. Amen.

28 September

READ AND UNDERSTAND

Proverbs 9:18. Foolishness leads to death. So don't be foolish, learn from the Bible and become wise.

Proverbs 23:31-32. Don't let the sparkle and taste of wine lie to you, the next morning you will feel like you have been bitten by a poisonous snake. Don't get drunk, it is sin, the consequences of getting drunk can also be very dangerous.

LOOK AT YOURSELF

Have you see a drunk person before? People get drunk from alcohol like wine. They drink too much and it makes them do funny things. A drunk person cannot think properly and does not act properly. When they wake up in the morning they often feel terrible. So remember that it is foolish to get drunk. Don't ever think that it is fun to get drunk. It is a sin and God is displeased when people get drunk. You should always want to live a life that pleases God.

PRAYER

Thank you, God, for giving me the Bible so that I can learn about things that are foolish so that I don't do them. Dear Jesus, please help me to remember how foolish it is to get drunk. Please help me to live a life that pleases you in everything that I think, say and do. Amen.

29 September

READ AND UNDERSTAND

Proverbs 19:3. Being foolish will bring problems. Some people ruin their own lives because of their foolishness and then they get angry with the Lord and blame Him. Remember to be wise. Remember that there are consequences to your actions.

Proverbs 14:17a. People who get angry quickly do foolish things. So don't get angry.

Proverbs 3:34a. God will laugh at those who don't respect Him. You must respect God.

LOOK AT YOURSELF

Do you get angry quickly? Do you get cross when someone is horrible to you? God says that it is foolish to get angry. It is a sin to get angry. Remember how Jesus showed love to the people who killed Him. He did not get angry with them and start fighting them. He prayed for them and He asked God to forgive them. Do you want to be like Jesus? Do you want to show love to others. Ask God to help you to become more like Him.

PRAYER

Thank you, God, that Jesus died on the cross so that my sins can be forgiven. Dear Jesus, please forgive me for the times when I have disobeyed you and I have gotten angry. Please help me to show love to people, even to those who are horrible to me. Please help me to change and to become more like you. Amen.

30 September

READ AND UNDERSTAND

Proverbs 21:16. If you turn your back on wise and godly living, it will result in death. If you leave the company of wise people you will find you are in the company of dead people. Don't be a fool, live in a way that pleases God and brings glory to Him.

Proverbs 27:10. You must not forget your friends; you must remember how important good friendships are. Then, if you are going through a difficult time you can ask your friend for help. You won't have to ask your family who might live far away; you will have someone to help who is close. Choose your friends wisely and be a good friend.

LOOK AT YOURSELF

Are your friends Christians? Do your friends love God and want to live a life that pleases Him? Remember that your friends will influence your character. So if you want to be wise and not foolish, you must make sure you choose wise friends and not fools. If you have good Christian friendships, those friendships will last for a long time. You will be able to help each other in difficult times and you will be able to encourage each other to live a godly life.

PRAYER

Thank you, God, for friends. Thank you for warning me in the Bible about how important it is to have godly friends. Dear Jesus, please help me to have friends who love you and want to obey you. Please help me to be a good friend. Please help me to show love and to become more like you. Amen.

WEEK 40

THE IMPORTANCE OF WISDOM

This week we are going to study wisdom again. Wisdom is one of the most important things taught about in the book of Proverbs. This week we are going to study Proverbs 8:17-21 as well as Proverbs 5:1-2. If you are a Christian you can ask God to give you wisdom as you study the Bible. Wisdom has many benefits and it will help you a lot in life. Remember that even though with wisdom you may get riches, honour, wealth and prosperity; we also read that wisdom itself is worth a lot more than gold and silver.

TIME TO REMEMBER

Proverbs 5:1-2. "My son, pay attention to my wisdom, listen well to my words of insight, that you may maintain discretion and your lips may preserve knowledge."

1 October

READ AND UNDERSTAND

Proverbs 8:16. You will be a good ruler if you have wisdom. The Bible teaches rulers how to be wise.

Proverbs 8:17. Wisdom will reward those who want it. If you want wisdom you can get it.

LOOK AT YOURSELF

Do you think that the Bible is only for adults? Do you think you can be wise? If you are a Christian you can get wisdom. If you ask God to give you wisdom and you spend time learning from the Bible, you can get wisdom. Wisdom is available to all people. Wisdom will help leaders rule well and it will help children live well. Wisdom will help you to live a life that pleases God. Isn't that great?

PRAYER

Thank you, God, that wisdom is available to all Christians. Thank you for giving me the Bible so that I can learn how I must live. Dear Jesus, please forgive me for the times when I have not obeyed you. Please help me to change and to live a life that pleases you. Amen.

2 October

READ AND UNDERSTAND

Proverbs 8:18. Wisdom will often give you money and honour; things as well as righteousness. With wisdom you will get everything you need. So this does not mean that every Christian will be very rich. But we can know that God will provide for His children.

Proverbs 21:11. If you punish a mocker, people who don't know any better can learn a lesson. If you instruct a wise person they will learn and get more wisdom. So be wise and learn when you are taught.

LOOK AT YOURSELF

Do you listen when you are being taught? Do you pay attention and try to understand as much as possible? Do you ask questions about things that you don't know? You must listen and learn when you are taught. Then you will be able to become wise and you will be able to learn more and more. You must also learn from things that happen to other people, and then you will be able to do things that are good and stay away from things that are bad. If you desire to live a life that pleases God, He will look after you and He will provide for you.

PRAYER

Thank you, God, that you look after your children. Thank you for everything that you have given me. Dear Jesus, please forgive me for my sin. Thank you that you died on the cross so that I can be forgiven. Please help me to learn from the Bible and to listen when I am being taught. Please help me to learn more about how I must live. Amen.

3 October

READ AND UNDERSTAND

Proverbs 8:19. What you get if you have wisdom is better than gold and silver. So learn from the Bible and become wise.

Proverbs 24:23. It is wrong to show partiality and say that the guilty person is innocent because he is your friend, or to say that an innocent person is guilty because he is your enemy. Don't show partiality to people, it is a sin and God hates it.

LOOK AT YOURSELF

Have you ever lied to get someone who you do not like into trouble? Have you ever lied to get a friend out of trouble? It is wrong to lie; God wants you to always be honest. You must also remember to treat everyone with love, not just someone who you think that you can get something from. Remember that living a life that is pleasing to God and obeying Him is much more important that having money and things.

PRAYER

Thank you, God, for everything that you have given to me. Thank you that you showed love to me even though I did not obey you. Thank you that Jesus died on the cross so that my sins can be forgiven. Dear Jesus, please help me to show love to everyone. Please help me to always tell the truth. Please forgive me for the times when I have not obeyed you. Please help me to change. Amen.

4 October

READ AND UNDERSTAND

Proverbs 8:20. If you have wisdom you will be righteous and just. So learn from the Bible and become wise.

Proverbs 29:21. If you give the people working for you everything they want, and you don't expect them to do their job properly, you will see that they will think of themselves as family and that they don't have to do their job at all. So remember that people must do the job they are paid for.

LOOK AT YOURSELF

Did you know that only Christians can live a righteous life; a life that pleases God? If people who are not Christians do things that are good, it is still not pleasing to God because they are not doing it for God. But if you are a Christian, you can read and study the Bible and you can become wise. You will be able to know what is right and wrong and you will be able to live a life that pleases God. The only reason you can please God is because Jesus died on the cross so that your sins can be forgiven. There will always be sin in your life, but you must repent of your sins and you must ask God to help you to change.

PRAYER

Thank you, God, that Jesus died on the cross so that my sins can be forgiven. Thank you that I can learn in the Bible about how I must live to please you. Dear Jesus, please help me to be wise and to know how to live. Please help me to live a life that pleases you. Please forgive me for the times when I have not obeyed you. Please help me to change. Amen.

5 October

READ AND UNDERSTAND

Proverbs 8:21. Often wise people will have money and things. So learn from the Bible and become wise. Remember that not all Christians will be rich, but God looks after Christians and that means that He will provide what you need.

Proverbs 31:25. A godly wife is strong and she is respected. Because of her wisdom she does not have to worry about the future. Boys - you must find a wife who is godly. Girls - you must be women who are godly.

LOOK AT YOURSELF

Do you trust in God for everything? If you are a Christian you can know that God will provide you with what you need. You don't have to be afraid of the future. You can know that God is in control and everything that happens to Christians will be for their good. Remember that God wants you to ask Him for your daily bread. He wants you to remember that everything that you have is from Him.

PRAYER

Thank you, God, for everything that you have given to me. Thank you that I have a place to sleep and clothes to wear. Thank you that I have food to eat and that you have given me so many other things as well. Dear Jesus, please help me to be more thankful for what I have. Help me to remember that you have given me everything. Please help me to trust in you. Amen.

6 October

READ AND UNDERSTAND

Proverbs 5:1. Pay attention to wisdom and listen to understanding. The Bible can teach you how to be wise and have understanding, so you must learn form it.

Proverbs 16:1. People can plan things in their heart, but God is in control. When you are planning something, remember that God is in control.

LOOK AT YOURSELF

Have you ever had a special day planned for the family? Maybe there has been a trip to the zoo or to the beach planned? Whenever we make plans we must remember that God is in control. So if something happens that you can't do what you had planned, you must not get upset or angry. You must thank God that He is in control and that He knows what is best. It is difficult when you don't get to do something that you were looking forward to, but you must trust God and be thankful for what you have.

PRAYER

Thank you, God. You are in control of everything. Thank you that you know what is best. Dear Jesus, please help me to trust you when things don't happen the way I wanted them to. Please help me to thank you for what I have and not to get upset about what I don't have. Please help me to trust you more. Amen.

7 October

READ AND UNDERSTAND

Proverbs 5:2. The Scriptures will help you to act and speak wisely. So you must study it and obey it.

Proverbs 27:3. It is not wise to get into an argument with a fool. Even if he is being stupid you must not make him angry or become angry yourself because of what he is doing. That will do more damage that the weight of a huge stone or a big load of sand. So don't get into arguments with a fool.

LOOK AT YOURSELF

Has anyone tried to fight with you about what the Bible says? Has anyone told you that it is not God's word or that it is not important? Maybe someone has said that they don't believe what the Bible says and they argue about it and tell you that it is not true? You must remember to not fight with them. You know that the Bible is God's Word. You know that everything that it says is true. You must tell them the truth, but if they don't want to believe then you must leave it and not argue with them. You must pray for them; pray that God would show them the truth and that they would believe the Bible.

PRAYER

Thank you, God, for giving me the Bible. Thank you that the Bible is your word and it is true. Dear Jesus, please help me to be wise and to have speech that is wise. Please help me to remember not to argue with people about what I know is true. Please help me to obey what I have learnt from the Bible. Please help me to become more like you. Amen.

WEEK 41

SHARING WHAT WE HAVE

This week we are going to look at how bad it is to be a greedy person. A greedy person is someone who thinks that having money and things is the most important thing in life, and just wants more and more. You will see that if you are a Christian you should be a thankful person and a person who shares, not someone who is always thinking of themselves and always greedy for more.

TIME TO REMEMBER

Proverbs 23:4-5. "Do not wear yourself out to get rich; have the wisdom to show restraint. Cast but a glance at riches, and they are gone, for they will surely sprout wings and fly off to the sky like an eagle."

8 October

READ AND UNDERSTAND

Proverbs 11:26. People will not like you if you are greedy. So share what you have.

Proverbs 14:31. If you are mean to poor people, you insult the God who made them. But kindness shown to the poor is an act of worship to God. So be kind to poor people.

Proverbs 30:13. There are people who think that they are so good, they think that they are the best. This is pride and God hates pride, you must be humble.

LOOK AT YOURSELF

How important are money and things to you? Do you keep all your money or all your sweets for yourself? Or do you share some with others? If you want to live a life that pleases God you will show kindness to others and you will share what you have. You need to be kind to all people, and that includes people who are poor. There are a lot of people who have a lot less than what you have. So you must remember to share with the poor and show kindness to them. If you think that you are too important to share with poor people you are being proud and God hates pride. So be humble and share.

PRAYER

Thank you, God, for everything that you have given to me. Thank you for the place I have to sleep and the clothes that I have to wear. Thank you for providing food for me every day. Dear Jesus, please help me to share what I have. Please help me to show love and kindness to others and to live a life that pleases you. Amen.

9 October

READ AND UNDERSTAND

Proverbs 14:4. The value of things is not how nice they look; it is how much they help you. So don't just spend money on things that look nice.

Proverbs 31:3. You must not spend your strength on impure relationships those relationships can destroy kings. So remember how important marriage is.

Proverbs 5:18. Be happy with your marriage and find your joy in the one you married.

LOOK AT YOURSELF

Have you ever spent your money on a toy or sweet that looked really nice? Was it worth all the money that you spent? You must be careful that you don't just spend all your money on things that look nice. You must think about what you are going to buy. You must find out if it is worth it.

Remember how important marriage is and remember that it is a special relationship for a man and a woman for the rest of their lives.

PRAYER

Thank you, God, for creating marriage. Thank you that it is a good relationship, please help me to remember what I have learnt about it. Dear Jesus, please help me to be wise with how I spend the money that I have. Please help me to think about what something is worth and not just how nice it looks. Thank you for giving me so much. Please help me to be more thankful for what I have. Amen.

10 October

READ AND UNDERSTAND

Proverbs 14:30. If you are happy with what you have, you will probably be healthy. But if you are jealous for lots of things, you may become sick. So be thankful for what you have.

Proverbs 22:28. You must not steal. In Israel's time they marked the border of their farms with big stones; some people would move the stones and take some of their neighbours land as their own. God says that this is stealing. It is sin, just like any other stealing and so you must never take something that belongs to someone else.

LOOK AT YOURSELF

Are you happy with what you have? Or have you ever wished you could have what your friend has? Have you ever taken something that belonged to your friend because you wanted one yourself? God hates stealing and He wants you to be happy with what He has given to you. If you are always looking at what others have and wanting what they have, you won't be thankful for what you have. God has given you so much, you need to be thankful and not jealous of others.

PRAYER

Thank you, God, for giving me so much. Thank you for my home and my clothes and the food that you give me every day. Dear Jesus, please help me to be more thankful. Please help me to remember that there are a lot of people in the world who have a lot less than what I have got. Please help me to remember that it is a sin to steal. Please help me to live a life that pleases you. Amen.

11 October

READ AND UNDERSTAND

Proverbs 21:17. If you love luxuries, having fancy things and eating fancy foods, there is a chance that you will become poor. Remember to be thankful to God for what you have and know that having the best things in this life will not make you rich.

Proverbs 17:5. If you laugh at poor people, you are insulting the God who made them. If you are glad when bad things happen to other people, you will be punished. You must show love to those people who are poor or are going through a difficult time, then you will be pleasing God.

LOOK AT YOURSELF

Do you think that the most important thing is to have a lot of things and to have the best and most expensive things? Do you think that people who have less than you are less important than you? Remember that everyone is equal before God. It does not matter how much money people have, everyone needs Jesus as Saviour and Lord. To be a Christian is the most important thing in life, not money.

PRAYER

Thank you, God, that Jesus died on the cross so that my sins can be forgiven. Dear Jesus, please forgive me for my sins. Please help me to show love to all people. Please help me to change and to live a life that pleases you in everything that I think, say and do. Amen.

12 October

READ AND UNDERSTAND

Proverbs 23:4-5. You must not overwork to be rich, working just so that you can have more money. Remember that money and things can disappear, as though they had grown wings like an eagle and flown away.

Proverbs 18:1. A person who always wants to be alone is selfish and only cares about what he wants. If you do this you are not obeying all the wise advice that the Bible gives. So obey the Bible and have fellowship with other people.

LOOK AT YOURSELF

Some people will spend a lot of time at work and be very busy. Often they do that so that they can have a lot of money. Other people do that so that they can be alone at work and not have to be with other people. Remember that money is not the most important thing and that relationships with other Christians are very important. Don't let money be too important to you, it can disappear so quickly. Rather make sure you have good Christian friendships that will last forever.

PRAYER

Thank you, God, for giving me so much. Thank you for all the things that I have and for all the friends that I have. Dear Jesus, please help me to be a good friend. Please help me to remember that money is not the most important thing in life. Please help me to live a life that pleases you in everything that I think, say and do. Amen.

13 October

READ AND UNDERSTAND

Proverbs 27:20. Hell is ready for every sinner that dies, and it does not get full, wanting more and more to die and to go to hell. In the same way greedy people who just want more and more, are never happy with what they have. Don't be like that, thank God for what you have and be grateful, not always wanting more.

Proverbs 19:8. If you get wisdom you love your soul, if you remember what you learn you will find good. So remember how important wisdom and understanding are.

LOOK AT YOURSELF

How do you think your mum would describe you? As someone who is greedy and always wants more, or as someone who is thankful for what you have? God wants you to be thankful for what you have. Remember that if you are greedy, you will probably never be satisfied with what you have. As soon as you have what you want, you will probably just want more. So remember what the most important thing to get is. It is not money, food, toys or any other stuff. The most important thing to get is wisdom.

PRAYER

Thank you, God, for all the things that you have given to me. Thank you for my home and for my clothes and for the food that you provide every day. Dear Jesus, please help me to be more thankful for what I have. Please help me to learn from the Bible and become wise. Please help me to live a life that pleases you. Amen.

14 October

READ AND UNDERSTAND

Proverbs 30:15-16. Being greedy is like a leech that has two mouths; both mouths say "more", "more". There are four things which are always greedy for more. The grave, people will die and the grave is never full; a woman that does not have a child, she will always want to have a child; a desert, that will never have enough water; and a fire, that wants to carry on burning everything in its way. Don't be greedy, you will never have everything that you want, you will always want more.

Proverbs 11:29b. Foolish people will always be servants to the wise. So learn from the Bible and become wise.

LOOK AT YOURSELF

Are you a greedy person? Are you greedy for money or for anything else? If you are a Christian you should be thankful and not greedy. Share what you have and do not keep everything you get for yourself. You must think about other people as more important than yourself and then you will be able to show them love as God has commanded you to. If you are always thinking about yourself, you will not be able to show love to others.

PRAYER

Thank you, God, for showing so much love to me in that Christ died for me. Thank you that because of Christ my sins can be forgiven. Dear Jesus, please help me to be thankful for what I have. Please forgive me for the times when I have been selfish and greedy. Please help me to change and to become more like you. Please help me to show love to you and to others. Amen.

WEEK 42

DON'T BE LAZY - DO YOUR BEST

This week we are going to look at how bad it is to be a lazy person. God wants you to do your work well and to also do your work when it needs to be done. Most of the Israelites were farmers, and so if they were lazy and did not do the work on the farm, they would become poor. Sometimes people today also become poor because they do not work. So remember not to be a lazy person, but to do your work and to do the best job that you can.

TIME TO REMEMBER

Proverbs 28:19. "He who works his land will have abundant food, but the one who chases fantasies will have his fill of poverty."

15 October

READ AND UNDERSTAND

Proverbs 6:11. If you don't want to work you might become poor. Don't be lazy, work hard.

Proverbs 29:1. A person who does not repent and stop sinning when he is shown his sin over and over again, will be punished and will not have an opportunity to repent again. So listen when you are corrected, look at your life and stop sinning.

LOOK AT YOURSELF

If your mum or dad shows you that something that you are doing is wrong, do you listen to them and change? Do you listen to your mum when she says that you are being lazy, and that you need to work harder? Are you lazy, or do you do the best job that you can? God wants you to do all your work for Him. You should want to do the best job that you can do so that God will be pleased.

PRAYER

Thank you, God, for my parents. Thank you that they can help me to know how to live a life that pleases you. Dear Jesus, please help me to listen when I am corrected. Please help me to see when I am sinning and when I need to change. Please forgive me for the times when I have sinned against you. Please help me to become more like you. Amen.

16 October

READ AND UNDERSTAND

Proverbs 10:4. Being lazy can make you poor, but hard work can make you rich. So work hard.

Proverbs 16:33. God is in control of everything. There is no such thing as luck.

Proverbs 19:10. It isn't right for a fool to live in luxury or for a slave to rule over princes. They do not have the character to be able to use their things or responsibility wisely.

LOOK AT YOURSELF

Do you always work hard when you have work to do? Do you do the best job that you can? When your mum asks you to help with something in the house, do you quickly go and help her? Do you do as much as you can for her? Everything that you do you should be doing for God. When you help your mum, or do your schoolwork, if you do those things for God, and you do the best you can, you are pleasing God.

PRAYER

Thank you, God, for being in control of everything. Thank you that I can always put my trust in you. Dear Jesus, please forgive me for the times when I have complained and not done my best with something that I had to do. Please help me to do everything for you. Please help me to live a life that pleases you in everything that I think, say and do. Amen.

17 October

READ AND UNDERSTAND

Proverbs 15:19. If you are lazy, life will be difficult. If you are righteous, you will not have those troubles. Work hard and don't be lazy.

Proverbs 25:28. If you don't have self-control, you are in danger, like a city that does not have walls around it. You can get into trouble quickly and you don't have anything protecting you from sinning. So be self controlled and do not sin.

LOOK AT YOURSELF

Do you have the self-control to stop yourself from doing something? If you know that you need to get something done, do you have the self-control to do what you need to and to not put the TV on, or to not just go and play? If you don't have self-control, it will be more difficult to stop yourself from sinning when something tempts you to sin. So try and have self-control even in areas where it is not sinful. For example, not eating a biscuit before lunch, but rather going to help your mum get the food ready. Or not watching your favourite TV programme so that you can spend time reading your Bible. There are many situations were you can have self-control and not be lazy. Think about how you can use your time wisely and not be lazy.

PRAYER

Thank you, God, for helping me to know when something is wrong. Dear Jesus, please help me to do what is right and to not sin against you. Please help me to have self-control and to not be a lazy person. Please help me to change and to live a life that pleases you. Amen.

18 October

READ AND UNDERSTAND

Proverbs 20:4. If a farmer is too lazy to work on his fields, when it is time to gather the crop there will be nothing. If you don't work you might not get food. So remember to not be lazy, work when there is work that needs to be done.

Proverbs 16:2. You may think that everything you do is right, but God looks to see why you are doing it. Even if you do what is right, if you are not doing it to glorify God, it is sin.

LOOK AT YOURSELF

Are you a Christian? Only Christians can please God because only Christians will want to do what is pleasing to God, they are the only ones who know who the only true God is. Do you do everything for God? Do you do what is right so that God would be glorified and pleased? If you have work to do, you must not be lazy but rather you must do the best job that you can, so that God would be pleased. Remember that when you do things for other people, you are also doing it for God.

PRAYER

Thank you, God, that you know everything. Thank you that you know everything about me. Dear Jesus, please forgive me for my sin. Please help me to live a life that pleases you. Please help me to do everything for you, and to do the best that I can. Thank you that Jesus died on the cross so that my sins can be forgiven. Please help me to change. Amen.

19 October

READ AND UNDERSTAND

Proverbs 21:25. Lazy people who don't want to work are only killing themselves; if they do not work they might have no food and could starve. Don't be lazy.

Proverbs 22:7. Be careful of borrowing money. Just like rich people have poor people working for them, so if you borrow money you could become like a salve to pay that money back. Be thankful to God for what you have and try to live with what you have. Don't borrow money just to have things that other people have.

LOOK AT YOURSELF

Is there anything that you would like to buy? You should try not to borrow money to get what you want. It would be better if you could do work to earn money and then save your money until you have enough. Remember that if you borrow you must pay back. So rather work and earn your money. Then if you want to buy something you know if you have enough or not. You will also be careful of what you spend your money on because you know how long you have worked to earn it.

PRAYER

Thank you, God, for everything that you have given to me. Thank you for my home, for my clothes and for the food that you provide every day. Dear Jesus, please help me to be thankful for what I have. Please help me to not always want what other people want. Please help me to remember to work hard and to do the best job that I can. Please help me to live a life that pleases you. Amen.

20 October

READ AND UNDERSTAND

Proverbs 24:30-34. This is teaching us that if you are lazy and say "I just want to sleep a little" and you never do the work that you need to, then you will have a field like that described in verse 30-31. Most of the Israelites were farmers and if they did not do their work then the weeds and thorn bushes would grow and there would be no space for the plants that were for food. So if they were lazy they would become poor because they had no food. So don't be lazy, work hard and do your work when it needs to be done.

Proverbs 6:18a. The Lord hates those who think up wicked plans. Be careful what you think about. Never think about wicked things.

LOOK AT YOURSELF

Do you like to sleep a lot? Do you go and sleep in the afternoon when you know there is something that you need to do? Remember that there will be consequences for being lazy. You must do your work when there is work to be done. You must do everything in a way that will be pleasing to God. That means that you must do what is right and that you must have the right thoughts. God knows what you think, so you must not think about wicked things, but rather about what is true and right.

PRAYER

Thank you, God, that you know everything. Thank you for giving me the Bible so that I can know how to live a life that is pleasing to you. Dear Jesus, please forgive me for my sins. Please help me to have thoughts and actions that are pleasing to you. Please help me to change. Amen.

21 October

READ AND UNDERSTAND

Proverbs 28:19. A hard-working farmer has lots to eat, but a stupid person will waste time doing things that are useless, and he will have nothing to eat. So work hard.

Proverbs 31:6-7. Wine and strong drinks were used to help people who were dying and in a lot of pain, the alcohol would help them cope with the pain as does pain killers in our day. So these verses are telling us again that getting drunk is not right, it is not for anyone to get drunk any time they want. So don't get drunk.

LOOK AT YOURSELF

Remember that getting drunk is a sin and it is also a waste of time and money. There are some people who do not work, and when they get some money they spend it on alcohol. They are wasting their time doing things that are useless and they often have nothing to eat. You must look at your day and see if you spend time doing other things that are useless. Do you do your work when it needs to be done? Do you work hard and do the best job that you can? You know that if you do it will be pleasing to God.

PRAYER

Thank you, God, for teaching me this week about how important it is to do my work and that I do the best job that I can. Dear Jesus, please help me to not be lazy. Please help me to remember what I learn and to live a life that pleases you. Please help me to change. Amen.

WEEK 43

THINK BEFORE YOU SPEAK

This week we are going to look at speech. We are going to see that it is foolish to talk too much and to always want people to listen to you. We will see that if you are wise you will think before you speak.

TIME TO REMEMBER

Proverbs 18:2. "A fool finds no pleasure in understanding but delights in airing his own opinions."

22 October

READ AND UNDERSTAND

Proverbs 12:18. If you speak without thinking it can hurt someone like a sword can hurt, but wisely spoken words can heal. So think before you speak. And speak words that will be kind to others.

Proverbs 10:19. The more you talk, the more likely you are to sin. If you are wise, you will keep quiet.

Proverbs 7:3. Always remember what the Bible says, and obey what it says.

LOOK AT YOURSELF

Have you ever been cross with someone and said something that you knew would hurt them? Has anyone ever said something hurtful to you? What people say can really hurt and so you need to be careful and think before you speak. God wants you to show love to others and you can't show love if you are saying hurtful things. You should rather be saying things that are kind and showing love to that person, even if they have done something horrible to you. So remember that God commands you to love others, you need to show love to everyone.

PRAYER

Thank you, God, for showing love to me in letting Jesus die on the cross so that my sins can be forgiven. Dear Jesus, please forgive me for not showing love to other people. Please help me to change and to obey you. Please help me to be careful about what I say, and let me have speech that is kind and loving. Please help me to become more like you. Amen.

23 October

READ AND UNDERSTAND

Proverbs 13:3. Be careful of what you say and it could protect your life. Careless talkers destroy themselves. So think before you speak.

Proverbs 16:32a. It is better to be patient and not get angry than to be a powerful warrior.

Proverbs 19:2. It is not good to be without knowledge. If you are not patient you could go the wrong way. Remember to be wise and patient.

LOOK AT YOURSELF

Have you ever gotten angry when things did not go your way? Or when someone did not do what you wanted them to do? The Bible says that you should be patient and not get angry. Remember to always have speech that is kind and gentle. If someone is horrible to you, you must be patient and not get angry, you must show love to them. This is sometimes a difficult thing to do, but we must copy Christ who is our example, He was not even angry with the people who killed Him.

PRAYER

Thank you, God, that Jesus died on the cross so that my sins can be forgiven. Thank you that you showed so much love to me by allowing Christ to die for me. Dear Jesus, please forgive me for all my sins. Please help me to be a patient person, someone who is gentle and kind. Please help me to show love to others and in everything to become more like you. Amen.

24 October

READ AND UNDERSTAND

Proverbs 15:28. Righteous people think about how to answer a question. Evil people talk without thinking, their evil words pour out of their mouth. Think before you speak.

Proverbs 16:4. Everything that the Lord made has its purpose. The wicked will be destroyed. So obey God and don't be wicked.

Proverbs 9:7b. If you try and tell a wicked person that what they are doing is wrong, they will say bad things about you.

LOOK AT YOURSELF

Do you do horrible things to other people? Do you say horrible things to other people? Remember that a Christian will not be a wicked person. A Christian will be someone who wants to obey God and live a life that pleases Him. God will punish wicked people. So don't disobey God. Don't be wicked but rather love God and obey Him. If you obey God you will show love to other people as well.

PRAYER

Thank you, God, that Christians will not be punished in hell because Jesus died for their sins. Thank you that my sins can be forgiven. Dear Jesus, please help me to obey you. Please help me to love you and to love others. Please forgive me for the times when I have said or done horrible things. Please help me to change and to become more like you. Amen.

25 October

READ AND UNDERSTAND

Proverbs 17:27. Wise people think before they speak. People who can control themselves have understanding. So be wise and understanding, control yourself and don't talk too much.

Proverbs 21:9. It is better to live in a small and cramped corner, where there is peace and quiet, than to live in a big house with a wife who wants to argue and fight. Women should not be quarrelsome; it is wrong to look for things to fight about.

LOOK AT YOURSELF

Do you talk a lot? Do you look for things to fight and argue about with your brother or sister? If you are wise you will remember to think before you talk. You will know when you need to be quiet. You will also know how wrong it is to argue and fight. God is not pleased if you are quarrelsome. So remember to be careful of what you say today. Try to have speech that is pleasing to God.

PRAYER

Thank you, God, for given me the Bible so that I can learn about how you want me to live. Dear Jesus, please forgive me for sinning against you. Please forgive me for the times when my speech has not been pleasing to you. Please help me to remember to think before I speak. Please help me to change and to become more like you. Amen.

26 October

READ AND UNDERSTAND

Proverbs 17:28. It is wise to not talk too much; even a fool will look wise if he keeps quiet. When a fool closes his lips he looks like he understands. So don't talk too much.

Proverbs 26:17. In the Bible's time dogs were not tame, so think about walking past an angry dog that you don't know, and think about how stupid it would be to go to that dog and pull his ears. I am sure the dog would bite you. It is just as stupid to get involved in an argument that is none of your business; you will only bring trouble for yourself. So don't get involved if you don't know anything about a situation and if it has nothing to do with you.

LOOK AT YOURSELF

Do you listen to other people talking and always try to make a comment? Do you like to tell people what you think about a situation? Remember that a fool will even look wise if he keeps quiet, so you should rather keep quiet. It is wrong to push your way into other people's conversations. So remember to be wise and think before you talk.

PRAYER

Thank you, God, for being all wise. Thank you that I can learn to be wise if I study the Bible. Please help me to become wise as I learn from your Word. Dear Jesus, please help me to think before I speak. Please help me to always have speech that is pleasing to you. Please help me to remember that it is wrong to always want to give my opinion. Please help me to change. Amen.

27 October

READ AND UNDERSTAND

Proverbs 18:2. A fool does not care if he understands a thing or not, he only wants to give his own opinions. Don't be a fool, make sure you understand and don't just want to talk.

Proverbs 18:19. You must do all you can to make sure that you do not fight and quarrel with family or close friends. It is more difficult to make that relationship right than it is to break into a strong city or to get through a strong gate. So don't quarrel and fight.

LOOK AT YOURSELF

If someone starts to fight and argue with you, what do you do? Do you argue and fight back? Or do you try to make peace. Often the things that we fight about are really not very important. If you only had one day left with that person, would you fight with them? Or don't you think it would be better to rather be at peace? If you have done something that has hurt them, you should ask them to forgive you. You must show love to others and if you fight you are not showing love.

PRAYER

Thank you, God, for showing so much love to me by sending Jesus to die for me. Dear Jesus, please forgive me for my sins. Please help me to change and to remember how wrong it is to fight and argue. Please help me to think before I speak so that I don't say things that can hurt other people. Please help me to love you more and to show love to others as well. Amen.

28 October

READ AND UNDERSTAND

Proverbs 29:20. It is very foolish to speak without thinking; you must not answer before you have listened properly. You are worse than a fool if you don't think before you speak.

Proverbs 18:17. The first person to speak in court always seems right, until another person comes and asks questions and gives the other side of the story. Remember to listen to all the people involved before thinking you know what happened.

LOOK AT YOURSELF

Imagine your mum comes and asks your brother if he knows who has taken the money off the table. And he says that it was you. How would you feel if your mum punished you without even asking you what happened? Wouldn't it be better to ask everyone first? Maybe your dad took it and put it away. It is always better to listen properly and to listen to everyone before you say something. You can also say something that afterwards you realise was not right. So remember to be wise and think before you speak. Remember also how important it is to listen.

PRAYER

Thank you, God, that you know everything. Thank you that you hear my prayers even if I don't say anything out loud. Dear Jesus, please forgive me for sinning against you. Please forgive me for the times when I have said things that I should not have. Please help me to think before I speak. Please help me to listen carefully when people talk to me. Please help me to live a life that pleases you in everything that I think, say and do. Amen.

WEEK 44

THE IMPORTANCE OF TRUTH

This week we are going to see how important it is to tell the truth. We will see that it is wrong to lie and that lying can hurt other people.

TIME TO REMEMBER

Proverbs 20:17. "Food gained by fraud tastes sweet to a man, but he ends up with a mouth full of gravel."

29 October

READ AND UNDERSTAND

Proverbs 13:7. *It is wrong to pretend to be rich if you are poor. It is wrong to pretend to be poor if you are rich. Don't be a liar, be honest.*

Proverbs 25:27. *Just as it is not good to eat too much honey, as it will make you feel sick. So it is not good for you to think about all the praise you deserve. You must not think you are so good, and everyone must tell you how good you are. That is being proud. You must rather be humble.*

LOOK AT YOURSELF

Are you happy with what the Lord has given to you? Do you thank the Lord for His provision? He has given you a lot of physical things; a home, food and clothes. He has also given you talents. Everything that you can do is because God has given you that ability. So don't be proud and want people to praise you. God must get the praise for things that you can do well. So don't think about praise that you deserve; you don't deserve it, God does.

PRAYER

Thank you, God, for everything that you have given to me. Dear Jesus, please forgive me for my sins. Please help me to remember that everything that I can do is because you have created me. Please help me to live a life that is pleasing to you in everything that I think, say and do. Amen.

30 October

READ AND UNDERSTAND

Proverbs 13:15b. Liars are slaves to their sin. So don't lie, always be honest and tell the truth.

Proverbs 15:12. Proud people do not like to be corrected; they will not ask advice from people who are wiser than they are. You must be humble and ask advice.

Proverbs 26:13. Lazy people are always giving excuses why they don't work, they say "If I go outside, there might be a lion and I would be killed", even if he had never seen a lion in his life. So don't make excuses, you must work when there is work to be done.

LOOK AT YOURSELF

Have you ever lied so that you would not be corrected because you knew you had done something wrong? Have you ever lied to get out of doing your work? Or lied about why you have not done the work you should have done? God hates lying. You must always tell the truth. If you have done something wrong, you must be honest about it and get the correction or punishment that you need. It would be much worse to lie. Remember that God knows everything; you cannot lie to Him.

PRAYER

Thank you, God, that you know everything. Dear Jesus, please forgive me for sinning against you. Please forgive me for the times when I have lied. Please help me to always tell the truth. Please help me to live a life that pleases you in everything that I think, say and do. Amen.

31 October

READ AND UNDERSTAND

Proverbs 20:14. Some people will always complain that the price of a thing is too high, but then they go off and tell everyone that they got it at such a good price. They will lie to the person selling so that they can get a better price. Remember that lying is a sin and God hates it, so never lie.

Proverbs 21:8. Guilty people walk on a crooked path, innocent people walk on a road that is straight. Remember to do what is right and to live in a way that pleases God and brings glory to Him.

LOOK AT YOURSELF

Are you a Christian? Do you believe that Jesus Christ died on the cross so that your sins can be forgiven? If Jesus is your Saviour and Lord then you will want to obey Him. You should want to live a life that pleases Him in everything that you do. That means you will never tell a lie and try to deceive people. God hates lies, you should always tell the truth.

PRAYER

Thank you, God, that you never lie. Thank you that I can trust everything that I read from your Word. Dear Jesus, please forgive me for my sins. Please forgive me for the times when I have lied and been displeasing to you. Please help me to always tell the truth and to live a life that pleases you in everything I do. Please help me to change. Amen.

1 November

READ AND UNDERSTAND

Proverbs 20:17. If you get something being dishonest you might enjoy it like the best food, but sooner or later it will be like a mouthful of sand. Remember that God hates lies and there are consequences for sin.

Proverbs 27:4. Angry people can be cruel and people who are cross can do as much damage as a flood. But the damage that can be done by someone who is jealous is much worse than both. It is the most uncontrollable sin. So don't be jealous for what other people have.

LOOK AT YOURSELF

Have you ever been jealous of something that your friend has? Would you lie to be able to get one for yourself? Remember that God hates lies and even if you get what you wanted, you would know that you have disobeyed God. It is much more important to obey God than to have anything in this world.

PRAYER

Thank you, God, for all the things that you have given to me. Please help me to be happy with what I have, and not to be jealous of what other people have. Dear Jesus, please help me to always be honest. Please help me to remember that it is better to obey you than to have everything that I want. Please help me to change and to become more like you. Amen.

2 November

READ AND UNDERSTAND

Proverbs 25:18. Telling lies about someone will hurt them. It will damage their reputation (what people think about them) like weapons damage the body. So don't tell lies.

Proverbs 18:20. The words that you say will affect your character and conscience. Remember that you will have to live with the consequences of what you say. So think before you speak. Let your speech bring glory to God.

LOOK AT YOURSELF

If you tell lies, people will learn that they cannot trust what you say. One day you could be telling the truth and they might not believe you. If you tell lies about other people, it will hurt them and they will not want to be friends with you. So remember to think before you speak. You must never lie. Lying can hurt other people and it can cause problems for you as well. So remember to always tell the truth.

PRAYER

Thank you, God, that Jesus died on the cross so that my sins can be forgiven. Dear Jesus, please forgive me for all my sins. Please forgive me for not obeying you and for not always telling the truth. Please help me to change and to think before I talk, so that I will not lie but will tell the truth. Please help me to become more like you. Amen.

3 November

READ AND UNDERSTAND

Proverbs 26:18-19. Can you think how dangerous it would be for a mad man to have a bow and arrows, the arrows having fire on the end, and he shoots them anywhere he wants? That is how dangerous it is to lie to a friend and then to say "I was only joking". You must never lie, it is serious and you must not think that you can joke about it.

Proverbs 17:17. To be a true friend you must always show love, even if your friend is having a difficult time. Family support is there for difficult times. Remember to be a good friend and brother or sister.

LOOK AT YOURSELF

Have you ever lied and tried to cover your lie by saying that you were only joking? Today you have learnt that this is very dangerous and it can cause problems between friends. God wants you to be a good friend, showing love all the time. And if you want to show love to God and to others, you will always tell the truth.

PRAYER

Thank you, God, for your love to me. Thank you that Jesus died for me. Dear Jesus, please help me to love you more and to love others more as well. Please forgive me for my sins and please help me to change. I know that you can never lie, please help me to become more like you, always telling the truth. Amen.

4 November

READ AND UNDERSTAND

Proverbs 26:28. If you lie, you are someone who hates other people. This is because your lies will hurt those people who you lie to, or lie about. Someone who always says nice things that they don't mean will only cause trouble. So don't lie, you must always tell the truth.

Proverbs 23:12. You must desire to be wise and you must be diligent in becoming wise, you must pay attention and listen carefully when you are taught. So read your Bible and become wise.

LOOK AT YOURSELF

Have you learnt this week how important it is to tell the truth? Even if you say nice things, if it is a lie, it is wrong. Lies are displeasing to God and they can hurt other people. You must keep studying the Bible and keep asking God to give you wisdom. Then you will learn about how God wants you to live and you can pray and ask God to help you to obey Him.

PRAYER

Thank you, God, for giving me the Bible so that I can learn about you and become wise. Dear Jesus, please help me to be wise. Please help me to think before I speak so that I will not lie and will always tell the truth. Please forgive me for the times when I have disobeyed you. Please help me to change and to live a life that pleases you. Amen.

WEEK 45

THE IMPORTANCE OF WISDOM

This week we are going to study wisdom again. We will study Proverbs 8:32-36 and 9:3-4 and learn more about the important topic of wisdom in Proverbs.

TIME TO REMEMBER

Proverbs 8:33. "Listen to my instruction and be wise; do not ignore it."

5 November

READ AND UNDERSTAND

Proverbs 8:30-31. God used wisdom to design and create the earth and people. God is the source of wisdom.

Proverbs 8:32. Young people must be wise. God will bless the people who obey the Bible. If you obey God, you will be given wisdom, and will be able to live a life that pleases Him.

Proverbs 19:25. If you punish a mocker, people who don't know any better can learn a lesson. If you correct a wise person they will learn and get more wisdom. So be wise and learn when you are corrected.

LOOK AT YOURSELF

Do you obey what you learn in the Bible? Do you listen and learn when someone corrects you? If you are wise you will want to obey God and you will always want to learn more. Remember that God is the source of wisdom, and if you want to be wise you must study the Bible and ask God to give you wisdom. Having wisdom will help you in so many ways.

PRAYER

Thank you, God, for being all wise. Thank you that you know everything and that you have given the Bible so that I can learn more about you. Dear Jesus, please help me to obey you. Please help me to spend time in the Bible, learning more about how you want me to live. Please help me to change and to become more like you. Amen.

6 November

READ AND UNDERSTAND

Proverbs 8:33. You must be wise and listen to what you are taught. It is important.

Proverbs 23:6-8. Don't eat with people who are selfish, they say to you "eat and drink, come and have some more", but every bit you take they are thinking about how much it costs. If you find out how they really feel it will make you feel sick. All the time that you were thanking them for their kindness, you were wrong, they were not being kind at all. Don't desire fine foods; desire rather to have a simple meal with good friends.

LOOK AT YOURSELF

If someone takes you out to eat at a restaurant and they tell you that you can order whatever you want; don't order the most expensive thing on the menu. You should try and wait and see what they order and not order something a lot more expensive. If they say that they are having something, would you also like that; then even if it is expensive, if you would like it then it is fine. But don't just order something expensive, you might find they have to order something very cheep for themselves because they don't have enough money. So be careful about how important expensive food is to you. It is better to have something cheaper and have a good time with your friends.

PRAYER

Thank you, God, for everything that you give to me. Thank you that I have food to eat every day. Dear Jesus, please help me to not be greedy for expensive food. Please help me to remember that friendships are more important that fancy food. Please help me to be kind to others and think of them as more important than myself. Amen.

7 November

READ AND UNDERSTAND

Proverbs 8:34. If you are wise you will be blessed. It is good to spend time reading and studying the Bible every day. So learn from the Bible as much as you can and become wise.

Proverbs 16:26. When we have to work for our food then we will work hard because we are hungry.

Proverbs 18:16. Giving a gift to someone may help you to get what you want. But remember that God hates bribes and it is sinful to bribe someone or to take bribes.

LOOK AT YOURSELF

Some people are always looking for a quick way to make money. They don't want to have to work hard to earn the money that they need, they want to get rich quick. You need to be careful of this, because you might be tempted to do something that is not right so that you can get money. So remember how important it is to study the Bible, and then you will know what is right and what is wrong.

PRAYER

Thank you, God, for giving us the Bible. Thank you that it can help me to know how to live a life that pleases you. Dear Jesus, please forgive me for my sins. Please help me to be someone who does my work well and does the best job that I can. Please help me to remember that obeying you is much more important than having money. Please help me to obey you in everything that I do. Amen.

8 November

READ AND UNDERSTAND

Proverbs 8:35. Wisdom gives life and it will make God happy with you. So learn from the Bible and become wise.

Proverbs 26:1. To have snow in the summer is not normal, it does not come at the right time and it would do damage to the farmers crop. For the Israelites it was also damaging to have rain in the harvest. This proverb tells us that if a fool is put in an important place or if given praise, this is also out of place, not normal, and may do damage to people who look to him as an example. So don't be a fool.

LOOK AT YOURSELF

Do you live a life that is an example to other people? If someone had to look at your life and try to be more like you, would it be a good thing for them to do? At different times in your life, different people will look at your life and you will be an example to them. So remember that you should be a good example and not a fool who will be a bad example to others. If you don't want to be a fool, you must read your Bible and you must ask God to give you wisdom and understanding.

PRAYER

Thank you, God, for giving me the Bible so that I can learn about you and about how I should live. Dear Jesus, please help me to be a good example to other people. Help me to be an example of someone who is wise and who obeys you. Please help me to live a life that pleases you in everything that I think, say and do. Please help me to change. Amen.

9 November

READ AND UNDERSTAND

Proverbs 8:36. If you don't want wisdom you hurt yourself. If you hate wisdom you love death. So you must want and love wisdom.

Proverbs 17:12. It is safer to meet a mother bear who is angry because her cubs have been stolen than to meet a fool who in his anger can do so much damage. Don't be a fool and get angry.

LOOK AT YOURSELF

Do you get angry? Do you get cross with people? If you are wise you will not get angry. A person who gets angry is a fool. If you want to be wise you will want to learn from the Bible and you will want to obey God. A fool does not care about God's word and he does not even care if he hurts himself in his foolish behaviour. So don't be a fool. Love wisdom and want to live a life that pleases God.

PRAYER

Thank you, God, for the wisdom that you have given to us in the Bible. Dear Jesus, please forgive me for the times when I have gotten upset and angry. Please help me to remember how foolish it is to get angry. Please help me to be wise and to live a life that is obedient to you. Amen.

10 November

READ AND UNDERSTAND

Proverbs 9:3. Wisdom is offered to all people. You must learn from the Bible and become wise.

Proverbs 10:26. Never get a lazy person to do something for you, they will be as irritating as vinegar is on your teeth or smoke in your eyes. Don't be lazy, work hard.

Proverbs 26:15. Some lazy people are so lazy that they put their hand in a bowl of food, but are too lazy to bring it to their mouth. Don't be lazy. Work hard and always do your best.

LOOK AT YOURSELF

If your mum asks you to help her with something, do you do the best job that you can for her? Or are you lazy, walking slowly, working slowly and not doing a good job at all? If you want to please God you must not be lazy, you must work hard. Everything that you do must be done for God. You should want to obey and help your mum so that God will be pleased.

PRAYER

Thank you, God, that Jesus died on the cross so that my sins can be forgiven. Dear Jesus, please forgive me and help me to change. Please help me to remember that everything that I do must be done for you. Please help me to live a life that pleases you in everything that I think, say and do. Amen.

11 November

READ AND UNDERSTAND

Proverbs 9:4. If you are not wise you must and can become wise. Learn from the Bible and you will become wise.

Proverbs 20:28. Mercy and truth will keep a ruler in his position. Mercy makes his position sure. Remember to show love to other people.

Proverbs 29:26. People want rulers to like them so that they will be treated fairly, but you don't know if the ruler will do what is right. We do know that God always does what is right and just, so we must rather want to please God and obey Him.

LOOK AT YOURSELF

Everyone likes to have a leader who is fair. Would you like to have a leader who punished you for something you did not do? Nobody would like that. God is the ruler over the whole world and He is always fair. God is also so merciful that He does not punish us for things that we should be punished for. Because Christ died on the cross, you won't have to be punished for your sins. If Jesus Christ is your Saviour and Lord, then your sins are forgiven, and you will not be punished but will be given eternal life.

PRAYER

Thank you, God, for salvation. Thank you that you are merciful and gracious and you allowed Jesus to pay for my sins. Dear Jesus, please forgive me for my sins. Please give me wisdom so that I can know how to live a life that pleases you. Please help me to obey you. Thank you for everything that you have done for me. Amen.

WEEK 46

HOW TO LIVE A GODLY LIFE

This week we are going to study Proverbs 3:1-11. We are going to learn about how to live a godly life. You will see how important it is to have wisdom and to obey God in everything that you do.

TIME TO REMEMBER

Proverbs 3:5-6. "Trust in the Lord with all your heart and lean not on your own understanding; in all your ways acknowledge Him, and He will make your paths straight."

12 November

READ AND UNDERSTAND

Proverbs 3:1. You must remember your parents teaching, and be obedient. Remember you must honour and obey your parents.

Proverbs 3:2. Obedience will bring blessings and peace. So obey God.

Proverbs 20:30. Physical punishment in not to just make you painful, it is to stop you from sinning. Such discipline can help to purify and cleanse our hearts that are full of sin and need to be cleaned.

LOOK AT YOURSELF

Do you get punished if you do not obey your parents? It is good to get punished because it will help you to remember how important it is to obey God. If you obey God, you will obey your parents, whose job it is to help you to live a life that pleases Him.

PRAYER

Thank you, God, for my parents. Thank you that they can help me to know how to live a life that pleases you. Please help me to remember what I have learned form the Bible and please help me to obey you. Please forgive me for the times when I have sinned and not obeyed you. Please help me to change. Amen.

13 November

READ AND UNDERSTAND

Proverbs 3:3. Always be kind and tell the truth. This is what God commands you to do, you must obey Him.

Proverbs 3:4. Obedience will make God and man happy. So obey God.

Proverbs 11:13. Someone who is always talking about other people will not keep a secret. But an honest person can keep a secret. Always be honest.

LOOK AT YOURSELF

When last did you tell a lie? When last did you say something horrible about someone else? If you are a Christian you must want to obey God. God hates lies and He wants you to be an honest and a kind person. God commanded us to love Him and to love others. If you love God you will obey Him. And if you love others you will be careful of what you say.

PRAYER

Thank you, God, for always telling the truth. Thank you that you can never lie. Thank you for the love that you showed by sending Jesus to die for sinners. Dear Jesus, please forgive me for sinning and not obeying you. Please help me to change and to always tell the truth. Please help me to show love to others in what I think, say and do. Please help me to become more like you. Amen.

14 November

READ AND UNDERSTAND

Proverbs 3:5. Trust in God with all your heart. Never rely on what you think you know, but ask God to help you and trust what the Bible says.

Proverbs 30:1-3. Agur wrote the proverbs in chapter 30 and he knew that the only way to be wise is if God gives you wisdom. He says that on his own he was more stupid than any man, that he did not have any understanding. On his own he had no wisdom and knew nothing about God. Only when you humbly go to God and ask Him to teach you, will you be able to be truly wise.

LOOK AT YOURSELF

Do you think that you are special and important because you know things in the Bible? Remember that everything that you learn is because God has allowed you to learn it. All wisdom is from God, so you must not think that you are important. You must keep reading the Bible and you must keep asking God to give you wisdom. On your own you will not be wise at all.

PRAYER

Thank you, God, that you are all wise. Thank you that you know everything and that you gave the Bible so that I can learn about you. Dear Jesus, please help me to remember that all wisdom is from you. Please help me to become wise as I learn from the Bible. Please help me to rely on you in everything. Amen.

15 November

READ AND UNDERSTAND

Proverbs 3:6. Remember the Lord in everything you do, and He will show you the right way.

Proverbs 3:7a. Don't think you know everything. You will always have more to learn.

Proverbs 3:7b. Fear God and stop doing evil. If you know how holy God is, you will fear Him and you will want to obey Him.

LOOK AT YOURSELF

Do you know how holy and pure God is? He can never sin and He hates sin. If you are a Christian you will want to obey God. You will want to please Him. Knowing how holy God is can help you to stop sinning. So remember who God is and try and live a life that pleases Him. Keep reading your Bible and asking God to give you wisdom to know what is right and what is wrong.

PRAYER

Thank you, God, that you cannot sin. Thank you that I can read in the Bible and learn about how holy and perfect you are. Dear Jesus, please forgive me for sinning against you. Please help me to change and to live a life that pleases you in everything that I do. Please help me to always keep learning from the Bible so that I can learn more and more about you and how you want me to live. Amen.

16 November

READ AND UNDERSTAND

Proverbs 3:8. If you are obedient it will be like good medicine, healing your wounds and easing your pains. So obey God.

Proverbs 15:32. If you do not want to learn and be corrected, you are hurting yourself. If you accept correction, you will become wiser and get understanding. So listen to and obey your parents.

LOOK AT YOURSELF

I am sure there is nobody who likes it when they are sick or when their body is in a lot of pain. If people are very sick or in a lot of pain they take medicine to help their body get better. If you are a Christian you will not want to be disobedient. Just as much as you would want to feel better, so you would want to obey God and learn about what you are doing that is wrong, so that you can change. Keep reading your Bible and asking God to show you how you must live. And if someone corrects you, you must listen and learn, so that you can learn how to live a life that is obedient to God.

PRAYER

Thank you, God, for giving me the Bible so that I can learn how to live a life that pleases you. Thank you for the people in my life who can help me to know how to obey you. Dear Jesus, please forgive me for the times when I have disobeyed you. Please help me to change. Please help me to obey you in everything that I do. Amen.

17 November

READ AND UNDERSTAND

Proverbs 3:9-10. Thank the Lord by giving back to Him. If you give to the Lord, He will always provide for you. Remember that everything you have has been given to you by God.

Proverbs 3:32b. God loves those who obey. So learn from the Bible what God wants you to do, and obey Him.

LOOK AT YOURSELF

Do you receive pocket money? Or do you get money for work that you do? Do you give some of that money to God, in thanks for what He has given to you? This is what God wants you to do. He wants you to remember that everything you have is from Him. So don't just think about what you can buy for yourself. Think about giving some to your church, maybe using some to buy something for a child who does not have a lot. If you don't have money, you could give some of your time in helping other people and serving in your church.

PRAYER

Thank you, God, for everything that you have given to me. Dear Jesus, please help me to not be selfish. Please help me to do things for other people and to remember to share what I have with others. Please forgive me for the times when I have just thought about myself. Please help me to change and to show love for others. Amen.

18 November

READ AND UNDERSTAND

Proverbs 3:11. Don't hate God's instruction and discipline. God instructs and disciplines us for our good.

Proverbs 24:17-18. You must not rejoice when your enemies have trouble, you must not be happy when they have difficult things happen. God says that He hates this and that He will see you being happy and will be unhappy with you. God will then be cross with you instead of being cross with your enemy. So remember that if people do things that are mean to you, God will see and He will judge them. You must not be glad if something bad happens to them, you must give good even if bad is given to you.

LOOK AT YOURSELF

Have you ever said "Serves you right" when someone who did something horrible to you, is having something horrible happen to them? This is not living in a way that is pleasing to God. God is pleased when we show love to others. He wants us to trust that He knows when people are horrible to us. He will correct and discipline them. You need to focus on showing love to that person, helping them when you can, and wanting the best for them.

PRAYER

Thank you, God, that you can see everything that happens. Thank you that you know when someone has been horrible to me. Dear Jesus, please help me to show love to all people, especially to those who are horrible to me. Please help me to change and to live a life that pleases you in everything that I think, say and do. Amen.

WEEK 47

VIOLENCE IS WRONG

This week we are going to see how bad it is to be a person who is violent and who does evil things. We will see that wicked people love violence and evil and we will see that they will be punished for their wickedness.

TIME TO REMEMBER

Proverbs 3:29. "Do not plot harm against your neighbour, who lives trustfully near you."

19 November

READ AND UNDERSTAND

Proverbs 1:11. The wicked will attack and kill people for the fun of it. Don't be a part of that. It is wicked to hurt people.

Proverbs 20:26. A wise king will be able to find out who is doing wrong, and he will punish him. So remember to obey God and not to be wicked, the wicked will be punished.

LOOK AT YOURSELF

Have you ever gotten cross with someone and hit them? Have you ever just wanted to hurt someone and so you hit them or kicked them? Only wicked people will want to hurt other people. If you are a Christian you will remember that God wants you to show love to other people. It is very wrong to hurt people, and if you do, you will be punished. Also remember that if someone hurts you, you must not hurt them back. God will punish them for what they do to you.

PRAYER

Thank you, God, that wicked people will be punished. Thank you that you know everything that happens and you know if someone hurts me. Dear Jesus, please help me to never hurt people. Please help me to remember to show love and not hate. Even if someone hurts me, please help me to remember that it is wicked to hurt other people. Please help me to obey you and to show love. Amen.

20 November

READ AND UNDERSTAND

Proverbs 2:14. The wicked enjoy evil, they think it is fun. That is wrong. You must not be wicked, you must hate evil.

Proverbs 12:10. A righteous person takes care of their animals, but wicked people are cruel to theirs. So be kind to God's creatures.

Proverbs 30:14. There are people who are like horrible animals, with teeth that are like sharp swords and knives; they just want to kill the poor and needy. They are wicked and God will judge them.

LOOK AT YOURSELF

Are you kind to animals? Are you kind to all the people in your life? God created life and you must remember to be kind to people and to animals. If you are cruel to any of God's creation, He will not be pleased with you. Being cruel and hurting others is wicked and it is displeasing to God. So remember that God wants you to show love to other people. And you must also look after the animals that He has given to you to look after.

PRAYER

Thank you, God, for creating the world and everything that is in it. Thank you for creating me and all the people in my life. Dear Jesus, please forgive me for the times when I have been cruel and not shown love. Please help me to obey you and to please you in everything that I do. Amen.

21 November

READ AND UNDERSTAND

Proverbs 3:29. Do not plan anything that will hurt your neighbour, he lives beside you, and he trusts you. God commands us to love our neighbour.

Proverbs 4:16. The wicked love to do evil, they love to cause others to stumble. Don't be wicked, obey God.

Proverbs 12:6. The words of wicked people are murderous, but the words of the righteous rescue those who are in trouble. So make sure your words are kind and not wicked.

LOOK AT YOURSELF

Has anyone every hurt you and so you think about something horrible that you can say to them? That is being wicked and not showing love. God want us to always show love. No matter what people have done to us. People who plan to hurt others and who enjoy hurting others are wicked and are disobeying God. So make sure you are showing love to others, in what you think, say and do.

PRAYER

Thank you, God, for showing love to me in sending Jesus to die for my sins. Dear Jesus, please forgive me for the times when I have not obeyed you. Please help me to love you more and to love others more. Please help me to have speech that is kind and not wicked. Please help me to change and to become more like you. Amen.

22 November

READ AND UNDERSTAND

Proverbs 4:17. Evil men love wickedness and violence. Don't be evil, obey God.

Proverbs 14:7. Stay away from foolish people; they have nothing to teach you. Choose your friends wisely.

Proverbs 19:29. People who mock will be judged and the backs of fools will be beaten. So don't mock people and don't be a fool.

LOOK AT YOURSELF

Do you have friends who are wise, who love God and want to learn more about God? Or do you have foolish friends, who don't care about God and how He wants them to live? If you are wise, you will choose friends who are Christians. Then you will be able to help each other to live lives that are pleasing to God. Remember that fools will be punished. And if you want to obey God you will stay away from people who love wickedness.

PRAYER

Thank you, God, for giving me the Bible so that I can learn about God and how you want me to live. Dear Jesus, please help me to choose friends who love you. Please help me to want to obey you in everything and help me to not be a fool or a wicked person. Please help me to live a life that pleases you in everything that I think, say and do. Amen.

23 November

READ AND UNDERSTAND

Proverbs 1:19. When you use violence to get things, violence will take your life. Violence is sin, you must never be violent.

Proverbs 1:8-9. Listen and remember the good lessons and the laws that your father and mother give. They will improve your character as nice clothes or jewellery improves your appearance.

Proverbs 28:26. It is foolish to trust in yourself. If you are wise and you listen when you are taught then you will be safe. So be wise, don't be a fool.

LOOK AT YOURSELF

Do you listen when your parents teach you? Do you want to learn and become wise? It is so much better to be a wise person who wants to learn, than a fool who thinks that he knows everything. So keep learning from the Bible and from your parents. They will help you to learn about how to please God. One thing that does not please God is a person who gets things by being violent. So remember that it is wrong to hurt people, violence is sin.

PRAYER

Thank you, God, for my parents. Thank you that they can help me to learn about how you want me to live. Dear Jesus, please forgive me for the times when I have not wanted to listen and learn. Please help me to remember that I have so much to learn. Please help me to obey you and obey my parents. Amen.

24 November

READ AND UNDERSTAND

Proverbs 12:12a. All that is important to wicked people is evil. Don't be wicked, obey God and hate evil.

Proverbs 30:18-20. Here we see four things that are hidden and cannot be followed. A bird that flies in the sky does not leave a trail. A snake that slithers over a rock does not leave a trail. A ship that travels on the ocean does not leave a trail. A man that has an impure relationship with a woman does not leave a trail, he knows that he is sinning and so he hides it. The woman sins with the man and then says "I have done nothing wrong". But remember, God knows all things; you cannot hide from Him. God says that impure relationships are sin and you will be punished for it.

LOOK AT YOURSELF

It is wrong for a man and a woman to live together and act as if they are married if they are not. God created marriage and it is special. God will know if people are disobeying Him. You can't hide your sin from God. Remember that a Christian will want to obey God. A Christian should not enjoy evil, they should enjoy obeying God.

PRAYER

Thank you, God, for creating marriage. Thank you that you know everything and that nothing is hidden from you. Dear Jesus, please forgive me for my sins. Please forgive me for not obeying you. Please help me to hate evil and to do what is right. Please help me to obey you in everything that I think, say and do. Amen.

25 November

READ AND UNDERSTAND

Proverbs 16:27. Evil people look for ways to hurt others and even their words burn with evil.

Proverbs 17:20. If you think and speak about evil things you will probably not find any good, only trouble and disaster. So be careful of what you think about, your speech will be like your thoughts.

Proverbs 13:17. Wicked messengers cause trouble, but those who can be trusted bring peace. So don't lie, always tell the truth and then people will trust you.

LOOK AT YOURSELF

Did you make sure that you did not hurt anyone this week? Now you need to check if your thoughts were also pleasing to God. God does not only want you not to hurt others, He also wants you not to think about hurting others. You must not only have the right actions, you must also have the right speech and thoughts. So it is not good enough just to stop hitting your sister. You also need to make sure that you are speaking to her in love and thinking about her in love.

PRAYER

Thank you, God, that you have given me the Bible so that I can know how I must live. Dear Jesus, please help me to obey you. Please forgive me for the times when I have not had thoughts and speech that is pleasing to you. Please help me to change and to be a person who shows love in what I think, say and do. Amen.

WEEK 48

HOW TO BE A GODLY PERSON

This week we are going to look at Proverbs 31:17-23. This section is telling us about how a godly woman will live. This is a lesson to all of us though. We all need to live godly lives. It will help the girls to know what kind of a woman they should be, as well as helping the boys to know what kind of a woman they must marry.

TIME TO REMEMBER

Proverbs 31:20. "She opens her arms to the poor and extends her hands to the needy."

26 November

READ AND UNDERSTAND

Proverbs 31:17. A godly wife is a hard worker, she is strong.

Proverbs 6:7. Learn from the ants, they work even when there is nobody telling them what to do. You must work hard even if there is nobody telling you what to do.

LOOK AT YOURSELF

Do you work hard? Do you always do the best job that you can when you have something to do? If you want to please God, you will be a hard worker, working when you know there is work to be done. You should be able to work hard even if your mum is not watching and making sure that you work. You should be doing all your work for God, who sees everything.

PRAYER

Thank you, God, that you see everything and that you always know what I am doing. Dear Jesus, please help me to always obey you and live a life that pleases you. Please help me to be a hard worker and to do my work for you. Please help me to please you in everything that I do. Amen.

27 November

READ AND UNDERSTAND

Proverbs 31:18. A godly wife knows that she has good things for her family. She uses her time wisely and works before the sun is up and works till after the sun goes down. She also plans well so that her lamp does not run out of oil in the night.

Proverbs 26:14. Just like a door swings back and forth on its hinges and does not move any further, so a lazy person turns over in bed, he does not want to get out of bed to do any work. So don't be lazy.

LOOK AT YOURSELF

Are you lazy? Do you stay in bed as long as you can? Or do you get up early to make sure that you get everything done that you need to? A godly person will not be lazy. If you are a Christian you will want to please God in the way that you do your work and in the way that you spend your time.

PRAYER

Thank you, God, for each day that you have given to me. Dear Jesus, please help me to use my time well. Please help me to not be lazy, but to be a hard worker, always doing my work for you. Please help me to please you in all that I do. Amen.

28 November

READ AND UNDERSTAND

Proverbs 31:19. A godly wife makes clothes and keeps her hands busy.

Proverbs 15:8. The Lord is pleased when righteous people pray, but He hates the sacrifices that wicked people bring Him. God is not pleased if someone says he is a Christian but lives a wicked life. Your righteousness is important to God; you must obey Him in everything.

Proverbs 10:8. Wise people will listen to good advice, but a fool will not stop talking so that he can learn. So be wise and listen when you are taught.

LOOK AT YOURSELF

Do you learn from the Bible? Do you want to change when you see that something that you are doing is not pleasing to God? If you are a Christian you will want to please God. You will want to obey Him. Remember that we will never be able to obey God fully, but we must try to as much as we can. God will forgive us for the times when we sin, but we must try to obey.

PRAYER

Thank you, God, that Jesus died on the cross so that my sins can be forgiven. Dear Jesus, please forgive me for the times when I have sinned and not obeyed you. Please help me to learn more about you and how you want me to live. Please help me to change and to become more like you every day. Amen.

29 November

READ AND UNDERSTAND

Proverbs 31:20. A godly wife cares for those who are in need, she cares for the poor.

Proverbs 19:17. When you have pity on the poor and give to them, it is like lending to the Lord. The Lord will pay you back. Remember to give to the poor, help where you can, be kind and unselfish.

Proverbs 15:30. Smiling faces make people happy, and good news makes people feel better. So be friendly (with your face) and be kind (with your words) and you will bring happiness to other people.

LOOK AT YOURSELF

Do you show kindness to other people? Do you show care to people who are poor and who are in need? Are you prepared to share some of what you have with people who don't have as much as you? God wants Christians to show love. He showed so much love to you in saving you, and you need to show love to others. If other people see you showing love, you might be able to tell them about God's love and how they can be saved.

PRAYER

Thank you, God, for the love that you showed in sending Jesus to die for my sins. Dear Jesus, please help me to show more love. Please help me to obey you and to be kind and friendly. Please help me to tell other people about your love and how they can be saved. Amen.

30 November

READ AND UNDERSTAND

Proverbs 31:21. A godly wife does not worry about cold weather because she has made warm clothes for her family.

Proverbs 19:26. A child who mistreats his father or chases his mother away is a disgraceful person, bringing embarrassment to the people who know him. So remember the command to honour your parents.

LOOK AT YOURSELF

If you are a Christian you will care for the people in your family. You must always speak nicely to your parents and remember that God commands you to honour and obey them. If you honour your parents, you will respect them and you will listen to them when they talk to you.

PRAYER

Thank you, God, for my parents. Dear Jesus, please forgive me for my sin. Please help me to always show respect to my parents and to always obey them. Please help me to live a life that pleases you in everything that I do. Please help me to remember that I must care for the people in my family, and always show love to them. Please help me to change. Amen.

1 December

READ AND UNDERSTAND

Proverbs 31:22. A godly wife is blessed by God and is able to have nice things for herself as well as for her family.

Proverbs 27:21. Fire is used to test how good silver and gold are. To test a person, praise is used. If you think you deserve lots of praise and are so happy when someone says something good about you, you are a proud person. But if you accept praise humbly, you show that you are not self-centered and proud. So don't be proud and think that you are more important or special than others.

LOOK AT YOURSELF

Are you thankful to God for everything that you are able to do? Are you thankful to God for everything that you have? Or are you proud? Do you think that you are special because of what you do and because of what you have? If you are a Christian you will remember that everything you have is from God. If people praise you and say something good about you, you must give glory to God for what He has done.

PRAYER

Thank you, God, for everything that you have given to me. Dear Jesus, please forgive me for the times when I have been proud and enjoyed being praised. Please help me to be humble and to always give you the glory. Amen.

2 December

READ AND UNDERSTAND

Proverbs 31:23. A godly wife will help her husband be respected and will help him do well.

Proverbs 19:14. Parents can provide their sons with an inheritance of houses and money, but only the Lord can give a wife that is wise.

Proverbs 5:6. Impure relationships are unrighteous and will lead to death. God created marriage and it is a good relationship.

LOOK AT YOURSELF

The Bible teaches us a lot about what kind of a person we should want to marry. One day you might want to get married and you must remember how important it is to have a godly husband or wife. You must also try to be a godly person yourself. Then you will be a blessing to the person that you marry.

PRAYER

Thank you, God, for creating marriage. Thank you that it is a good and special relationship. Dear Jesus, please help me to be a godly person. Please help me to obey you. Please forgive me for my sins and please help me to change. Amen.

WEEK 49

MARRIAGE AND PURITY

This week we are going to study Proverbs 7:19-27. This passage is talking about how terrible it is to have a relationship outside of marriage. It talks about a lady who is married but she does not care, she is looking for other men. Remember that God created marriage for one man and one woman, and it is for the rest of their lives.

TIME TO REMEMBER

Proverbs 7:22. *"All at once he followed her like an ox going to the slaughter, like a deer stepping into a noose."*

3 December

READ AND UNDERSTAND

Proverbs 7:19-20. The wicked will promise that if you join them in their sin, you will not get caught. That is a lie. God knows about all sin and He will punish sinners.

Proverbs 6:13. Worthless, wicked people try and trick others. Don't be wicked, always tell the truth.

Proverbs 14:22. The people who plan evil will get destroyed. If you plan to do good things, you will get respect, trust and kindness from others. So don't plan evil, plan to do good.

LOOK AT YOURSELF

Have you ever planned to do something that you knew was sinful? Remember that God knows everything, so you can never hide your sin from God. If you are a Christian you will want to please God in everything that you do and so you will not plan to do evil and sinful things. Ask God to help you to live a life that pleases Him.

PRAYER

Thank you, God, that Jesus died on the cross so that my sins can be forgiven. Dear Jesus, please forgive me for my sins. Please help me to change and to live a life that pleases you in everything that I think about, say and do. Please help me to become more like you. Amen.

4 December

READ AND UNDERSTAND

Proverbs 7:21. The wicked will give you many good reasons to sin with them. Don't. It is never good to sin. God will punish sin. You must obey God.

Proverbs 7:1. Remember what the Bible says and never forget what it tells you to do.

Proverbs 28:1. Wicked people know that they have done wrong and so they think that people are chasing them, even if nobody is. But someone who loves and obeys God does not have to be afraid; they are as brave as a lion.

LOOK AT YOURSELF

Has anyone ever asked you to do something that you knew was wrong? Did they tell you that it was fine to do it, that it is really nice and that it was worth it? It is never worth it, if you disobey God. Nothing is worth more than living a life that is pleasing to God. People who sin will often be worried about being caught, so they might not really enjoy life at all. You must remember what the Bible has taught you, and you must obey it.

PRAYER

Thank you, God, for giving the Bible so that I can learn about how I need to live. Dear Jesus, please help me to remember what I have learnt about how you want me to live. Please help me to obey you in everything and to remember that sin is not worth disobeying you. Please help me to change and to become more like you. Amen.

5 December

READ AND UNDERSTAND

Proverbs 7:22. Sin will lead to death. So you must not sin, you must obey God.

Proverbs 21:14. A secret gift will help to stop someone being cross with you, a bribe will help calm someone who is very angry with you. But remember that giving a bribe, so that you can get away with something, is sinful, and God hates it.

Proverbs 22:8. If you are wicked you will only get trouble. A person who rules others with anger will not be a ruler for long. So don't be wicked, don't be a person who gets angry.

LOOK AT YOURSELF

Have you ever gotten angry and said something horrible to someone? If you are sorry for hurting them, and you want to ask them for forgiveness, there is nothing wrong with doing something nice for them to show that you are sorry. But it is sinful if you do something nice for them or give them a nice gift, just so that you don't get into trouble. So don't sin and sin again. You must ask God to forgive you when you sin and you must ask forgiveness from the person that you sinned against. And if you get punished for your sin, you must accept it and know that it is fair.

PRAYER

Thank you, God, that my sins can be forgiven because Jesus died on the cross for me. Dear Jesus, please forgive me for sinning against you. Please help me to live a life that is pleasing to you. Please help me to show love to other people. Thank you for the love that you have shown to me. Amen.

6 December

READ AND UNDERSTAND

Proverbs 7:23. If you are tempted by sin, you are like a bird going into a net, you don't realise that it will cost you your life. So when you are tempted to sin, you must resist and you must obey God.

Proverbs 12:13. Wicked people are trapped by their own words, but honest people get themselves out of trouble. Always be honest and tell the truth.

LOOK AT YOURSELF

Have you ever told a lie because you thought that you would get into trouble if you told the truth? You must remember that you will be in more trouble if you lie. God knows everything and you cannot hide the truth from Him. So remember how foolish it is to sin and to disobey God. It is like being trapped in a net. So don't sin. Obey God and always tell the truth.

PRAYER

Thank you, God, that you know everything. Dear Jesus, please forgive me for sinning against you. Please help me to remember that I can't hide my sin from you. Please help me to always tell the truth and to always have speech that is pleasing to you. Amen.

7 December

READ AND UNDERSTAND

Proverbs 7:24. Listen to what the Bible says. Pay attention to its teaching.

Proverbs 7:25. Do not get involved in impure relationships. God created marriage and it is good.

Proverbs 5:16. It is not good to have children outside of marriage. Children are a blessing from God to a married couple.

LOOK AT YOURSELF

God created the first family and has told us how He wants the family to be. God designed marriage for one man and one woman for their whole lives. He also planned that children would be born to married couples, so that the children would have a mummy and a daddy to look after them and teach them about God. It is sad that people don't always obey God. But we know what is right; what is pleasing to God.

PRAYER

Thank you, God, for creating marriage and for giving children to married couples as a blessing from you. Dear Jesus, please help me to remember what I learn from the Bible. Please help me to always remember how important marriage is to you. Please help me to obey you in everything that I do. Amen.

8 December

READ AND UNDERSTAND

Proverbs 7:26. Impure relationships trap many people, and it has ruined their lives. Marriage is created by God and it will bring happiness.

Proverbs 18:22. When a man gets a wife he gets a special jewel, it shows that God is being good to him. God created marriage and it is good.

Proverbs 5:20. Do not look for love outside of your marriage.

LOOK AT YOURSELF

Some people don't care about what God says. They don't care that what He says is the truth. They don't care about marriage and how important and special that relationship is. So remember how special marriage is, and that the promises that a man and woman make when they get married are for as long as they live. Make sure you are living a life that pleases God in everything. Then you will be able to be a godly wife or husband if you get married some day.

PRAYER

Thank you, God, that you created marriage and that it is good. Dear Jesus, please help me to remember what I learn in the Bible. Please help me to live a life that pleases you in everything that I think, say and do. Amen.

9 December

READ AND UNDERSTAND

Proverbs 7:27. Impure relationships lead to death. God created marriage and it is good.

Proverbs 16:22. Wisdom is a fountain of life to the wise, but trying to educate stupid people is a waste of time.

Proverbs 1:22b. Those people who mock the Bible must stop mocking and learn from it. The Bible teaches us everything we need to know, it is important.

LOOK AT YOURSELF

Is the Bible important to you? Do you want to learn about God and what is pleasing to Him? If you are a Christian you will want to learn from the Bible and you will want to obey God. Ask God to help you to be a wise person and not a fool.

PRAYER

Thank you, God, that Jesus died on the cross so that my sins can be forgiven. Dear Jesus, please forgive me for my sin. Please help me to stop sinning and to obey you in everything. Please give me wisdom and help me to remember what I have learnt from the Bible. Please help me to obey you. Amen.

WEEK 50

WISDOM AND MONEY

This week we are going to look at Proverbs 9:8-13 and learn again about wisdom. We will also see a lot of passages that tell us about signing surety, which means promising to pay what someone else owes. We will see that it is foolish to sign surety and the Bible tells us that we must not do it.

TIME TO REMEMBER

Proverbs 9:10. "The fear of the Lord is the beginning of wisdom, and knowledge of the Holy One is understanding."

10 December

READ AND UNDERSTAND

Proverbs 9:8a. If you try and correct someone who mocks the Bible, he will hate you.

Proverbs 9:8b. If you are wise you will love the people who tell you when you are doing the wrong thing.

Proverbs 6:1. Do not promise to pay what someone else owes.

LOOK AT YOURSELF

Do you listen when someone tells you that you are doing something wrong? Or do you get cross with that person, and not want to listen? The Bible says that if you are wise you will listen when others correct you. Then you will be able to learn more about how to live a life that is pleasing to God.

PRAYER

Thank you, God, for the people in my life who can help me to live a life that is pleasing to you. Dear Jesus, please help me to be wise and to listen to correction. Please forgive me for the times I have sinned against you. Please help me to change and to please you in everything that I do. Amen.

11 December

READ AND UNDERSTAND

Proverbs 9:9a. Teach a wise person and that person will become more wise.

Proverbs 9:9b. Teach a righteous person and that person will get more knowledge.

Proverbs 6:2. Do not promise to pay what someone else owes. You will be trapped by your words.

LOOK AT YOURSELF

Do you listen when you are taught? Do you want to become wise and to get more knowledge? Keep reading and learning from your Bible and ask God to give you wisdom, and then you will be able to become wise.

PRAYER

Thank you, God, for giving me the Bible so that I can learn more about you. Dear Jesus, please help me to become wise and to learn from the Bible about you and how you want me to live. Please help me to remember what I learn and to always want to learn more. Please help me to obey what I learn in the Bible and to live a life that pleases you. Amen.

12 December

READ AND UNDERSTAND

Proverbs 9:10a. To be wise you must first fear the Lord.

Proverbs 9:10b. If you know God, you have understanding. So read your Bible and get to know God.

Proverbs 6:3. If you have promised to pay what someone else owes, you should not have promised, you must humble yourself and ask to be released from that promise.

LOOK AT YOURSELF

Do you know that God is holy and that He can never sin? Do you know that nobody can live a life that is pleasing to God? We are all sinful and we all disobey God. The only one who did not sin was Jesus, because He is God. What is wonderful is that Jesus died on the cross so that your sins can be forgiven. If you are a Christian you have the Holy Spirit living inside of you and He will help you to live a life that pleases God. We will never be able to live a perfect live, but we must always keep trying to stop sinning and obey God.

PRAYER

Thank you, God, that you are holy and can never sin. Thank you that Jesus died on the cross so that my sins can be forgiven. Thank you that Christians are given the Holy Spirit to help them to obey you. Dear Jesus, please help me to obey you in everything that I do. Please help me to stop sinning and to live a life that pleases you. Amen.

13 December

READ AND UNDERSTAND

Proverbs 9:11. Wisdom will add years to your life. So learn from the Bible and become wise.

Proverbs 21:7. Wicked people will get destroyed by their own wickedness. They know what the right thing to do is but they refuse to do it. Obey God and do what is right, don't be wicked but be a person who loves others.

Proverbs 6:4. If you have promised to pay what someone else owes, get out of that promise quickly if you can.

LOOK AT YOURSELF

Have you ever done something that you knew was wrong? You know what the right thing to do is, but you choose to disobey and sin against God. Ask God to forgive you for your sin and ask Him to help you to choose to do what is right.

PRAYER

Thank you, God, that my sins can be forgiven because Jesus died on the cross. Dear Jesus, please forgive me for my sins. Please help me to change and to live a life that pleases you in everything that I think, say and do. Please help me to obey you. Amen.

14 December

READ AND UNDERSTAND

Proverbs 9:12a. It will be good for you if you are wise. So learn from the Bible and become wise.

Proverbs 22:26-27. Don't promise to be responsible for what someone else's owes; don't promise to pay if they don't. If they don't pay you will have to pay. And if you don't have the money they will take your things to pay for it, they will take even your bed and you will have to sleep on the floor. You must be wise with your money.

LOOK AT YOURSELF

You won't be allowed to sign surety until you are older. But you must remember that it is wrong. The Bible says that you must be careful and wise with your money. Everything that you have is given to you by God and it is God's. So you must use what you have wisely. Ask God to give you wisdom and ask Him to help you to be wise with your money.

PRAYER

Thank you, God, for giving us the Bible. Thank you that it teaches us so much about how to live in a wise way. Dear Jesus, please help me to be wise with my money. Please help me to always remember what I have learned in the Bible, so that I can always live a life that is pleasing to you. Amen.

15 December

READ AND UNDERSTAND

Proverbs 9:12b. It will be bad for you if you are not wise. So rather learn from the Bible and become wise.

Proverbs 20:16. Anyone who is foolish enough to promise to pay what a stranger owes will probably never pay the money back. So you would have to take his own property to make sure that he pays. It is foolish to promise to pay what someone else owes.

LOOK AT YOURSELF

Have you ever been asked to lend someone money? You must be careful of lending money to someone that you don't know well. You might never get paid back. You must also remember not to ask someone to lend you money if you don't have the money at home to pay them back. You must be wise with your money and remember not to pay what someone else owes.

PRAYER

Thank you, God, for everything that you have given to me. Dear Jesus, please help me to be happy with what I have and not always want more. Please help me to be wise and to think about what you want me to do in every situation. Please help me to become more and more like you. Amen.

16 December

READ AND UNDERSTAND

Proverbs 9:13. If you don't have wisdom you will be foolish and you will know nothing. So don't be foolish, learn from the Bible and become wise.

Proverbs 11:15. If you promise to pay what a stranger owes, you will regret it. You will be safe if you don't get involved.

Proverbs 17:18. Only a fool will promise to be responsible for someone else's debts. Even if he is your friend, you must not.

LOOK AT YOURSELF

We have seen a lot of verses this week that have told us how foolish it is to promise to pay what someone else owes. Remember this important lesson from Proverbs. One day you might be asked to sign surety and you will be able to quickly say no, because you know that it is a foolish thing to do.

PRAYER

Thank you, God, for warning me about things that are foolish and that can cause trouble for me. Dear Jesus, please help me to remember what I have learned so that I can always live a life that is pleasing to you. Please help me to please you in everything that I think, say and do. Amen.

WEEK 51

WISDOM AND FAMILY LIFE

This week we are going to see how happy and joyful parents will be if they have godly children. So if you live a life that is pleasing to God and you are wise, you will bring so much joy to your parents.

TIME TO REMEMBER

Proverbs 23: 24-25 "The father of a righteous man has great joy; he who has a wise son delights in him. May your father and mother be glad; may she who gave you birth rejoice!"

17 December

READ AND UNDERSTAND

Proverbs 15:20. Wise children make their parents happy. Only foolish children will not respect their parents. Remember the command to honour and obey your parents.

Proverbs 28:7. If you obey God you are wise and you will bring joy to your parents. But if you are someone who eats too much you are foolish and you will embarrass you parents. So be wise, don't eat too much.

LOOK AT YOURSELF

Are you a Christian? Do you want to obey God and live a life that pleases Him? If you obey God and live a wise and godly life, you will bring joy to your parents and it will be pleasing to God. So remember what you have learned and obey it. Ask God to forgive you for the times when you have not obeyed and ask Him to help you to obey.

PRAYER

Thank you, God, that Jesus died on the cross so that my sins can be forgiven. Dear Jesus, please forgive me for my sins. Please help me to obey you and to obey my parents. Please help me to be wise and to live a life that pleases you in everything I do. Amen.

18 December

READ AND UNDERSTAND

Proverbs 17:6. It is a joy and honour for parents to live long enough to have grandchildren. It is an honour for children when they have wise and godly parents. Be thankful to God for your parents.

Proverbs 17:19a. If you love to quarrel and fight you show that you love sin. Quarrelling will only end in trouble.

Proverbs 21:19. It is better to live in a desert, where there is peace and quiet, than to live in a big house with a wife who wants to argue and fight. Women should not be quarrelsome, looking for things to fight about.

LOOK AT YOURSELF

Do you like arguing with people? Do you look for things to fight about? If you want to please God you will not do that. You must rather have speech that is kind and gentle. You must show love to other people and you must consider them as more important than yourself.

PRAYER

Thank you, God, for my parents. Dear Jesus, please help me to be wise and godly so that I can bring joy to my parents. Please forgive me for the times when I have argued and fought. Please help me to show love to others and to have speech that is kind and gentle. Please help me to become more and more like you. Amen.

19 December

READ AND UNDERSTAND

Proverbs 15:31. If you pay attention when you are corrected you will become wise. So listen to and obey your parents.

Proverbs 11:14. When there is no one guiding, the people will fall. But when there is lots of advice there is victory. So don't be proud, be humble and ask for advice.

LOOK AT YOURSELF

Are you proud, thinking that you are always right? Do you think that you never make mistakes? You must be humble and listen when people correct you and help you. You must also be humble and ask for advice. If you are wise, you will be humble and know that you always need to learn more.

PRAYER

Thank you, God, that Jesus humbled himself by becoming a man. Thank you that he died on the cross so that my sins can be forgiven. Dear Jesus, please help me to be humble. Please forgive me for the times when I have been proud. Please help me to change and to become more like you. Amen.

20 December

READ AND UNDERSTAND

Proverbs 23:15-16. If you learn from your parent's discipline and instruction and become wise, your parents will be very happy. They will thank God and rejoice that you are wise, and they will know that you are wise because you speak about things that are right. So learn from them and become wise.

Proverbs 17:2. Everyone knows that a son in a family is more important to the father than a servant. But sometimes a wise servant, who is a blessing to the family, will rule over a foolish son, who is a burden and a shame to the family, and the servant will share in the inheritance as if he was a son.

LOOK AT YOURSELF

Do you speak about things that are right and pleasing to God? Or do you have speech that is not right? Do you lie, argue or speak in a horrible way? If you are wise you will always tell the truth and you will have speech that is kind and gentle. Ask God to help you to be wise so that you can be a blessing to your parents.

PRAYER

Thank you, God, for my parents. Dear Jesus, please help me to listen and obey my parents. Please help me to be wise and to have speech that is pleasing to you. Please help me to be a blessing to my parents. Please help me to live a life that pleases you in everything that I think, say and do. Amen.

21 December

READ AND UNDERSTAND

Proverbs 6:22. Your parent's instruction will guide you, protect you and help you know what to do. So remember that command to honour and obey your parents.

Proverbs 15:15. The life of the poor is difficult, but if you are happy you will always enjoy life. It does not matter if you are rich or poor, you must be happy with what you have.

LOOK AT YOURSELF

Do you moan about not having things? Do you complain if you don't get everything that you want? You must remember that God has given you so much and you should be grateful for what you have. Thank God for what you have and be happy with what you have.

PRAYER

Thank you, God, for my parents and all that they teach me. Thank you for everything that you have given to me. Dear Jesus, please help me to be happy with what I have. Please help me to remember how much you have given to me. Please help me to listen and obey my parents so that I can live a life that pleases you. Amen.

22 December

READ AND UNDERSTAND

Proverbs 23:24-25. Parents who have godly and wise children are very happy, they are proud of their children. So you can make your parents glad and bring them joy by being wise and living a life that glorifies God.

Proverbs 13:16. Wise people always think before they act, but fools show you how foolish they are. So think before you do something.

Proverbs 5:8. Stay away from impure relationships. God created marriage and it is good.

LOOK AT YOURSELF

If you want to do something, do you ask "Is it something that God would be pleased with?" If you are wise you will think before you do things. You will be able to live a life that pleases God and you will bring joy to your parents. In everything that you do, you should want to obey God and do what is pleasing to Him.

PRAYER

Thank you, God, for giving me the Bible so that I can learn about what is pleasing to you. Dear Jesus, please help me to obey you and to please you in everything that I do. Please help me to think before I do something, so that I will not do it if it is not pleasing to you. Please help me to be wise and to bring joy to my parents. Amen.

23 December

READ AND UNDERSTAND

Proverbs 27:11. If you are wise your parents will be happy. If people tell them that they are not good parents then they will be able to say, "we have got wise children" and it will prove that they have done what God wanted. So listen to your parents and become wise.

Proverbs 12:25b. Kind words will cheer people up. So be kind to others. Think about what you say, and try and be kind to others in your speech.

LOOK AT YOURSELF

Have you said something horrible or rude to anyone in your family? God wants you to be wise and to think before you speak. Then you will remember to have speech that is kind and gentle. So ask God to help you to have speech that is pleasing to Him. Ask God to help you to show love to others.

PRAYER

Thank you, God, for the love that you showed to me in sending Jesus to die on the cross for me. Dear Jesus, please forgive me for the times when I have had speech that was not kind. Please help me to change and to have speech that is kind and gentle and that shows love to others. Please help me to change and to become more like you. Amen.

WEEK 52

OUR WONDERFUL WISE GOD

From now to the end of the year we are going to learn about God and how wonderful He is. We will see that He made everything, He is in control of everything, and He knows everything.

TIME TO REMEMBER

Proverbs 18:10. "The name of the Lord is a strong tower; the righteous run to it and are safe."

24 December

READ AND UNDERSTAND

Proverbs 20:12. God has given us eyes to see with and ears to listen with; they are a gift from Him who created them. Remember to use your eyes to read and learn and your ears to listen to instruction and teaching. Then you will be able to glorify God with the use of your eyes and ears.

Proverbs 21:24. A proud and arrogant person thinks that they are better than others; they mock other people, look down on them and think that they are so much better. This pride is hated by God and will be punished. Don't be proud, it is sin.

LOOK AT YOURSELF

Do you think that you are special and that you deserve to have everything that you want? Do you think a lot about all the things that you would like to have? You must remember to think about other people. You must also remember how much you have been given. Not only did God create you, He also sent Jesus to save you. If you are a Christian you will be able to be with God in heaven one day. Now that is something to be thankful for.

PRAYER

Thank you, God, for creating me. Thank you for everything that you have given to me. Dear Jesus, please forgive me for my sins and help me to obey you. Please help me to live a life that pleases you in everything that I do. Amen.

25 December

READ AND UNDERSTAND

Proverbs 16:6a. Because of God's love and truth, our sin's can be forgiven. Christ died so that our sins can be forgiven. Trust in Christ as your Saviour and Lord and you will be forgiven of your sin.

Proverbs 20:27. God has given us a conscience that searches our heart and shows that we are sinners. So think about yourself and you will see that you are a sinner. All people are sinners.

LOOK AT YOURSELF

Jesus humbled Himself and became a man. Today a lot of people in the world celebrate Christmas, the birth of Christ. But there are not that many people who really know how wonderful it is that Jesus Christ became a man. Jesus came to earth so that, as God, He could live a perfect life and die on the cross to pay for our sins. As a lot of presents are given out for Christmas, you must remember the most important present. John 3:16 "For God so loved the world that He gave His one and only son, that whoever believes in Him shall not perish but have eternal life."

PRAYER

Thank you, God, for giving your only Son so that I can be saved. Dear Jesus, thank you for humbling yourself and becoming a man. Thank you for dying on the cross so that I can be saved. Please forgive me for my sins and help me to change. Amen.

26 December

READ AND UNDERSTAND

Proverbs 30:4. Only God can go to heaven and come back again, only God can control the wind, only God can control the seas, it is God who created the whole earth. Do you know of anyone who can say that they can do all that and are like God? The only person is Jesus Christ, because He is God.

Proverbs 25:25. Good news is so nice to get, it is as nice as getting cold water when you are really thirsty.

LOOK AT YOURSELF

Not only did God make everything, He is also in control of everything. While Jesus walked on earth He was controlling the weather and everything else as well. So if you ever hear someone say that Jesus is not God, you will be able to tell them that they are wrong. Jesus is God, and He came to earth to die for the sins of His people. The only person to never sin was Jesus, because He is God and He can never sin. So think about how wonderful it is that God became man.

PRAYER

Thank you, God, that Jesus became a man so that He could die on the cross for my sins. Dear Jesus, please forgive me for my sins. Thank you that I can be forgiven because of what you have done. Please help me to change and to become more and more like you. Amen.

27 December

READ AND UNDERSTAND

Proverbs 19:21. People might plan all kinds of things, but the Lord's will is going to be done. Remember that God is in control of everything.

Proverbs 15:16. It is better to be poor and fear the Lord than to be rich and be in trouble. The fear of the Lord is the most important thing in life.

LOOK AT YOURSELF

Are you a Christian? Do you know that you are a sinner and that you cannot please God on your own? Jesus Christ died on the cross so that your sins can be forgiven. If you are a Christian you will be given the Holy Spirit who will help you to live a life that pleases God. Knowing who God is is the most important thing. If you know how wonderful and perfect and holy God is, you will want to obey Him and live a life that pleases Him.

PRAYER

Thank you, God, for giving me the Bible so that I can learn about you and how wonderful and perfect you are. Dear Jesus, please forgive me for sinning against you. Please help me to remember that you hate sin and that you want me to obey you. Please help me to change and to obey you in everything that I think, say and do. Amen.

28 December

READ AND UNDERSTAND

Proverbs 15:3. The Lord sees what happens everywhere, He is watching us, whether we do good things or evil. So you cannot sin in secret. God knows everything you do.

Proverbs 26:23. Someone who has evil in his heart might try to sound happy and excited, but he is lying. Just like taking a normal pottery pot and putting expensive decoration on the outside, it is lying about what it really is. So don't be wicked, don't have evil in your heart.

LOOK AT YOURSELF

Have you tried to hide your sin from God? Have you ever thought that you can sin and that no one will know? God knows everything and you cannot hide from Him. You must obey God and do what is right, showing love to others and not hate. If you have evil and hate in your heart, you must ask God to forgive you and you must start obeying Him in all that you think, say and do.

PRAYER

Thank you, God, that you know everything. Dear Jesus, please forgive me for my sins. Please help me to obey you and to remember that you know when I don't obey you. Please help me to live a life that is pleasing to you in everything that I do. Please help me to change. Amen.

29 December

READ AND UNDERSTAND

Proverbs 17:3. Fire tests the purity of silver and gold, but the Lord tests our hearts. God knows what you think and why you do things. You cannot hide your sin from God.

Proverbs 10:20. A good person's words are like pure silver, but a wicked person's ideas are worth nothing. Your words come from your mind, so make sure you are not thinking wicked things.

Proverbs 6:19a. The Lord hates people that tell lies. You must always tell the truth.

LOOK AT YOURSELF

Do you have godly speech; speech that is pleasing to God? Do you have thoughts that are pleasing to God? Remember that God knows what you are thinking and He knows if you have wicked and sinful thoughts. If you want to do what is pleasing to God, you must make sure your thoughts are pleasing to Him as well.

PRAYER

Thank you, God, that you know everything and that you know what is in my heart. Dear Jesus, please help me to remember that you know what I am thinking. Please help me to have thoughts that are pleasing to you. Please also help me to have speech that is pleasing to you. Help me to always tell the truth. Help me to obey you in everything that I do. Amen.

30 December

READ AND UNDERSTAND

Proverbs 18:10. The name of the Lord is like a strong tower that can protect us. If we are Christians we can go to God in faith, prayer and devotion to Him and we can depend on Him. Always remember to place your trust in God.

Proverbs 1:3b. The Proverbs will teach you to do what is right. God tells us how to worship and love Him and we must do what He says.

LOOK AT YOURSELF

If you are having a difficult time, do you go to God in prayer? If you are a Christian you can know that everything will work together for your good. So you can pray to God to help you and you can trust in Him to be in control. You must keep reading your Bible so that you can learn more and more about who God is, and then you will know more and more about how wonderful He is.

PRAYER

Thank you, God, that I can always trust in you. Thank you that you are in control of everything. Dear Jesus, please help me to trust in you when something that is not nice is happening. Please help me to remember that you will work all things to the good of your children. Please help me to learn from the Bible about who you are and how you want me to live. Please help me to change and to become more like you. Amen.

31 December

READ AND UNDERSTAND

Proverbs 21:30. There are no human plans, even if they are clever, that can stop God's plan. God is in control of all things and we cannot change His plan. We must trust in God who is all powerful.

Proverbs 12:25a. Worry can rob you of happiness. So don't worry, trust in God.

Proverbs 27:7. Sometimes a person with lots of things does not appreciate them because he takes them for granted. But a person who only has a little will appreciate every thing that he gets. So remember to be thankful and appreciative of everything that you have.

LOOK AT YOURSELF

How wonderful it is that we can trust God in everything. We don't have to worry about things because God is in control of everything. Are you thankful to God for all the good things that He has given to you? You must thank God for what you have, even if you are having a difficult time. If you are a Christian He will work everything for your good. So remember to put your trust in Him.

PRAYER

Thank you, God, for everything that you have given to me. Thank you that you are in control of everything and that I can trust in you. Dear Jesus, please help me to not worry about things but to trust in you. Please help me to be more thankful for what I have. Please help me to show love to you by obeying you in everything that I do. Amen.

AUTHOR'S COMMENTS

This book was written because of a need I have to raise our little girl in a home where God's word is important and where the lessons of Proverbs have an important role in our job to "bring (her) up in the discipline and instruction of the Lord" (Ephesians 6:4). As Tedd Tripp said in his book "Shepherding a Child's Heart": *Your children need a framework in which they can understand life. King Solomon's Proverbs are a rich source of information about life. The child who begins to understand the Proverbs' characterization of the fool, the sluggard, the wise man, the mocker and so forth will develop discernment about life. I was amazed to see my children interact with their high school experience with a depth of insight and perception I never knew at their age. They have been able to evaluate their responses in ways I could not do until my mid-twenties. The reason? Instruction in the ways of God has given them biblical wisdom.*[1]

His comments on Family Worship have also played a part. *"Reading the Proverbs daily is of great benefit to children (and to adults). Our daily practice was to read one third of a chapter of Proverbs before school each day. This was a rich source of wisdom and encouragement for our children. We have seen them learn and then later internalize the principles in this practical section of the Word of God. The Proverbs are like an owner's manual for life. Proverbs confronts a child with every aspect of true spirituality."*[2]

I have sometimes found it a bit difficult to read through from chapter to chapter with younger children. Sometimes I did not understand what a Proverb was saying, and at other times I was not sure how to explain it to a child. Sometimes the whole chapter was dealing with one issue and at other times every verse was challenging different issues and it was a bit overwhelming. So the desire for something easier to use with children has been on my mind for many years.

In John MacArthur's "Successful Christian Parenting", my attention was drawn to the different themes that Proverbs deals with. After dealing with what the Proverbs teach on the different themes, he writes: *Parents, if you fail to teach your children to **fear God**, the devil will teach them to hate God. If you fail to teach them to **guard their minds**, the devil will teach them to have a corrupt mind. If you fail to teach them to **obey their parents**, the devil will teach them to rebel and break their parent's hearts. If you fail to teach them to **select carefully their companions**, the devil will choose companions for them. If you fail to teach them to **control their lusts**, the devil will teach them how to fulfil their lusts. If you fail to teach them to **enjoy their own spouses**, the devil will teach them to destroy their marriages. If you fail to teach them to **watch their words**, the devil will fill their mouths with filth. If you fail to teach them to **pursue their work**, the devil will make their laziness a tool of hell. If you fail to teach them to **manage their money**, the devil will teach them to* *squander it on riotous living. And if you fail to teach them to **love their neighbours**, the devil will teach them to love only themselves. We have a great responsibility to this generation and the next.*[3] *(Emphasis mine)*

He also makes the comment that "Wisdom is the theme throughout the Book of Proverbs. The word wisdom dominates the book.... Note carefully that true wisdom includes not simply intellectual content, but practical conduct as well. Wisdom encompasses not only what we *know* but also what we *do* and sometimes what we *don't do*."[4]

My desire in writing the Proverbs Family Devotional was to allow the emphasis of the Book of Proverbs to dominate, and to spread the themes throughout the year so as to have a book that is easier to use with children and which has practical application every day.

I pray that the Lord would use this book to help parents in their job of instruction and training their children. That it would help Christian children to know how to live a life that is pleasing to God, and for those who are not saved to be reminded over and over again about their need for a saviour.

[1] Tedd Tripp, *Shepherding a Child's Heart,* (Wapwallopen, PA: Shepherd Press), 1995. p 108.
[2] Ibid., 74.
[3] John MacArthur, *Successful Christian Parenting,* (Nashville: Word Publishing), 1998. pp 103-104.
[4] Ibid., 74.

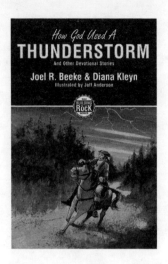

BUILDING ON THE ROCK

Five devotional books by Joel Beeke

How God used a Thunderstorm
Living for God and the Value of Scripture
ISBN: 1-85792-8156
How God stopped the Pirates
Missionary tales and remarkable conversions
ISBN: 1-85792-8164
How God used a Snowdrift
Honoring God and dramatic rescues
ISBN: 1-85792-8172
How God used a Drought and an Umbrella
Faithful witnesses and childhood faith
ISBN: 1-85792-8180
How God sent a Dog to save a family
God's care and childhood faith
ISBN:1-85792-8199